Also by Mark St. Amant

Committed: Confessions of a Fantasy Football Junkie

Just Kick It

Tales of an Underdog, Over-Age, Out-of-Place, Semi-Pro Football Player

MARK ST. AMANT

SCRIBNER

NEW YORK   LONDON   TORONTO   SYDNEY

SCRIBNER
1230 Avenue of the Americas
New York, NY 10020

SCRIBNER and design are trademarks of
Macmillan Library Reference USA, Inc., used under license
by Simon & Schuster, the publisher of this work.

For information about special discounts for bulk purchases,
please contact Simon & Schuster Special Sales:
1-800-456-6798 or business@simonandschuster.com

Designed by Davina Mock
Set in Berling Roman

Manufactured in the United States of America

1 3 5 7 9 10 8 6 4 2

Library of Congress Cataloging-in-Publication Data

St. Amant, Mark, date.
Just kick it : tales of an underdog, overage, out-of-place, semipro football player /
Mark St. Amant.
p.   cm.
1. St. Amant, Mark, date. 2. Football players—United States—Biography. 3. Boston
Panthers (Football team) 4. Football—Massachusetts—Boston. I. Title.
GV939.S67A3 2006
796.332092—dc22   2006044376
[B]

ISBN-13: 978-0-7432-8675-6
ISBN-10:   0-7432-8675-8

To my teammates and everyone else
who toils away at this level of football across the country.

CONTENTS

Contents

PROLOGUE:
OUTSIDE THE LINES

WHEN I DELVED into the history of semi-pro football, I discovered that trying to dig up the roots of football at this level could quite possibly cause me an aneurysm. Stalin's Russia—Winston Churchill famously described it as "a riddle wrapped in a mystery inside an enigma"—had nothing on semi-pro football. Records were spotty and contradictory. Accurate statistics were virtually nonexistent. But I needed to clear this up (as much as possible, anyway) and try to find out just where semi-pro football leagues came from and to whom we owe a debt of gratitude for sustaining it over the decades.

Enter Steve Brainerd.

Steve, a member of the Minor League Football Hall of Fame and the United States Football League Association Hall of Fame, is widely considered one of the foremost historians and researchers on semi-pro/minor league/amateur football (see, there are even three names for it). Whatever the name, he knows all about the approximately 800 teams and 70-odd leagues currently playing semi-pro ball from Maine to Hawaii, and where their roots were planted.

Thirty years ago Brainerd and his wife, Wisconsin natives, perhaps tired of harsh midwestern winters, packed up their car and headed for California. Along the way, they planned to visit friends in Tucson. Their car, however, had a different itinerary. Somewhere in the deserts of New Mexico, it broke down, forcing the Brainerds to use up all their money getting the car repaired, after which they limped into Tucson. "But then we thought, 'Hmm, this seems like a nice place,'" Steve tells me, "Why don't we just stay here?" So they did. And they've been there for three decades, happy with their decision not to continue on to California.

"LA is a great place to visit," he says, "but I now know I wouldn't want to live there. Although, if we're talking about semi-pro football, they've got it all over California. They've got teams coming out of their ears—LA, Orange County, San Diego, up north. And they had some great minor league teams back in the thirties and forties. I hope that if LA ever gets an NFL franchise back, they call them the 'Bulldogs.'" The Bulldogs, he explains, were a minor league team who, in the late thirties, played exhibition games against NFL teams, the supposed cream of the American football crop, the best of the best, teams perpetually stocked and restocked with Heisman-winning talent from the Harvards, Yales, Notre Dames, Armys, and Navys of the eastern football world. The results? The minor league Bulldogs of the Pacific Coast Professional Football League won five, lost four, and tied three. "They were a very, *very* good football team," Steve says, with obvious admiration.

Why were they were so good? Thanks to their location, the Bulldogs and other big-name teams like the Hollywood Bears had a virtual monopoly on all the California football talent. Remember, the westernmost outpost of pro football in those days was Chicago, home of the Bears and Cardinals. There was no San Francisco 49ers, no Oakland Raiders, no San Diego Chargers. As far as football was concerned, Southern California might as well have been Neptune. This was long before ESPN and *SportsCenter*'s Top 10 plays, scouting combines, rankings services, streaming video feeds, and other invaluable cogs in the massive, unstoppable, worldwide football recruiting machine with which today's football scouts and recruiters can find even the most obscure football talent in Mountain Goat, Oregon, or Cow Pasture, Texas, unearth that diamond in the rough, and, in minutes, deliver everything from his yards-per-carry, to his 40-yard-dash splits, to his DNA and Wunderlic scores straight to the BlackBerry of the head coach at, say, University of Miami, all with the pinpoint accuracy, speed, and precision that would make Jack Bauer and his CTU pals on *24* envious. But in Southern California, in the 1930s, as the Bulldogs exemplify, even the most talented, deserving players flew under the NFL's radar.

That said, the stockpile of local talent couldn't all be blamed on undeveloped technology. While deserving West Coast white players were also no doubt ignored or simply not discovered by what would eventually become the NFL, race also played a major role in the lack of western players in the eastern-dominated pro ranks. In 1920, the owners/representatives of 13 midwestern football teams, including future Chicago Bears legend George Halas (then player/coach of the Decatur Staleys) and Pittsburgh's Art Rooney, assembled at an automobile showroom in Canton, Ohio, to form an organized league so the area could have a true champion. Thus the American Professional Football Association (APFA) was born.

The admission fee for the APFA was $100 per team. They also agreed not to use any player who still had remaining college eligibility, in part to preserve the "gentlemanly" integrity of the college game, a drastic difference from today's standards.

Mostly hoping to capitalize on his notoriety, they named Jim Thorpe the league's first president. And notoriety was the extent of what Thorpe brought to the table. "Thorpe was a terrible administrator," writes author Bill Crawford in his Thorpe autobiography, *All-American: The Rise and Fall of Jim Thorpe*. "He just did not give a rat's ass about finances or social niceties necessary to grease the wheels . . . in the rough and tumble new league." However, Thorpe served during more open-minded times, racewise. Initially, talented black players were commonplace in the APFA: Robert "Rube" Marshall of the Rock Island Independents; Paul Robeson and Frederick Douglass "Fritz" Pollard for Akron; Fred "Duke" Slater with the Chicago Cardinals; Jay Mayo "Inky" Williams with the Hammond Pros. After all, one of the goals of the league was to put the best product on the field, sell tickets, and make money. (In fact, Pollard became the first African-American professional head coach when he took the reins at Akron in 1920.)

But then, in 1933, in the midst of the Depression, the relatively young NFL drew the color line. Another black player did not appear on an NFL field until after the Second World War. Just like its counterpart in baseball, football had closed the door to talented black athletes. NFL owners feared they would be harshly criticized, and their games possibly boycotted, if black men were allowed to collect football paychecks while white men stood in bread lines and lived in shantytowns. (In later decades, George Preston Marshall, the innovative yet closed-minded owner of the Washington Redskins, the last team to break the color barrier, would famously remark, "We'll start signing Negroes when the Harlem Globetrotters start signing whites.") This meant that even one of the biggest football stars in the country at the time, Kenny Washington, the UCLA two-time consensus All-American, was barred from playing in the NFL because of skin color. Later, another UCLA football star (who was also a pretty good baseball player) was prohibited from joining the NFL ranks: Jackie Robinson. Today these two would be no-brainer first-round NFL draft picks; in the 1930s and 1940s, however, they were forced to toil in the relative hinterlands of the minors and semi-pros for the Bears and Bulldogs.

While these are extreme examples from a distant past, one thing remains constant: there is always a margin. There will always be players who strive to "make it," whether that means making the proverbial leap from high school football to college, or college football to professional. But there are far more who fail to make it. Whether by choice or circumstance, there will always be players who end up toiling away on the gritty fields of football's most anonymous yet ubiquitous level, and doing so purely for the love of the game.

That's what semi-pro football is all about, and that's where my story begins.

NO CRYING IN FOOTBALL

IN JUNE OF 2004, I joined a semi-professional football team. This was strange for three reasons.

First, I was nearly 40 years old.

Second, I stood about five feet eight and weighed 160 pounds. After a full meal.

Third, I had never played a single down of real football—helmets, pads, referees, possible pain, humiliation, and broken bones—in my life.

Pray for me.

While I wasn't exactly hooked up to an iron lung when I decided to start playing football, I was still too old to be picking up new hobbies that involved physical violence. In the 15 years since playing soccer in college, aside from the occasional jog along the Charles, I had morphed into a primarily couchbound mammal—an advertising copywriter turned author who was better suited to noncontact activity. Something, say, from a continuing-education catalog. Like origami. Far as I knew, no one had ever gotten a concussion while folding little paper swans.

Instead, not only had I chosen to play football, I also set my sights on the most make-or-break position there was: placekicker. A curious choice if you knew that in my earlier life the only skill I'd mastered in sports seemed to be choking when it counted most: clanking last-second free throws, striking out with the bases loaded, missing easy breakaways. I had always been fairly talented, but I wouldn't have ever called myself a "money player."

Take Pomfret Soccer Camp. I was 12, and it was my first real sleep-away camp. On the final two days of the week, they held the campwide championship, only the most important event of my young life. My team, the Purple team, mostly made up of kids from the 'burbs of Boston, had advanced to the finals against the Gold team, which consisted of some tough-talking, elbow-throwing, under-13's from somewhere in the Mafia burial ground swamps of Jersey. Compared to my skinny, prepubescent self, these "kids" looked like full-grown adults. Gold chains. Deep baritone voices. One of them had a five-o'clock shadow, I kid you not. I think another one wore a wedding band.

Anyway, we were losing a chippy, penalty-filled game 2–1 with only a few seconds left when my best friend at the time, Kenny Keyes, and I executed a perfect give-and-go around the lone remaining defender who stood between us at the top of the goalie box. I passed the ball to Kenny and sprinted to the right of the hairy, muscle-bound defender, who now turned to take on Kenny; Kenny, meanwhile, just as Rocky Balboa Jr. reached him, reared back for a shot, which drew the goalie out toward him to cut down the angle—Kenny was the best player in camp and had a blistering left-footed shot that all goalies feared—but instead, skillfully deflected the ball back to me. I was now all alone, with the goalie hopelessly out of position, staring into a completely open net.

Now, most kids with any sort of athletic composure and/or internal fortitude would have relished an open net, grinned confidently, and tapped the ball in for the heroic, game-tying goal. But me? As I wound up for my shot, images of failure flashed before me: shots going wide; shots hitting the posts; balls smashing through windows, knocking over flowerpots, flying out into highways, and being run over by 18-wheel trucks; shots that never were; words I'd misspelled in spelling bees; you name it. As I wound up, I felt like a golf ball had been jammed into my trachea. My mouth went Mojave Desert–dry, my salivary glands reduced to sandpaper. The net, which should have looked massive and welcoming, appeared to have shrunken down to the size of your average loaf of bread. Worst of all, I suddenly felt the urge to vomit, or black out, or both. I may have indeed blacked out, because to this day I can't even remember kicking the ball. The next thing I *do* remember was an audible groan from my sideline (and surprised, jubilant, mocking cheers from the opposing sideline) as my would-be hero-making goal fluttered clumsily high over the crossbar by a good 10 feet. The ref blew his whistle. We had lost.

Head down, I walked over to our sideline. On the way, one of the Sopranos-in-training sidled up next to me. "Way to choke, ya little fuckin' pussy," he said, leering. He then condescendingly patted me on the back with his hairy knuckles and went off to celebrate with his teammates, who were probably lighting up victory cigars and chugging beer they'd bought without needing fake IDs.

If I had any balls, or fight left inside of me, I would have—should have—punched this smug asshole in the face. But I'd only been in one "fight" in my entire life, in fourth grade, and that merely consisted of my taking one wild swing at Steven Scott as we played on a snow bank—why I felt the need to eliminate Steven and commandeer the snow bank, I have no idea—barely grazing him, and yelping as the awkward momentum sent me tumbling down from my lofty arctic perch. Steven pointed and laughed . . . until our mutual, prepubescent love interest, Kristin Yeradi, comforted me on the ground below. (Hm, I guess I *do* know what we were fighting about.) Translation: I was a lover, not a fighter.

So, naturally, instead of sticking up for myself on the soccer field that day, I just walked to the far end of the bench area and sat down hard in the grass, far away from my teammates, some of whom glared at me as if I'd been caught molesting their dogs. Pretending to be in pain, I pulled my right leg back, tucked it behind me, and stretched an "aching" quad, leaning back against the grass, trying to breathe, staring up at the sky. Kenny, who was our best player and therefore immune to any persecution for associating with me, the new team pariah, soon appeared above me. He asked me if I was okay. I nodded. He knew I was lying, and told me not to worry about it. "We wouldn't have scored the first goal without you," he added, referencing the perfect, lofting corner cross I'd chipped to him in the first half that he'd deftly one-timed for our first and only score. He slapped me on the shoulder and walked off. And that's when I started crying— quiet, internal hiccups at first, which soon morphed into those borderline hyperventilating gasps that you try your damndest to choke back down into your stubborn lungs, but simply can't. I shifted so no one could see me. And that, my friends, was the single worst moment in my athletic history.

While I'd certainly had my high points over the subsequent years of playing various sports in high school and college—I was typically one of the better athletes, but never had what it took or made the necessary sacrifices to be the best—I knew that somewhere deep inside me there was that little 12-year-old who cried on the sideline that day. What I guess I'm saying is, considering all of this, I was the last guy who should have been potentially putting himself in the position of having to, say, kick a field goal with seconds left on the clock, the game on the line. No one had ever confused me with Larry Bird. I didn't want to take that last shot. Let someone else do it.

But it wasn't like I went into this planning to *actually play* football. I was researching semi-pro football, on a hunch that I might come across some prime material for a second book. Through a series of contacts and Google searches, I tracked down Reggie Murphy, 37, general manager and offensive lineman for my local semi-pro team, the Boston Panthers of the Eastern Football League (EFL), and a 14-year semi-pro veteran. At one point during our interview, I casually mentioned my soccer experience and—ding!—I could almost hear the lightbulb turn on over his head. "Hey, we need a kicker," the outgoing Mattapan resident told me. "You should come try out at practice tomorrow night." Before I could stop myself, the words were already out: "Sure. Why not?"

Sure. Why not? Did I have a death wish? Was I—in the immortal words of *Fast Times at Ridgemont High*'s Ray "Mr. Hand" Walston—*on dope?*

I never once considered playing Pee Wee football (ages nine, 10, 11). My brother played, but Doug was three years older, taller, and more filled out than I would ever be—my chest was practically concave, my arms and legs like swizzle sticks—and he had the biting, sarcastic wit and attack-when-cornered mentality indigenous to the common suburban preteen smart-ass that often caused other kids (and even some parents) to want to kick his ass. Which meant he was also very fast, running in long, gangly strides, like a prepubescent antelope. So when he joined the Wellesley Junior Red Raiders, he became the first and only St. Amant to ever play any level of organized football.

While Doug never took sports too seriously, and only played them because his friends did and it was just something to do when not making out with trashy chicks and smoking cigarettes with his delinquent buddies, I was hooked on sports right from the start. While he dove into music and got hooked on Stones, Police, Ramones, and Sex Pistols albums, I devoured NBA, NFL, NHL, and MLB yearly encyclopedias, memorizing stats, scores, records, player bios. My bedroom was littered with baseball and football cards, team hats and pennants, you name it. While Doug was off running with his mini *Outsiders* gang, I was busy recruiting our little sister, Leslie, to underhand baseballs to me. A little athlete herself—she would eventually be an all-state gymnast and earn a scholarship to a Division I college—she pitched willingly, probably amazed that either of her two idiot older brothers had noticed she was even there. She only stopped being my personal batting practice machine when I almost poked out her eye when a broomstick I was moronically using as a bat slipped out of my hands.

But while baseball was fun, and I always played Little League, the game was a little too slow for me. Like Doug, I could run like the wind, and was good at kicking things (balls, tables, occasionally my siblings). So I gravitated toward soccer, which was far more free-styling and frenetic, perfect for a kid who, by his elementary school years, was borderline hyperactive. (Our pediatrician, Dr. Strauss, once even suggested that I be put on some prehistoric pharmaceutical forefather to Ritalin. My mom refused, perhaps hoping I'd just spontaneously combust one day and leave them with one less mouth to feed.)

Soccer was more or less in its infancy in the late '70s when I started playing, and it wasn't considered, shall we say, the manliest sport. It was Europe's game. The one where the refs blew the whistle if a player so much as *breathed* on another player. The one where there was no hitting allowed, no tackling (unless it was of the "sliding" variety), and to use one's hands was a punishable offense. Soccer, to most, was duller than Ben Stein reading Herman Melville. Worse, it was considered downright un-American. The country was fresh off OPEC and the Ayatollah. Blaring, double-neck–guitar-soloing arena rock provided our nation's collective sound track. And the manly, blue-collar, shaggy-bearded Pittsburgh Steelers, fresh off a handful of Super Bowl titles, represented not only everything sports were supposed to be, but also everything *America itself* was supposed to be: bigger, stronger, and more resilient than anyone else on Earth. And soccer players? They wore little satin shorts. They pratfalled and faked injuries like little divas. Could you ever imagine Jack Ham, "Mean" Joe Greene, Mel Blount, or Jack Lambert faking an injury? Didn't think so.

Soccer's "wimpy" stigma relented a bit as the country and I moved into the '80s. Translation: I wasn't downright embarrassed to play it anymore. Brazilian legend Pelé had become an American sensation, joining the New York Cosmos of the upstart North American Soccer League. Indoor soccer was fast becoming popular, with the creation of the Major Indoor Soccer League (MISL). But still, while football remained the manliest sport this side of boxing or crocodile wrestling, and was exploding in popularity to—gasp—even rival baseball, it wasn't even on my radar as I attended Belmont Hill (an all-boys school outside of Boston, coat-and-tie, all that), followed by Westminster School (a coed boarding school to which I transferred after my family moved to Simsbury, Connecticut). I do, however, recall the Westminster football players calling us soccer players "soccer bunnies," something I always found odd, considering that Westminster Martlet football—has there ever been a *less* imposing school mascot than the "Martlet," a mythical footless bird?—was a hapless, unimposing program that finished with maybe one or two wins per season, and whose biggest defensive lineman was about the size of our all-state goalie. Still, the football players, if not literally, remained the figurative big men on campus. And despite its less-than-rugged reputation, and though I dabbled in other sports throughout high school (hockey goalie), soccer remained my number-one game.

I went on to play four years of NCAA soccer at Franklin and Marshall College in Lancaster, Pennsylvania. We were called the "Diplomats." Continuing a disturbing trend in my scholastic/athletic life, our college mascot was, yes, a diplomat, specifically some poor freshman trying to maintain his balance in a 60-pound plastic Ben

Franklin head and wearing goofy 18th-century garb—ruffled puffy linen shirt, waistcoat, knee-length topcoat, breeches, buckled boots, the whole bit. The F&M Diplomat ran a close second to the podiatrically mutilated Westminster Martlet on the wimpy mascot scale. After all, there was probably nothing more intimidating for our opponents than squaring off against a 275-year-old, bifocal-wearing, original Declaration-signer with gout. Worst of all, our name was often shortened to the "Dips"; might as well have just called us the F&M Eunuchs.

F&M was only Division III soccer, so I certainly don't claim to have been a predecessor to Freddy Adu. But play was competitive and obviously required a certain amount of skill and foot-to-ball coordination that luckily, for my eventual football tryout, I would always retain. Best of all, I didn't have to be big to play. I entered F&M at a positively Mary Kate Olsen-esque 135 pounds, and thanks mostly to constant soccer-playing, had *maybe* reached Ashley's size by graduation, despite a four-year diet of pizza, beer, and anything deep fried and Cheez Whizzed. And even though I immediately gained an ungodly 40 or so pounds postcollege due to sudden inactivity and a salary that would only cover fast food and even cheaper/worse beer than I'd had in college—a jowly era my brother *still* refers to as my "Brando" stage—I never grew into any sort of body that one might consider football-ready.

But there I was anyway, joining a semi-pro team in June of 2004—too small, too old, too inexperienced . . . and, just maybe, too white.

I'm not talking Marshall Mathers/Eminem "white guy raised in an 8 Mile trailer park" white, or even "suburban white kid wearing a Wu-Tang shirt" white, also commonly referred to as "Kevin Federline." No, I'm talking *white* white: French-Canadian descent (with some mutt-like Norwegian mixed in); blond hair and blue eyes (Malcolm X's proverbial "blond-haired, blue-eyed devil"); prone to sunburns; basically, the whole suburban preppy boy starter kit.

More glaring, I currently lived on Beacon Hill, a historic neighborhood located practically in Boston's geographical center on, you guessed it, a hill. During the Revolutionary War, it was a strategic post that overlooked both Boston Harbor and the Charles River and allowed Colonial forces to keep watch on British ships. Today it is easily the most Wonder Bread–white neighborhood in the city. Many of Boston's multimillionaires and blue bloods make up the brownstone-dwelling residents who park their Range Rovers, Mercedes, and

Beamers on cobbled, brick-sidewalked, lantern-lit streets, particularly Louisberg Square, only the most expensive square mile of property in New England. Let's just say when you live a quarter mile (and several million dollars) away from John Kerry and Teresa Heinz, it doesn't exactly ramp up your street cred.

Admittedly, there weren't many black kids at the schools I attended. Belmont Hill and Westminster were almost all white back in the day. And F&M, an idyllic, finely manicured liberal arts college in central Pennsylvania Amish Country with barely 2,000 students, was more or less just a *slightly bigger* version of my prep schools. While there were, of course, black students with whom I was friendly at all three schools, I wouldn't say we were *friends*, and rarely crossed paths on a social level. This wasn't to say that my white friends and I were out wilding like neo-Nazi skinheads, or that the black students were bow-tie-wearing Farrakhan disciples. I'm just telling the truth about the racial balance of my life, which to that point had been: I'd always been predominantly surrounded by white people. Period.

And the icing on my vanilla cake? I grew up in Wellesley. A tony, idyllic suburb 15 minutes west of the city, Wellesley makes Beacon Hill look like Compton. It boasts a median family income of almost $135,000, seventh-richest in the state, and is 90 percent white. Along with being the home of fun-loving poet Sylvia Plath, *SNL* alum Jane "You Ignorant Slut" Curtin, the late sports broadcaster Curt Gowdy, Judge Arthur Garrity (who infamously ordered the integration of Boston public schools in 1974, leading to racial violence and chaos), and, most impressive of all, 1980's "Stroke Me" rocker Billy Squire, Wellesley was also famous for an incident that took place in September of 1990.

A young black man was sitting in his car with his fiancée, opening his mail, when seven Wellesley police officers surrounded him and ordered him onto the sidewalk at gunpoint. He complied, and they cuffed him as the suspect in a bank robbery that had just taken place across the street. There were just two problems, however: (1) any criminal worth his salt likely wouldn't have sat in a car right across the street from a bank he'd just robbed, let alone casually opening his mail; and (2) this "robber" didn't really need money—he was Boston Celtics' number-one draft pick and new NBA millionaire, Dee Brown. *Oops. Our mistake. Won't happen again, Mr. Brown. Um, good luck tonight against the Lakers, and real sorry to have jammed my knee into your back.* No, not one of my hometown's prouder moments.

Under the inevitable firestorm of (justifiably) bad press resulting from the incident, Wellesley selectmen subsequently gathered to examine the police treatment of Brown. While the officers defended themselves and were ultimately exonerated for following department procedure in such a case as robbery, the incident prompted several members of the black community to reveal that they had been frequently stopped by police for no good reason while driving through Wellesley. In short, they had been racially profiled long before that term was really in vogue. Add to that the fact that Jews and other minorities were not so secretly "discouraged" from moving into town well into the twentieth century and, well, you've got yourself a regular melting pot.*

However, along with millions of other things, my parents taught me this: never judge anyone by his or her background. And I hoped, when I first set foot on a Panthers' football field, that I would be afforded the same benefit of the doubt. But I secretly feared I wouldn't be.

Most of the Panthers hailed from Dorchester, Roxbury, Mattapan, and other predominantly black towns and neighborhoods in and around Boston. In 2004, the organization changed its name from the Roxbury Panthers to the *Boston* Panthers, in the hopes of attracting more players, and potential sponsors, from all over the city.

My goal was to try to belong as a nonfootball player entering a football players' world, not so much as a white man entering a black man's world. If I was able to do both over time and maybe get to know some of these guys as friends, then so be it, that'd be great. But I wasn't on a crusade for racial harmony or spontaneous "Ebony and Ivory" choruses. I just wanted to see if I could play football—a game I'd devoured as a spectator for so many years—despite my age, size, inexperience, and less-than-clutch track record. Plus, I wanted to write a book about it.

---

*That's not to say that Wellesley was, or is, a white separatist colony populated by bigots—it was a wonderful place to grow up—but it, like countless other American suburbs, right or wrong, just had its own way of doing things.

KICKING OFF

I ATTENDED MY FIRST Panthers' practice at Franklin Park not as a player, but as a writer—observing, taking notes, and secretly hoping Reggie had forgotten all about that whole *You played soccer? We need a kicker . . . Sure. Why not?* thing. But should I really have been worried? If anything, assuming I went through with it, I was only going to be the kicker. I mean, it's not like they'd want me catching passes across the middle.

Kickers have traditionally been outcasts in the football realm. Not *real* football players. Just practice nuisances, or nonentities, hanging out off to the side, wearing their Fisher-Price one-bar helmets and doing their weird kicking drills alone, grudgingly tolerated as a necessary evil because they might be called upon to win a hard-fought game, but certainly not respected. Like all petulant, precious Little Lord Fauntleroys, kickers are better seen and not heard. Kickers are usually only seen when they screw up, missing an extra point, hook-ing a field goal, or shanking a kickoff out of bounds. With 100-plus years of football history to draw from, only one player who was ex-clusively a kicker—Jan Stenerud—has ever been enshrined in the Pro Football Hall of Fame. Kickers, simply put, don't count.

Take Garo Yepremian, former Detroit Lions and Miami Dolphins kicker. While he wasn't the first soccer-style kicker in NFL history—that honor went to Pete Gogolak, a Cornell grad who signed with the Buffalo Bills in 1964—the little (five-foot-seven) Armenian estab-lished the kicker stereotype. Yepremian, originally signed by the Lions, remains the Dolphins' all-time leading scorer (830 points). He once made 110 consecutive PATs (points after touchdown, the fa-mous acronym that became the legal first name of one of football's other great kickers, George Allen "Pat" Summerall). In 1971, Yepremian also kicked one of the most memorable field goals in NFL history, a 37-yarder, 22 minutes, 40 seconds into overtime to defeat the mighty, defending Super Bowl champion Kansas City Chiefs, 27–24. Clocking in at 82 minutes, 40 seconds total, the game is the longest in NFL history, and one that, even more noteworthy, officially announced to the world that an upstart AFC dynasty had been born in Miami.

Despite these great accomplishments, Yepremian is primarily re-membered for two nationally televised laughs at his expense: (1) when he tried and failed miserably, awkwardly, and, for lack of a more gender-correct term, girlishly, to throw a pass that was easily returned by Mike Bass for a Redskins' touchdown (Washington's only score in the Dolphins' 14–7 Super Bowl win that completed their perfect 17–0 1972 season); and (2) when Garo's former Detroit Lions team-mate Alex Karras mocked his remedial English-speaking skills and football acumen in front of a nationwide audience on Johnny Car-son's *Tonight Show*, recounting the time the excited little kicker screamed "I keeek a touchdown!" after booting a meaningless extra point in a bad Lions loss. Uncoordinated, clueless, funny-looking, unathletic, quite possibly mentally challenged little freak shows—that is how the world perceives kickers.

I sat down in the grass and rested my back against a fence post near the parking lot and began to scribble in my little palm-sized spiral notebook. The field wasn't really a football field, per se, with sidelines, end zones, goalposts, et cetera; rather, it was more of an open, grassy space that lay between two baseball fields. The Boston Panthers had commandeered it for their own use. There was plenty of grass, but there were also several uneven peaks and valleys, and barren patches of dirt and rock. My ankles hurt just looking at it.

"Let's go, y'all, let's go!" one of the players yelled over to the guys who were still lingering in the parking area near their cars, putting their cleats, pads, and other equipment on, talking, laughing, taking their time. "Six o'clock means six o'clock! Stop fucking around and get out here, time to get to work!" Holding his silver helmet chest-level in his right hand, he banged the top of the helmet with his left palm—*Thwap! Thwap! Thwap!*—over and over, the football version of ringing a dinner bell, looking like he could smash right through the hard plastic shell if he wanted to. He wore black football pants and a green mesh jersey with yellow lettering on the back reading "D. Jones" and, below it, the number 54. A nearly shaved-bald head and thick neck poked out from his shoulder pads. I didn't need a team program to tell that this D. Jones was one of the alpha dogs here.

The parking lot guys quickened their pace a bit and jogged out to the field. A few guys glanced down at me as they passed. Some more than glanced, clearly wondering who I was and what I was doing there. I watched nonchalantly, pretending that hanging out at football practice in Dorchester was something I did every day.

As the other players began to circle around D. Jones, one of them stopped, turned around, and walked back over to me, holding his silver helmet down at his side. About five-foot-seven with slightly receding wavy brown hair, he approached with an energetic spring in his step, as if the momentum would cause him to topple forward at any moment. His was one of the few nonblack faces out there.

"Hey, how you doin'?" he asked with slight Latino accent.

"Good. Yourself?"

"I'm doing good." He studied me for a moment. "You a reporter?"

I briefly wondered what had given him that idea, and then remembered that I was holding a pen and a small spiral notebook and was taking notes.

I hesitated. What was I exactly? Until that moment I hadn't really thought about it. I wasn't a reporter; that was certain. I was possibly going to try out for the team, but I sure as hell wasn't a player; not yet, anyway. And I *was* planning on writing a book, but I didn't want to answer, "No, I'm an author," because that would have made me sound like, to put it bluntly, a pompous dick. And what if they didn't want their privacy invaded? What if they didn't trust reporters or writers or anyone of that ilk, especially white ones? Screw it, I thought, I *am* a writer. I *am* writing a book on semi-pro football, hopefully. So that's what I would tell him. Why start out lying?

"I'm writing a book on semi-pro football. I talked to Reggie last night and he told me to come on out," I added, feeling the need to explain that I hadn't just invaded their world uninvited.

The guy nodded. "That's cool. We've had reporters out here before." He paused. "I'm Elvis," he said, reaching down to shake my hand. I shook his and introduced myself.

"How long you been playing for the Panthers?" I asked.

"This is my first year. My boys Lenny and Gio play, too." He turned toward the practice field, squinted into the sun, and pointed to two almost identical short, stocky guys stretching out on the ground.

"What position do you play?"

He smiled. "Wherever they want me to. I'm one of the older dudes out here but I'm still a rookie."

I nodded. "How old are you?"

"Thirty-three," he answered. Wow, another guy on the north side of thirty who was making a foray into football. Glad I wasn't the only one. "I play special teams, some linebacker, whatever. I just like being out here and getting some run, keeping my old ass in shape, hanging with the guys, know what I'm sayin'?"

"Yo, E, you need an engraved invitation? Let's go!" D. Jones yelled over to Elvis, who chuckled, shook his head, and tugged on his helmet with both hands. "Captain Insano gets a little amped up sometimes, but he's a good dude. I better get out there before he kicks my Puerto Rican ass, though. Nice meetin' you."

I nodded and, for some stupid reason, gave him a thumbs up, and immediately felt like a total dork. A thumbs up? *Nice work, Roger Ebert.* And how about the fact that I was possibly going to join a team headed by a guy named Captain *Insano*? Good Christ—what was I doing here?

The Panthers ran through prepractice calisthenics: jumping

jacks, stretches, push-ups, short running exercises with high knees, high kicks, sideways "karaoke" sprints (like hockey players did, crossing left foot over right, right over left, front and back, et cetera), and, finally, full-out sprints. "Bring it in! Bring it in!" yelled a guy who was about six-foot-three with a broad, barrel chest and wearing a red, mesh number 92 Northeastern University football practice jersey. Like Captain Insano, this guy looked like he wielded some authority, since everyone seemed to listen and bring it in on his command. Nearby, the coaches, wearing their white Panther polo shirts, huddled on their own, with one in particular looking like the head coach: a stocky, neckless, broad-chested man of about 40 who was practically bursting out of his polo short, Incredible Hulk–style. While he said a few words, the three or four other coaches nodded and then broke away.

The players converged in a tight circle around Captain Insano, and raised their arms to the center, touching hands, finding someone else's shoulder, forming one tightly entwined group. I heard someone deep inside this human haystack—Captain Insano, I could only presume— saying a few words before yelling, "Panthers on three . . . Panthers on three . . . *one, two, three*!"

"*PANTHERS!*" the group responded, the booming voices echoing over the baseball fields. They then broke up into offensive and defensive units for drills, and headed over to their respective coaches.

For the next two hours, I took notes from an inconspicuous distance as they ran through passing plays, running plays, defensive schemes, blocking formations, tip drills, loose-ball and fumble-recovery drills, you name it.

Watching the workout, I couldn't believe that I had willingly put myself into a situation where I possibly had to try out for something. When was the last time I'd had to try out for *anything*? Sure, before I got married, I'd gone on the dreaded first dates, which are more or less tryouts of the worst kind: the player (i.e., the man) hopes that he'll show enough skill that the coach (i.e., the woman) will put him into the game, where he'll either score a glorious touchdown or, more likely, receive a penalty for illegal use of the hands. And yes, I've had my share of job interviews since graduating from college, which are another sort of tryout. But compared to a football tryout, even the most brutal job interviews were a breeze. Whenever I've had to sit across from some advertising executive creative director as he watched my reel to decide whether I'd be given a key to the Creative

Department clubhouse, I'd always at least had a concrete track record of success to lean on, some legitimate, rational reason why I was there interviewing in the first place: because I was an ad copywriter; that's what I did for a living. But "interviewing" for a football team? I had no frame of reference. I had no past experience to lean on. I had no "portfolio" of past kicking success to flip open, present to the coach, and say, "See this 43-yard field goal from the left hash mark into the wind during a blizzard with one second left on the clock? *This* is why you should hire me."

Lost in my own jittery daydream world, I hadn't noticed the little kid wearing a Tom Brady number 12 Patriots jersey standing in front of me. He just stared down at me, head cocked sideways, holding a football under his right armpit.

"Whatcha doin'?" he asked. He looked about eight.

"Watching practice." I held up my pen. "Taking some notes."

"Notes for what?"

"A book on football. Do you play for the Panthers?"

He shook his head, as if it'd been a totally serious question. "Nope. My dad does, though. My stepdad."

"Which one is he?"

Mini Tom Brady turned, scanned the field for a moment. "There," he said, pointing at a round, powerful, sturdy-looking player in royal blue football pants who, at that moment, was using his low center of gravity to block in a running drill. He was the fullback.

"What's his name?" I asked.

"Todd."

"What's your name?"

"DJ."

"Nice to meet ya, DJ." I held out my hand and, after looking at it for a moment, he shook it firmly, with conviction. "Do you play football?"

DJ shook his head. "Not yet. But I want to when I get older."

"You want to play for the Panthers like your stepdad?"

He shrugged. "Yeah, I guess so. I'm pretty fast. You gonna play football?" he asked.

Kid, I have no earthly idea.

"Maybe." I shrugged. "We'll see."

"Okay, then, bye." And just like that he ran off, the ball cradled in his armpit, ducking and weaving through imaginary defenders.

It was now almost dark. As the coaches and players made their way back to their cars, Reggie approached me with another player whom I assumed was team owner and veteran semi-pro receiver Delaney Roberts.

An Antigua native, Delaney, 36, moved to the States when he was 11 years old. When he got to Hyde Park High, where he and Reggie first met as freshmen, a football coach noticed the quiet yet blazing-fast Roberts running track and suggested he try out for the football team. And that was that; he was hooked. As a junior, he became the team's star punt returner and wide receiver. "I had never really played before, so I just played on instinct, and I had good speed," he says, a drastic understatement to Reggie. "He might move a little slow now," Reggie explains, "and back in the day, lots of guys might have been fast . . . but Delaney was *fast*."

By his senior year, Roberts was receiving so many recruiting letters that he sometimes never even opened them, all of them having started to look and sound alike. But one school stood out: Georgia Tech, coached then by Bobby Ross. "I really respected him," Delaney says of Ross. "He was a great guy, and said that even though I had only been playing for a short time, he saw my raw talent and thought I could play at the next level with the right coaching. I was all set to go on a full ride to Georgia Tech."

But then Fate intervened in his senior year: during a punt return in the late stages of a rain-soaked city championship game, he took a hit, landed awkwardly, and heard an unsettling "pop." "I knew right away it was bad," he says. "I had never heard nothing like that. And it hurt, too. When I tried to get up and walk on it, it felt like everything was just grinding together, fire was shooting up my leg."

Today, most college-bound recruits would have had the knee scoped to gauge the damage and likely rehab time. But Delaney never did, something he now regrets. "I was afraid to have surgery," he admits. "I seen lots of older guys in the neighborhood with these big, nasty surgery scars on their legs, so it just made me afraid of the hospital." More than the eventual surgery, he says, was the fear of hearing a doctor's diagnosis. He just didn't want to hear those dreaded words: your football career is over. "Yeah, I regret the way I handled that. I should have had it checked out, but I just shut down and pretended it never happened." He merely rested the knee for months afterward. Not surprisingly, it didn't quite heal right on its own. Also not surprisingly, the recruiters stopped writing.

"I called Coach Ross and told him that I'd hurt my knee," Delaney says. "He asked how bad it was, and I told him that I didn't know. He encouraged me to get it checked out, but I just never did it. And I never called him again. I just went on with my life. I sometimes think about what might have happened if I had the surgery and rehabbed—I know I could have played college, at least—but no sense getting stuck in the past." Delaney now had a successful plastering and blueboarding business, a small fishing boat he took out on weekends, a two-family home in Mattapan, a wife, stepdaughter, a baby son on the way, and his own semi-pro football team. Things were good. Perhaps it was his laid-back island upbringing, but he was all about living for today.

Fuller around the middle than in his speedster playing days, Delaney, dressed in carpenter's jeans, a white Boston Panthers T-shirt, paint-spackled Timberland work boots, cell phone clipped to his belt, walked up to me and held out his hand.

"Hey, Mark, wanna take some kicks?" Roberts asked with a deep, Barry White-ish voice.

I shrugged. "Sure." I felt the exact opposite of sure. But what else could you say when the owner asks you to kick? I had to purge my "sports wuss gene" at some point in my life, and it might as well have been in front of 30-odd Panthers standing nearby, unwinding, changing out of their cleats and jerseys into sneakers and street clothes. They had to be eavesdropping to see who I was and what I was doing there. I couldn't wimp out now. I had no choice but to kick.

I followed Delaney and Reggie out onto the battered turf. Reggie tossed me a ball. I meticulously set it on an orange, hard rubber tee. Donnie Williams, 41, the senior member of the Panthers who wore many hats—offensive lineman, holder for extra points and field goals, assistant general manager—headed downfield about 40 yards, turned, and waited in the darkness, ready to shag my kicks. Assuming I reached him.

"All right, Mark," Reggie said, nodding encouragingly.

This was really happening. No turning back now. I took a deep breath and started forward, slowly at first, and then speeding up as I approached the teed-up ball . . . five feet . . . three feet . . . one foot . . . and then, no foot—as in, no *left* foot planting into the turf and providing the necessary support to keep my idiotic body from falling. My stupid, no-good running sneaker, which was more than adequate for the cement jogging paths along the Charles River, proved to be less than suitable for this rocky, divot-filled turf. Hence, as if someone had yanked the entire park out from underneath my feet, I flew through the air legs-first like some sort of remedial superhero with vertigo and landed on my ass in a painful, humiliating thud, emitting a guttural "ooof" and sliding on said ass through the dirt, scraping the hell out of my left calf in the process.

No. No no no no no no. That did not *just happen. I did* not *just try to kick a football and fall on my ass in front of 30 men in the 'hood. Just sit here with your eyes closed and they'll all go away. . . . Don't move. . . .*

"You all right, Mark?" Reggie called over.

"I'm good," I said faux casually, bounding up, gathering the football, and jogging back over to the tee as if nothing had happened. I heard a few chuckles from the parking area.

"This place is a minefield," Reggie said, absolving me of any athletic sins. "Guys twist their ankles all the time. Just take your time." Delaney just stared at me, probably wondering if his childhood pal was playing a practical joke on him. What would Reggie bring him next time, a kicking mule? A legless midget on a skateboard?

I teed the ball up again, backed up, turned. *Screw this. I can kick a soccer ball. I can kick a stupid football, sneakers or no sneakers.* I ran ahead, mad, embarrassed, determined.

Contact.

The ball flew long and straight, sailing over Donnie's head. Reggie tossed me another ball; I teed it up and kicked again. And again. Most I hit well, sending Donnie back into the darkness to retrieve the ball; others I shanked, low, bumbling line drives. I was no Adam Vinatieri, but my old-guy leg at least hadn't detached from my torso, helicoptered into nearby power lines, and burst into flames.

Finally, after about 10 kicks, Reggie looked at Delaney and raised his eyebrows: *So, what do you think?* Delaney shrugged, his expression saying, *Better than what we got, I guess.*

"All right, Mark," Reggie said and grinned. "You're our new kicker."

Huh? *That* was my tryout? Shouldn't I have had to run with tractor tires tied to my waist? Had my vertical leap measured? Passed a urine test? Apparently not. Apparently the semi-pro kicking tryout process was, shall we say, informal.

Just like that, I was the new Panthers' kicker. I think I was, anyway. I mean, the head coach hadn't even seen me kick or given his blessing yet. Didn't his opinion mean anything?

"Pitt will be cool with it," Reggie said when I asked about the head coach. "And it's Delaney's team anyway, so . . ."

"What's his name?"

"Mike Pittman. We call him Pitt. Everyone's got a nickname. Hell, I don't even know half of these guys' real names, only their nicknames. Delaney doesn't either. Watch." He called over to Delaney, who'd been talking to Donnie and not listening to us. "D, what's Sugar Bear's real name?"

Delaney shrugged.

"What about Pee Wee?"

Delaney considered it for a moment. "William. I think."

"See?" Reggie smiled.

"Did Pitt know that you guys were bringing in a kicker tonight?" I asked.

Reggie shook his head. "I don't think he'll even know how to use a kicker. We've never really had one before. But Delaney and I will talk him into it. A good kicker is a real luxury in this league. Not many EFL teams have them. Last year, we left so many points on the field going for two after scoring, or having to go for it on fourth down even though we were in field goal range. If you have a good kicker you have a definite advantage."

"Hey, I never said I was a good kicker," trying to make a joke, but, honestly, feeling a little panicked, as if I'd somehow falsely advertised my skills. Damn Reggie for getting me into this! "I never even said I *was* a kicker."

"Football kicking, soccer kicking, same thing." Reggie shrugged. "You'll pick it up fast. I have faith in you, Mark. C'mon, let's go meet these little bastards. And I gotta introduce you to Pitt."

Great. The head coach didn't even want a kicker, let alone know how to use one. Imagine his surprise when he learned that he was getting one who had never *actually kicked* before. Throughout the entire practice, Pitt had looked like a serious, downright humorless guy who stood in the middle of live defensive drills, massive arms crossed at his even more massive chest, occasionally barking out a command or a criticism. Put a Smokey hat on him and he could have been a drill instructor at Parris Island.

Reggie, Delaney, and Donnie escorted me over to the parking lot. There were about two dozen guys still left, standing near their cars. A few sipped from beer cans, lowering them whenever a police cruiser skulked by, which one seemed to do every few minutes, a white cop and a black cop closely eyeing the group. A guttural, pulsating bass line pumped out of a low-riding, tricked-out Honda Accord straight out of *Pimp My Ride* central casting.

"Listen up, ya little bastards," Reggie announced. "This is Mark—our new kicker."

Most conversations stopped. Heads turned. I was suddenly front and center. There was a brief moment of trepidation—all I could hear was the bass line—*booph, BAM, booph, BAM!*—during which I feared they'd groan and ask why they couldn't get a *real* kicker, why they always had to scrape the bottom of the athletic barrel, or, worst of all, they'd ask what the hell I thought I was doing in their neighborhood, their field, their world. *Isn't there a polo team on Beacon Hill you'd rather play for, Opie?*

Number 54, Captain Insano, approached. He'd looked enormous in his pads, but now, while still big—about six-one, 245 pounds by my guess—he looked slightly less menacing. "Hey, Mark," he said, holding out his hand. His voice was soft, almost introspective, friendly. "I'm Darrell. Welcome to the Panthers, man."

I extended my own hand for a traditional handshake, only to discover that he was doing something different, something more elaborate. Our fingers got all tangled up, the grips all off-kilter, him still gripping my fingers when I was releasing, a total mess, like a remedial game of rock-paper-scissors. I'm surprised I didn't poke his eye out. We both chuckled . . . me nervous, him amused.

"Where'd you play before?" he asked.

A few heads turned to hear my response. I froze. *Shit. The one question I'd been dreading. Make something up . . . the Patriots . . . the Barcelona Dragons . . . a small school in the Niagara Falls area that they wouldn't know.* "Um, I've never played football before, actually," I finally admitted.

They stared.

"But I played soccer in college," I added quickly, as if that would make things better. I smartly left out the "Division III" part of my heroic sports history, however, and that I'd eventually quit, and that we were named the "Dips."

"You playing at Brockton this Sunday?" Insano asked.

I shrugged. "I think so. It's up to Coach Pitt, I guess."

"Cool," Insano nodded and then, before turning back around, added, "We finally got a full-time kicker." How I heard it: *We finally got a new mascot.*

I shook hands with a bunch of the other guys. Each handshake was also a bit awkward and fumbled, as neither I nor my "handshake partner" knew which type of handshake, exactly, the other pre-ferred—the more traditional "white-guy-businesslike" handshake or the more "urban hand-slap-followed-by-quasi-GI-Joe-with-the-Kung Fu-grip fingertip" thing that I'd just botched with Insano. Some went in for the soft rap of the knuckles, which I was utterly unprepared for, holding my open hand out for a shake when they were balled into a fist (paper-covering-rock), and, when they switched to the open-palm shake, I switched to a balled fist. Clearly, I was a moron. But we'd eventually iron that out.

So, okay, they didn't carry me on their shoulders and hail my arrival as the saving grace of the team. But honestly, the low-key manner in which they reacted was much better than that: they just went about their business as if I had been there since training camp, which had opened three months earlier, in April. One thought kept repeating in my head: *I'm the new kicker for a semi-pro football team? I'm the new kicker for a semi-pro football team! Wait, seriously . . . did I just say that I'm the new kicker for a semi-pro football team?*

And then, there he was: Coach Pitt.

Mike Pittman had a 20-inch neck. That pretty much summed up his football coaching credentials as far as I was concerned. But there's more. Even at 42 years old he was a rock-solid tank of a man. His bi-ceps were the size of my thighs. And that neck, which you'd have a hard time getting both hands around (should you be dumb enough to try to strangle him). Born in Baltimore, Pittman was one of 15 total children among his mother, father, and stepfather. In elementary school he moved with his mom, a social worker, and stepfather, a brick mason and jack-of-all-trades who worked on oil burners and fixed cars in his backyard, along with three younger siblings to the toughest projects of Greensboro, North Carolina. The Greensboro projects were rife with racial tension, drugs, and crime. Those projects were also where he started playing football in street pickup games when he was eight years old. He soon tried out for a Pop Warner team and has been involved in football ever since.

He eventually grew into a star high school defensive back and linebacker and moved on to Fayetteville State University, and, after a year, transferred to UMass-Boston in the early '80s. In 1984, at age 20, he tried out for the Boston Breakers of the United States Football League, which had a momentary heyday in the early-/mid-'80s with such high-profile signings as Herschel Walker (New Jersey Generals), Doug Flutie (Generals), Jim Kelly (Houston Gamblers), and Steve Young (LA Express). Out of the nearly 600 people who tried out, Pittman was one of the last players cut from the Breakers. Looking to stick with football, he discovered the Randolph Oilers of the EFL and began playing semi-pro. Pittman, a plumber, father of four, and grand-father of two, was still immersed in football, coaching three other teams besides the Panthers with his limited free time: he was an assistant at Norwood High School; he coached Pop Warner in the South End; and he also coached a local women's professional team, the Bay State Warriors. He was in his second year as head coach of the Panthers.

Maybe it was just that . . . *friggin' neck*. Or those keg-crushing biceps. Or maybe it was the fact that he was the only guy who was yet to so much as crack a smile that night. Whatever the reason, his mere presence made me nervous, looking at me as if I'd already screwed up somehow and needed to be scolded. With a slight aura of curiosity and skepticism he approached and spoke, his deep, serious voice somehow drowning out the bass beat of the hip-hop that *had* been blasting from the low-riding Honda. (Yes, even Tupac Shakur deferred to Coach Pitt.) Reggie introduced us and we shook hands. It felt like I stuck my palm into a catcher's mitt.

"Where you from, Mark?" he asked me.

Did he mean "from" as in, *Where is your family from?* or *Where did you grow up?* or *Where do you live now?* And why was I at such a loss to decode what was, essentially, under normal circumstances, a pretty simple question?

"I live up near the State House, near the Common." Even though those specifics made the location obvious, I just didn't want to say Beacon Hill.

"Ah," he replied with a nod and a barely perceptible grin. "A rich boy."

Shit! So there it was. He assumed I was a blue-blood, cosmo-sipping dandy.

"I wish," I answered. I was no rich boy, although I could virtually guarantee that I was the only guy here who used Kiehl's skin-care products for men. I pointed at my used 1999 Jeep Grand Cherokee. "My apartment's about as big as my car."

Pitt nodded, still staring at me, sizing me up. Having already reached his conclusion on one front—I was slumming it here in the 'hood, no matter what cute little jokes I made about my small apartment—he now moved on to pressing football matters. "Can you kick off into the end zone?"

"Sure," I answered way too eagerly. I wanted to sound confident. All it sounded like was a chirpy, blatant lie. So I thought it wise to backpedal a bit. "I think I can. I've never really—"

Pitt stared.

"Yeah, I can reach the end zone," I concluded, clumsily changing tack.

He cocked his head ever so slightly. "All right," he said finally, sighing, resigned to the fact that Reggie and Delaney had unearthed his new kicker from some crosstown scrap heap. "I'm not sure if you'll play this weekend, but come on down to Brockton and we'll see what happens. Khary's usually our kicker. But we don't kick that much, to be honest with you. We'll see, though. If you're any good, maybe we'll kick more."

Thanks a lot, Coach. No pressure or anything.

Along with kicking, Khary—about six-foot-one with a slightly lazy right eye and a close-shaven head, except for a tiny little samu-rai-looking ball of hair clinging to the back of his skull—was a defensive back and punter. He turned upon hearing his name and then went back to chatting with two guys in white tank top undershirts: a massive D-lineman, Derek, who had light brown stretch marks on his arms and chest, clear signs of hours spent lifting ungodly amounts of weights in the gym; and an even bigger guy whom everyone just called, appropriately enough, Big Paul. He was the team's center, easily six-foot-eight, 350 pounds. Dude practically had his own gravitational pull.

The Panthers' 2004 EFL season opener would be against the expansion Brockton Buccaneers that Sunday, just three days away. But I honestly didn't expect to play; after all, this had been my first "practice" with the team, and the season opener probably wasn't the time for Coach Pitt—clearly not the freewheeling, loosey-goosey type—to experiment with aging rookies who'd never played the game before. Christ, I didn't even own a helmet yet.

"If you can kick it into the end zone, we might be able to use you," Pitt reaffirmed, possibly challenging my earlier positive response. I tried to look him back in the eye, but I just wasn't able to hold his intimidating stare. So I looked at his shoulder, his eyes, the top of his head, the players behind him, the *Pimp My Ride* low-riding Honda, anywhere but his eyes as I responded.

"Cool," I said, trying to sound more at ease than I was. But not playing was fine with me. Let me watch for now. I obviously had a ton to learn.

Coach Pitt was the only one I received even the slightest skeptical vibe from that night. He was the only one who seemed to wonder what the hell I was doing there. Can't blame him; all he had to judge me on were a few kickoffs . . . in khaki shorts and way-too-clean running shoes. Kicking with a helmet and shoulder pads, in front of a hostile crowd, while angry grown men try to possibly kill me? That's a whole different story. *Should I waste my time with this guy?* Coach Pitt's squint and cocked head seemed to ask. *Can he possibly make my team better, help us win games?* It wasn't going to be a cakewalk making a believer of Coach Pitt. But while I had no empirical evidence upon which to base this conclusion, I knew that I wasn't any coddled, soft white boy from the 'burbs. I had a strange feeling that he *would* be able to count on me in the clutch at some point. I *would* play football. *Real*, American, honest-to-goodness football.

The season began in less than 72 hours.

THE VILLAGE IDIOT

I TOOK A LEFT out of Franklin Park onto busy four-lane Blue Hill Avenue, took a left onto Columbus Avenue, and headed back to Beacon Hill, 15 minutes and several worlds away.

At a stoplight outside Roxbury Community College, I dialed my wife.

"Hello, ma'am. Guess who you're talking to?"

"Matt Damon? Please let it be Matt Damon," she teased. Celia and I had a "dream hook-up" rule: if she ever miraculously had a chance to hook up with Matt Damon, she could do so, *once*, with no marital repercussions whatsoever. Ditto for me and *my* free sexual pass, miss Natalie Portman. Win-win.

"Close," I answered, "but no. You have the distinct pleasure of talking to the incredible athlete who was just chosen . . . as the brand-new kicker . . . for *the* Boston Panthers." I let the notion hang out there, letting her think for a moment that (a) I'd beaten out 20 other contestants based on feats of strength and cunning, and (b) the Panthers were as hard a team to make as the Patriots.

A long pause.

"What does that even mean?" she finally asked.

"It means I'm now a semi-pro football player. I'll have games most weekends. I'll be handling kickoffs, field goals, extra points. They had a guy named Khary doing it, but even though he's a great athlete—plays D-back—he's not really a kicker. He's the punter, but I think I'm a better kicker, probably, maybe."

"Wait, slow down."

"I was nervous at first, I mean, I only went there to interview guys. But they were all really cool. Reggie, Donnie, Delaney, Insano—"

"Insano?"

"His real name is Darrell—and there's Mohammad, Todd, Caleb, Jeremy, Brandon, all of them. Not sure what Coach Pitt thinks of me yet, though. Guy kinda scares me, actually. I don't think he thinks I can kick, which, I mean, *I* don't really know if I can do it yet, but I don't think he was buying me." I laughed. "And he called me a rich boy."

She chuckled. "I can show him a 500-square-foot apartment that proves you're not."

"I know, but I said I lived on Beacon Hill. Probably thinks we live next to Jack Welch. I don't know. He just looked kinda . . . skeptical. But I'm psyched. I mean, I have no idea what I'm in for, or whether I *should be* psyched, and I have to buy equipment and everything, but this'll be cool, you know? Being down on the sideline and on the field instead of just watching from the stands." Silence. "Hello?"

Still silent. I took a deep breath, realizing I'd rambled on like a kid on his first day of school—a kid who probably *should have* been on Ritalin all those years ago—telling his mom about all the new friends he'd met.

Her silence was understandable. I figured she was still trying to process the "I'm actually playing football because it might make for a better book" concept. After all, unless one is undercover with the Mob or interviewing Russell Crowe, being a writer was supposed to be pretty much safe and nonviolent. A noncontact vocation. Rarely had I ever been chop-blocked while writing ad copy. And it certainly didn't require wearing a cup and a mouth guard. Plus, as far as she'd known, I had only gone to meet Reggie and the other players, take some notes, et cetera. So the fact that I ended up *actually joining* the team was a shock. To her, this was probably like my going to a Sox game at Fenway and returning to tell her I'd been named the team's new center fielder.

"I'm gonna be honest with you," Celia finally said, laughing. "And don't take this the wrong way, but—you don't play football."

"I know. I'm just the kicker, though." I reassured the part of her that saw our insurance premiums skyrocketing. "It's not like I'm playing nose tackle."

"I have no idea what that means," she said. "Have you even kicked a football before?"

"Yes." *No.* I tried my best to explain. "Look, when Reggie, the guy I talked to yesterday, said that they needed a kicker it just hit me: Why just sit on the sidelines and watch a season of semi-pro football when I can actually *be a part of* a season in the semi-pros? You know, the whole George Plimpton *Paper Lion* thing. And he played quarterback! Guy weighed about a buck twenty and talked with a heavy Harvard accent. Could have been snapped in half. Plus"—now the lies were really flying—"I've always wanted to be a kicker."

"What?" She laughed. "Since when?"

She was right, I had never once considered being a football kicker. Ever. Still, to help her make sense of it all, I had to at least pretend that this had been a lifelong dream that—finally—had come true.

"Since forever," I lied. "I mean, who *wouldn't* want to be in that Adam Vinatieri position, lining up a kick to win the Super Bowl?" Until today, *me, that's who.* But if I didn't sound confident about this crazy little scheme of mine, and convince her that this would be beneficial to both Mark the Writer *and* Mark the Man Who'd Always Been Semi-emasculated in Sports, Celia would light my uniform on fire the first time I came home with so much as a scratch.

There was another long, pregnant pause. Sports references were lost on her. She knew who Adam Vinatieri was, this being Patriots country and all; but she probably didn't know what the Pats' kicker had to do with the facts at hand, which were as follows: her idiot husband had just semi-accidentally joined an inner-city team to play a violent contact sport he'd never played before. Which also meant that her idiot husband's midlife crisis had arrived approximately 10 years early. What was next, trading in the Jeep for a bitchin' Corvette?

"Look, if you're excited about it, I'm all for it," she conceded, perhaps secretly wondering if our meager freelancer's insurance plan covered such things as appendage replacement. "Congratulations."

"They have a cheerleading squad," I teased. "We can get you into a short skirt—"

"Yeah . . . I'll pass."

Over the next few days word of my new athletic career started to spread. My brother, Doug, the former juvenile delinquent who somehow avoided jail and became a responsible, successful banker with a wife and one son, a second on the way, living in the Jersey suburbs of Manhattan, was as baffled as Celia, but as clearly amused by my new quasi-career choice.

"Do you mean with actual helmets and everything?" he asked. My four-year-old nephew, Drew, chattered away in the background. "Hold on a second, buddy," Doug said to Drew, "I'm talking to Uncle Mark. He's gone insane."

I sighed. "Yes, with actual helmets."

"And shoulder pads?"

"Yup. It's real football."

"Do you get paid?"

"No," I answered. "Most players actually pay to play—team dues for uniforms, field rental, refs, all that. You have a couple semi-pro leagues down where you are. They're all over the place."

"Have you kicked before?"

"No. But it's not *that* different than soccer."

"So what kind of skill level is it? Like high school or college or . . ."

This was a good question. I had only been to one practice so far, but I told Doug that the guys looked pretty damn good to me, anyway. Some had played high school ball and were hoping to get noticed by college scouts. Others had played some college (typically Division II or III) and were staying in shape for a possible NFL or Arena tryout. Others had had pro tryouts, or played Arena I or Arena II, but despite having abandoned the pro football dream, kept playing because this was the closest thing they could find. One or two rare cases had actually made The Show and gotten the proverbial "cup of coffee" in the NFL—whether it was as "training camp bodies" or on practice squads—and were still chasing that dream. (Tommy, a stout, speedy cornerback, had reportedly been the last player cut from the Buffalo Bills' camp the previous summer.) Others, however, hadn't really played real football in their lives other than pickup games around the neighborhood or flag

football, and just wanted to see if they could compete at an organized level.

"Have you gotten hit yet?" he asked, chuckling. I could hear a
hint of concern that any big brother would show his younger sibling.
That said, we'd also watched way too many Monty Python skits
growing up, so any concern for my physical safety was far overridden
by a twisted, comedic curiosity that wanted to see my head removed
from my torso by a linebacker.

"I've only been to one practice, and that was just a couple kicks.
They say players *do* like to take potshots at the kicker, though. On
kickoffs and stuff I could get hit, you never know."

"You going to take steroids?"

"Probably should. You have any BALCO connections?"

"And, just so I understand this, because the image of you playing
football is just too friggin' hilarious, you'll be wearing an actual football helmet and—?"

"Jesus, yes—it's real football, with referees, helmets, everything."

"And the team's in Roxbury, and you're the only white guy."

"No, there's one other white kid, kid named Joe. The rest of the
team is black and Latino, mostly guys from Dorchester, Roxbury,
Mattapan, pretty much all over the city."

He laughed. "So it's not exactly Beaver Cleaver."

"More like Eldridge Cleaver."

"This is awesome," he said, laughing. "You . . . in a football helmet.
Remember the Great Gazoo from *The Flintstones*?"

"Yeah, I do. Thanks."

He laughed again. "This is just . . . *awe*some," he repeated.
"Drew . . . say 'bye to Uncle Mark, okay? He's about to start playing
football."

There was a rustle of the phone being transferred from father to
son, followed by heavy breathing, followed by, " 'Bye Uncle Mark play
fuh-ball."

Doug *had* to give me shit about it; that was his job. After all, he
(soon to have two sons), my sister Leslie (three daughters), and the
rest of my family had all long been wondering when Celia and I—
married for three years at that point—would finally settle down,
move to the 'burbs, get normal, secure jobs, buy a house, and start
trying to make a few kids of our own. So every time I called and excitedly started off a conversation with *Guess what?* I'd get their hopes
up only to smash them by finishing the sentence with something un-

expected and idiotic such as *I'm now the kicker for a semi-pro football team!*

Well, of course you are, they'd say with a sigh, as if I were telling them I was joining the circus, and wonder if, despite our suburban upbringing, I'd somehow managed to be kicked in the head by a mule as a child.

While this football thing might have been just more proof that I was still avoiding that logical progression into rational, safe, child-rearing adulthood, Doug and the rest of my family, while probably secretly throwing up their hands in confusion, were enthusiastic and encouraging, even though the subtext of all their comments was more or less, "You're clearly out of your mind, but good luck anyway." That's what my family has always given me: a wonderful combination of unconditional support to encourage me to succeed in whatever I wanted to do, and endless mockery to keep me in line in case that success got out of hand.

Even Celia—again, she knew virtually nothing about football—still knew instinctively that kickers were the bottom feeders of the football food chain. When I told her that many semi-pro teams didn't even have full-time kickers (but instead had guys like Khary who played other positions and kicked because no one else wanted to, or could), she considered this for a moment.

"Well, that *does* make sense," she finally surmised. "If someone's taking the time to play semi-pro football, they probably want to play a *real* position, don't they?" Ouch. *Et tu, Celia?* But she and Alex Karras were right: kickers were the redheaded stepchildren of the gridiron, and I was possibly, willingly (masochistically?), joining their ranks. I might as well have just worn a single-bar helmet.

Speaking of entertainment at my expense, our friends Ben and Holly bore witness to the most pathetic display of all. Up at Ben's dad's lake house in New Hampshire, I spent a beautiful early summer weekend *not* outside canoeing, hiking, or swimming, but rather *inside*, learning how to put on my brand-new equipment. I had to practice. Unlike most football players, I hadn't had years of "uniform-putting-on" experience to fall back on. And I sure didn't want to face the possibility of trying—and subsequently failing—to properly don everything for the first time in front of my new teammates. There were only 48 hours and counting before my (potential) kicking debut versus Brockton, and I'd have enough trouble earning my new teammates' respect without running onto the field with my shoulder pads on upside down.

Getting the pads on wasn't as easy as slipping on a pair of soccer shin pads, but it wasn't exactly brain surgery, either. (The helpful guys at Grogan-Marciano Sports in Mansfield—a store co-owned by former New England Patriots quarterback Steve Grogan—had shown me how when they virtually dressed me up like a life-sized Hasbro Remedial Football Guy doll.) I quickly mastered the shoulder pads, and spent the next few minutes lightly bashing my shoulders into doorjambs, support beams, even Celia, who was trying to read on the couch. While she certainly appreciated what a complete pinhead I looked like, she didn't appreciate the impromptu tackling drills, and kept shooing me away with her book, as if I were an overgrown mosquito.

The next step, however—getting the jersey on *over the shoulder pads*—was nothing short of tortuous. I tried every conceivable angle and approach: yanking, tugging, stretching, pulling, tearing, wiggling, all to no avail. This almost ended my football "career" before it began.

I pictured having to tell Reggie and the other guys, *Uh, sorry guys, I can't be your kicker after all—I couldn't dress myself like a big boy.* After I'd nearly ripped my arms out of their sockets in fruitless attempts and was about to throw the whole bag of equipment into the lake, Ben calmly suggested, "Why don't you just put the jersey on the pads *first*, and *then* put the pads on?"

Ben didn't watch sports. He didn't even really *like* sports, far as I knew. And he sure as hell had no experience with the intricacies of football equipment. Still, he was able to take one look at my pads and know exactly what to do, whereas I looked like an oxygen-deprived astronaut wannabe trying to pound a round peg into a square hole with my fist before flunking out of the NASA training program. I was officially doomed. But Ben's suggestion did the trick. I slipped the white mesh practice jersey onto the pads—which, believe me, is much easier to do when there's *not* a body inside them—and then merely lifted the whole apparatus up, put my head through the opening, and lowered it back onto my shoulders. Snug. Done. Perfect fit.

I stood in front of the mirror. Looking back at me was, to my shock, a football player—that is, if football players wore nothing but blue bathing suits, shoulder pads, and stark white protective shells on their heads. If I walked down Main Street in Ossipee at that moment, the locals would have just assumed the village idiot had broken free of his backyard tether wire and was roaming the town, dangerously unsupervised. I had to at least get the stark white football helmet looking more like, well, a football helmet and less like a medical safety precaution.

I'm not what you might call "handy" to begin with; removing nails from our walls with the curvy end of a hammer—see, I don't even know its proper name—is the extent of my home improvement acumen. Sadly, the helmet came in two parts: (1) the hard, round, smooth, plastic shell that, I wisely surmised, would protect my skull from being kicked in by a marauding opponent; and (2) the afore-mentioned black face mask that I'd have to attach by myself. Because I typically start convulsing at the mere sight of instruction manual line drawings or anything that requires more than one step, I was hoping that the guys at Grogan-Marciano Sports would attach the mask for me. But legally they weren't allowed to for fear of being sued if, God forbid, something malfunctioned and a customer got his face smashed in. So I was now stuck with a Philips head screwdriver and two bags of plastic clamps, nuts, bolts, screws, straps, and other random parts that I'd be lucky not to accidentally attach to my thigh and/or Ben and Holly's poor dog. On top of that, Grogan-Marciano didn't have any helmets left in metallic silver—the Panthers' color, like the Oakland Raiders—so I'd been forced to buy a shiny white one and a can of Krylon metallic silver spray paint in the hopes that, if I painted the thing up in New Hampshire on Friday night, it'd be dry by game time Sunday.

Shockingly, despite not having received the "do it yourself" gene from my forefathers, I handled the painting well. As Johnny Bench used to say in the old Krylon commercials, "No runs, no drips, no er-rors." I dried it in the toolshed, strategically positioning two house fans plugged into extension cords, and then went to work on attach-ing the mask. Despite the disconcerting presence of several line draw-ings and Steps A through G, I somehow screwed the right clamps into the right holes, attached the right chin thingies to the correct snap whatsits. Not a washer was out of place. Finally I was staring at a sleek, silver football helmet with a black face mask. In a few hours it had morphed from something a drooling half-wit might wear into something that Randy Moss would wear.

My uniform now complete, I put everything on—cleats, calf-length socks, tight white football pants with thigh, knee, and hip pads; abdominal-length undershirt; shoulder pads and practice jersey; metallic silver helmet with chin strap attached—and once again braved the kitchen peanut gallery. I clomped in on the hardwood floors and just stood there, arms defiantly crossed at my chest, saying nothing. It wasn't until I cleared my throat that they finally stopped preparing dinner, looked up, and soaked in my new image.

"Good Lord," Celia said.

"Sexy or what?" I asked her. "I'll keep this on when we go to bed if you want."

"Only if you wear the protective cup," she deadpanned.

"Jesus, what are you planning to do to me?"

Instead of laughing at me, they laughed *with* me. Laughing because they couldn't believe the transformation I'd undergone. No, I would never have the body, the muscles, or the neck to fill out a football uniform and look like the prototypical gridiron warrior. I would look like—well, a kicker at best. But hey, it was a start.

KICKOFF (SORT OF)

"YO, DO THEY GET any smaller than number 63?!"

That was the unimpressive best of the many one-liners, followed by hoots, hollers, and howls that were already raining down upon me as I took warm-up kicks on the Panther sidelines at Marciano Stadium in Brockton, just minutes before my first football game ever.

Of all the teams in the EFL, Brockton was the one most similar to the Panthers in terms of racial makeup (more black than anything else). In fact, several Buccaneers had at one point played for Boston/Roxbury, and lots of guys knew each other. This was the Bucs' first year in the league, and when the team was formed, several players from nearby teams—Boston, Randolph, Charlestown, Rhode Island—joined the expansion franchise. They were tough, athletic, and fast, just like Boston looked in practice. Like the man for whom

their stadium was named, Rocky Marciano, and Brockton's other boxing legend, "Marvelous" Marvin Hagler, they would be a tough team
to knock out.

*"Yo, 63, you sure you ain't supposed to be playing at the Pop Warner
game down the street?"*

The heckling continued as I warmed up, trying to ignore them. A
couple fans in their late teens, early twenties, tops, had shown up for
pregame, and were already half tanked. The only time they *weren't*
yelling something derogatory at me, in fact, was when they pressed
brown paper bag–wrapped bottles to their lips. I could only imagine
how they'd harass me once they got *fully* tanked. Empty cans, in the
wrong hands, can become projectiles. I found myself wishing for a
suit of armor instead of just the shoulder pads and helmet.

But I couldn't blame them for exploiting the whole "size angle"
with their jeers. After all, I still didn't really look like a football
player; I looked more like something you'd see tumbling out of a dangerously overcrowded clown car at the circus. For starters, there was
my game jersey. In the locker room, Delaney had rummaged around
and, finally, pulled out number 63. A number like 63 was typically an
offensive lineman's number, ideally designed for men the size of your
average Frigidaire. As such, I swam in it, even after I'd tucked it into
my black pants, which he'd given me to replace my tight white ones.
The pants were also clearly designed for a man who had three or four
of my asses. The kneepads barely clung to my knees, and more or less
just floated inside the loose fabric, closer to my shins than my
kneecaps. My silver helmet felt giant, as if I were wearing a satellite
dish on my head.

Despite my less-than-heroic look, and the nervous (bordering on
scared) energy coursing through my veins, there *had* been a few posi-
tives so far. My fellow Panthers didn't seem to be too taken aback by
my presence when I first entered the locker room a few hours before
game time. I was just another player, and no one really paid much attention, which was fine by me. Truth be told, I'd basically hidden in
my car in the parking lot for nearly an hour. Overeager and antsy, I
suppose, I'd left New Hampshire *way* too early and consequently arrived in Brockton way too early, and really didn't want to be the first
one there, mainly because I had no idea what to do or where to go.
Thus I killed time in the empty parking lot by listening to sports
radio and—how embarrassing is this to admit in public?—actually
pretending to make cell-phone calls. *Don't mind me, I'm just another*

football player on an important phone call, probably to my agent who has other teams interested in my booming leg. I'll be there in a minute, fellas, don't worry: the kicker is coming.

After about an hour of these shenanigans, players on both squads began to roll in, most of them commanding vehicles worthy of semi-pro football players: Ford F-250s, Mustangs, Dodge Rams, and the occasional Harley. They were large, beefy men wearing sleeveless tank top T-shirts and carrying their shoulder pads by face masks that they'd inserted up through the head hole. I made a mental note: *Carry your shoulder pads like that so you look like you know what the hell you're doing.*

I gathered my stuff out of the back of the Jeep—next to the pick-ups and the Harleys, I felt like I was driving a pink VW Beetle. I made my way through the front gates, where volunteer ticket takers were already setting up a card table, chairs, and a metal money box.

Following some other players under the grandstands on the near side of the field, I reached the visitors' locker room. I paused at the door and took a deep breath. *Okay, Mark, no turning back now. . . .*

Faster than I probably should have—I was so intent on not being hesitant that I totally overdid it in the "Point A to Point B" department—I scuttled into the locker room, head slightly down, eyes covertly up. But truthfully, I had no idea where, exactly, I should have been heading. Worse, never having carried all this equipment in a relatively confined space before, I clipped the shoulder, and part of the ear, of one player who was bent over and pulling on his socks.

"Dang, yo, watch it," the player said, sitting up, wincing, and rubbing his ear.

"Sorry." *Shit. Shit shit shit. Nice start, you clumsy tool.* "Sorry."

Red-faced, I made my way to the far corner (thankfully without giving anyone else a concussion) and sat down at the entrance to the bathroom/shower. The shower? Oh, God . . . showers. I hadn't even considered *that* little nugget yet! Horrifying images of my prepubescent middle school days of postgym class showers and self-conscious, hairless, nondropped testicles flashed before me. While it might not come off as very P.C., I defy any man to put himself in a testosterone-filled environment such as the football locker room, where one's physical strength and/or manhood are constantly being judged, tested, questioned, and put on the line, and *not* think about certain, shall we say, "physical stereotypes" that have been perpetuated over the centuries. Oh, come on, you know what I'm talking about; don't pretend that you don't, Mother Teresa. And as long as we're being uncomfortably honest here, while I had always felt more than content with the size of, well, my "personal belongings," and any right-thinking individual knows that these are just stereotypes—same as white men being unable to dunk and/or dance (okay, in my case, they're both true)—I simply couldn't help but flash-forward to postgame, when I'd slip into the showers, perhaps still wearing my underwear, and stand under the water spray for approximately 10 seconds, hands cupped over my crotch, before slipping back out again and power-walking to my car, a trail of water, shampoo suds, and shame in my wake.

The locker room was a sea of black faces, black jerseys, black eye paint. Everyone was more or less in the midst of their pregame rituals, that pregame "zone"—stretching; breathing deeply, purposefully, in through the nose, out through the mouth; lying on benches with headphones and nodding in rhythm to a blaring portable CD player; or outside, getting taped up by Kelly Walsh, the team's trainer.

Kelly, 27, was a short, red-haired, take-no-bullshit spitfire who had the athletic yet feminine build of a gymnast and a brusk, all-business demeanor. The fourth of six children in a California family full of athletes—one of her older brothers played Division II hockey, one older sister and younger sister were avid softball players, and her oldest sister was in her college's sports hall of fame for rowing—Kelly had moved east to attend Northeastern University. After graduating, she worked with several colleges and high schools in the area before two trainer friends who worked for the EFL's Clinton Irish Blizzard and Charlestown Townies told her that the Panthers needed a trainer. She jumped at the chance, mostly because she was having a horrible time in her current job with Marlboro High School. "I was getting burnt out there. Overworked, underpaid, the football staff when I started had very little respect for my profession, very little respect for the kids. And the kids, in turn, were miserable to work with. It made me dread having to go to football practice and games. I just didn't want to be there. I started to question whether I wanted to do this anymore, and I almost switched professions." But then trainer friends gave her Reggie's contact info, and the rest was history.

"When I came and worked with the Panthers I saw really quickly that they were just . . . fun. They'd do something stupid on the field and it was like, 'Eh, whatever, guess I owe you a beer later.' They made me laugh, and were just out for the fun of it, for the love of it.

They reminded me why I loved doing what I did. It put a smile on my face, having that kind of relationship with my athletes that I could joke around and have fun, but also have a mutual respect level."

Her positive Panther experience helped her stick it out at Marlboro High. And when a new football staff came in, everything turned around. "The staff was a dream to work with, it carried down to the kids, and I would have missed out on that experience if I hadn't joined the Panthers. I would have missed out on taking my hockey team to the state championship, and my volleyball team to back-to-back state championships."

I'd never heard a trainer refer to his or her team as "my team" before, but it only made sense. Like the kicker, the trainer was a small, sometimes barely noticeable, yet utterly vital part of the bigger football picture. I immediately felt an odd kinship with Kelly. We were both seemingly insignificant, white cogs in the larger machine, just hoping to help the team win however we could.

Tucked away in my far corner, I began to get undressed. No one told me to get the hell out. That was a plus. Only Delaney really noticed that I'd arrived. I waved when he happened to look my way. After a quick nod of the chin in my direction, he paused, and then, as if just then remembering who I was, leaned over and rooted through a large steamer trunk full of jerseys and other supplies that lay on the floor in front of him. After a few seconds he dug out that gigantic number 63 and tossed it over to me.

Catching it, I felt like the little kid in the classic Mean Joe Greene Coke commercial. *Hey, kid . . . catch. Gee, thanks, Delaney!*

I unballed it and held it up in front of me. My very first football jersey. Black. White numbers. White stripes running down each side and ending in sharp points, and smaller versions of the same on the shoulders. I don't know what I'd done to earn it—nothing, really; just a few kickoffs in the dark three nights before—but I hoped that at some point I'd prove myself worthy of it.

Not wanting to be the only loser on the field with a generic, naked silver helmet, I walked over to Delaney.

"Do you have any more of those Panther decals?"

"Yeah," he replied—so far, Delaney, while a nice guy, was a man of few words—and once again started rooting through the equipment trunk and pulled out a sheet of decals. He meticulously planted the bounding, snarling black-silhouetted panther on either side of the helmet and then the two black stripes that ran front to back, right down the middle of the silver dome. He handed my helmet back to me and smiled. "*Now*, it's a football helmet," he said.

I held it up in front of me, in the light, and couldn't help but grin. The stripes were appropriate; I felt like a new recruit who'd somehow survived basic training and was now being given his stripes as a buck private. Whether I'd even see the battlefield was still up in the air—Coach Pitt hadn't even acknowledged my presence yet. If I had to watch and learn tonight, or for a few games, I could accept that; I was in no position to demand playing time. But as I held my Panther helmet in front of me and stared at it, I realized this was not a drill. It was 100 percent, brought-to-you-in-Technicolor real.

My helmet may have just been a baby step, sure, but it was nevertheless one more step to becoming part of the team. I started digging through my duffel bag for my cleats, socks, Under Armour padded spandex shorts, and all the other equipment that I hoped to put on correctly.

Just as I snapped on my pads and adjusted them into place, Coach Pitt and the rest of the staff entered. Pitt looked just as serious as before—eyes narrow slits of concentration, every muscle in his body tensed, as if he, all by himself, was going to take on the entire Brockton team. After some chalk talk with both offense and defense, Captain Insano started pacing around the locker room like a caged lion, getting right in the face of whomever he happened to pass. Off the field he was Darrell Jones, soft-spoken, polite, quick with a smile, a devoted father and soon-to-be-husband. But now, at game time, he'd obviously flipped the Captain Insano switch. Slamming both Thanksgiving turkey–sized fists on guys' shoulder pads, he started yelling at anyone, everyone. "*They've been talkin' shit all week, y'all! An expansion team, talkin' shit to us! We gotta show them that we ain't havin' none of that, know what I'm sayin'?! It's about respect, y'all! They don't want to give us any, then we'll go take it from 'em!*"

Guys yelled back in approval, slamming their locker doors, a few of them leaving visible dents. Others belted out low, guttural *whoof-whoof-whoof*s, the frenetic barking of some mutant junkyard dog on the other side of the fence that you can never see, but you just *know* has a missing eye and blood dripping from its fangs, remnants of the last kid who foolishly dared to retrieve his stray baseball.

"What time is it, y'all?" cocaptain and fullback Todd Mathies asked quietly.

"GAME TIME!" everyone roared. Through it all, Coach Pitt watched from the back of the room. He leaned back against the chalkboard, his muscular arms folded across his chest, the stance he was probably in when he came out of the womb. There was the slightest trace of a smile, but his eyes were all business. He knew from his own linebacker-playing days that getting fired up before a game, on one's own, without a coach's motivation, was necessary. He knew that guys like Insano had to flip their internal switches and become, in many cases, totally different people. But he also knew there was a balance that needed to be struck.

So as the frenzy began to calm on its own, Pitt gently pushed off the chalkboard with his back and headed toward the front of the room. Parting the sea of black jerseys, he stopped and leaned into several players' ears—last-minute instructions, coverage assignments, motivation, inspiration, and (to my surprise) even a joke, as Khary nodded and grinned widely as Pitt whispered something to him.

Pitt reached the front of the room and turned around to face us, a human fire hydrant wearing a tight white polo shirt. "Okay, gentlemen, bring it in tight, take a knee, grab someone's hand," he said. "This is a not just a football team, it's a family."

Now, I'd never been a religious man. My family was "Creaster" Episcopalian (i.e., we only went to church on Christmas Eve and Easter). So praying usually made me uncomfortable or, even worse, made me giggle, especially when Doug and I would try to make Leslie crack up during Christmas Eve services. But I'd be damned if I was going to giggle during *this* prayer. It was clearly something the team did not take lightly. What 10 seconds earlier had been a roomful of individuals had suddenly become one indestructible unit, like Roman soldiers on the front lines who kneel, raise their shields in unison, and form an impenetrable wall of bronze and steel to fend off incoming arrows. This was my first time in a football locker room and man, it was something to see.

Assistant coach Mike O'Neal, who helped Pitt run the defense, stood in the middle of the pack. "Heavenly Father, we ask for Your blessing as we prepare to take the field of battle. We ask that You watch over these players, and guide them to compete to the best of their ability, with honor, pride, and self-respect. We ask that You keep them and their opponents safe and out of harm's way. Finally, we thank You for blessing us with this great game of football, one which we will always use to teach us to be better men, and pass on what

we've learned to our teammates, our families, and our communities.
Amen."

"Amen," everyone said in unison, and I was surprised to hear myself saying it, too. We all stood up, and, as quickly as the players had
shifted into solemn, respectful prayer, they morphed right back into
prebattle mode. Coach Pitt and his staff filed out of the room ahead
of us, leaving the final pregame words to the captains.

"Are you ready?" Captain Insano asked in a calm, almost serene
voice.

"Ready!" everyone responded as one. Except me. I guess you
could say that I wasn't quite . . . ready.

"*I said are you ready?*" Insano repeated, louder this time.

"*READY!*" we responded, my voice a deeper timbre than ever before.

Insano then started hopping up and down gently, nimbly on both
feet, a 245-pound ballerina bent on destruction. A couple of guys
nearby joined him, and in no time, five, seven, 10, 20 guys were hopping up and down in unison, growling, smashing each other on the
shoulder pads with the same fists that were so recently joined in
prayer. I could almost *hear* the testosterone and adrenaline flowing,
louder and louder as Insano and the other players kept screaming, like
a raging whitewater rapid barreling down a mountain after a long
winter's thaw.

"ARE MY PANTHERS READY?!" Insano screamed this time, his
eyes closed tightly, fists balled at his sides.

"*READY!!*"

"We couldn't hear you!" screamed Khary, who wore number 4.
His slightly lazy eye lolled around wildly as he looked back and forth
at everyone, challenging each player to channel the deepest, darkest
part of his natural aggression. "WE SAID, ARE . . . MY . . . PAN-
THERS . . . READY?!"

"*REAAAADY!!*" the room exploded.

"What time is it?!" Ace, a defensive lineman, now demanded in
his gruff, raspy voice, cocking his head and cupping one hand to his
ear.

"*GAME TIME!*"

"WHAT TIME IS IT?!" he asked again, turning his head in the
other direction and cupping his other ear.

"*GAAAAME TIME!*"

"HOW Y'ALL FEEL?"

"FIRED UP!!"

"I SAID, HOW Y'ALL FEEL?!"

"FIRED UP!!"

"DAWGS?"

"WHOOF!"

"DAWGS?"

"WHOOF!"

"DAWGS?"

"WHOOF!"

Then . . . nothing. Silence once again, before, seconds later, Insano brought it to a rousing conclusion.

"LET'S BUST THESE MOTHERFUCKERS UP! PANTHERS ON THREE, PANTHERS ON THREE," he bellowed. *"ONE, TWO, THREE . . ."*

"PANTHERS!"

As one violent, churning unit, the players bounded toward the exit, hopping up and down, practically mauling each other right then and there, one unstoppable force of nature in which I was swept up. I'm not even sure my cleats touched the floor as we moved toward the exit. My uniform and helmet temporarily hid my true identity as an interloper. My teammates had no idea that a totally clueless rookie was underneath; they just saw the pads, the jersey, a fellow Panther! They slapped my helmet like anyone else's—that is, harder than I've ever been hit before in my life.

Mercifully, I was finally carried out of the locker room, under the grandstands, and spat out onto the field. As my teammates rushed past and around me like a river dividing itself over a rock, I stopped to take it all in. I wanted to savor this first-ever football moment, my first time on the field as a real player. The stadium lights reflected off of the perfect green turf and padded, orange end zone markers. The crisp, white yard lines shone in the Brockton night. The stadium announcer's tinny, muted voice read off player names, numbers, and other announcements to the fans who were getting settled in their metal grandstand seats. I smelled popcorn and grilled hamburgers and breathed in the sweet, humid, early summer air. This was exactly how I'd always imagined football should look at its very core, how it should taste, smell, sound. Sure, I'd seen countless football games from the stands, and zillions more on TV. But this was like nothing I'd ever experienced.

The team broke into five rows of 10 or so players each, stretching from the 30-yard line back into the end zone, and started its pregame calisthenics. I ran over and took a spot in the most remote corner of the end zone, trying to stay out of the way, and just mimicked what everyone else did: jumping jacks, toe touches, stomach stretches, push-ups. When the team broke up into offense and defense, Brandon, a 23-year-old-defensive back, turned to me. "Yo, Kick."

I looked behind me. It took me a second to realize he meant me. I pointed to my own chest.

"Yeah, you." He grinned. "Wanna warm up?"

"Sure," I said too eagerly, but stood where I was. I had no idea where to take practice kicks or, really, what to do at all.

"All right," he said, looking at me a little sideways, and then ran over toward the sideline, but stopped and turned when he sensed that I wasn't following him. "What the hell, man . . . you comin' or not?"

Like a puppy dog, I nodded and scuttled over to the bench. I grabbed a ball and an orange kicking tee out of my duffel bag.

Brandon ran about 40 yards down past the end zone and turned to receive my first kick. Trying to look like I'd done this a thousand times before, I backed up the way I'd done during my tryout, only this time there was a big difference: a black face mask cut off portions of my visibility, a big ol' helmet engulfed my head, and my shoulder pads, while not *that* heavy, weighed down on me, all in all making for an awkward approach, which was made more awkward when I saw Coach Pitt, who'd flat-out ignored me to that point, watching my every move.

I reached the ball, swung my leg with all my might, let loose a kickoff and . . . it hooked left, badly, barely four inches off the ground, and after traveling about 20 haphazard yards, almost drilled Coach Pitt in the legs. He deftly sidestepped the bounding ball—as I said, he was a former linebacker and, from all I'd heard, a damn good one—and then watched it die on the turf a few feet downfield. He turned back around and glared at me, eyebrows raised, as if to say, *My ass you can kick it into the end zone.*

Brandon retrieved the ball and tossed it back to me. I quickly teed it up again, hoping that Coach Pitt would stick around for some good kicks. But he instead walked over to Coach O'Neal, conferred with his assistant for a moment, and then headed back to the defensive unit. That was it. He was going to cut my white ass. And on the heels of the worst kickoff in football history, that's when I heard my first official football heckling from the stands to my right, behind our own sidelines.

"Yo, do they get any smaller than number 63?!" Yup, they never got tired of that one.

I regrouped for some more kicks that flew long and straight, at least 50 yards, most of them clear over Brandon's head, one sailing over Brandon's head *and then* over some fencing that lay about 20 yards *beyond* him, where a little boy holding a soda in one hand happily chased after it. My confidence was returning. I was getting the hang of it. But each time I glanced over at Coach Pitt, he was working with the defense and oblivious to his budding kicking star over near the sidelines.

Pregame ended and the Panthers jogged over to our sideline. Walking out to midfield holding hands five-across, the captains—Insano, Todd, Khary, Mohammad (an offensive lineman who'd worn the red mesh Northeastern University jersey at that first practice), and Southie (the starting quarterback)—met the Buccaneers' captains and the referees for the coin toss. *Please please please let us win the toss and get the ball*, I pleaded. *Please don't make me have to kick off first.* Ignoring my pleas, the five Panthers returned from midfield and informed us that we'd be kicking off to the home-team Bucs. Hands shaking, knees buckling, I grabbed the orange tee and started trotting out to the field as faux confidently as possible. And that's when Coach O'Neal pulled me aside.

"Hey, Mark," he said, putting one arm around my shoulder in bigbrotherly fashion, guiding me back toward the sidelines and leaning in so I could hear him through my ear hole. "Coach Pitt wants Khary to kick off tonight, okay? Maybe next game, after we've had some time to practice. Just watch tonight, take it all in, and next week we'll start working on some kickoffs and stuff like that. Okay? All right." He slapped me on the helmet and jogged away down the sidelines.

So that was that. Like the boozers in the stands—only far goofier-looking and, worse, more sober—I would be a spectator. Admittedly, I was a bit relieved not to be thrown right to the sharks (or the Buccaneers, as the case may have been), but I also felt an odd wave of disappointment. Nerves or no nerves, I had gotten myself ready to look my lifelong fear of competition and athletic underachievement and game-time failure in the face once and for all and say, *You want a piece of me?* But not tonight. I would have to wait another week, at least. I mean, who knew when—if ever—Coach Pitt would have confidence in me?

But, it's not like he should have had much confidence in Khary's kicking, either. Clearly a talented athlete, Khary nonetheless toed the ball, an approach that, while sending the ball flying long and far when he hit it on the sweet spot, still left too much room for error—as opposed to the more reliable soccer-style kicking. So in our first possession, after Southie unleashed a perfect deep ball to Sam (one of our three speedy, gifted receivers) in the first quarter, putting us up 6–0, Coach Pitt opted to try for the two-point conversion rather than have Khary (or, worse, yours truly) attempt the PAT. Coach had zero confidence in the kicking game. But, we also failed to convert the two points when Southie underthrew receiver Kieve Robinson on a quick slant.

And, sadly, that 6–0 lead was the last one we'd have.

Though we dominated on both sides of the ball, mental mistakes killed us. Especially on offense. Whenever we got close to the goal line, we committed penalties, one after the other, that backed us up five, 10 yards at a time until we were practically at midfield again. Yes, it was only our first game, but still, the lack of concentration was mind-boggling even this early in the season. Our poor execution wasn't allowing us to utilize our greatest weapons: our greyhoundlike wide receivers. Jeremy Collins was the team's best all-around athlete. A former standout basketball player at Cambridge Rindge & Latin (alma mater of future NBA Hall of Famer Patrick Ewing and Michigan 1989 NCAA tournament hero Rumeal Robinson), Jeremy had played a few years of Division I hoops at the University of Rhode Island. Like older brother and outside linebacker Caleb—a math teacher at one of my high school alma maters, Belmont Hill—Jeremy, 27, was a polite, outgoing son of a preacher and was a Cambridge firefighter. Delaney's cousin Sam Baptiste, 24, had played football and run track at the University of New Haven—where he was a teammate of the aforementioned *almost*–Buffalo Bill cornerback, Tommy— and had recently played for the Manchester Wolves of the Arena II League. While Sam was maybe five-foot-nine, shorter and thicker than his fellow starting receivers, and, unlike the outgoing, loquacious Jeremy, was extremely quiet (albeit affable), his almost sleepy demeanor was deceptive: his powerful sprinter's legs allowed him to burst off the line and kick into an extra gear. Jeremy was shifty and freakishly athletic; Sam, who also possessed nifty moves, was mostly straight-ahead burst, and was hoping to turn this season of semi-pro ball into a tryout with NFL Europe. Kieve Robinson, 24, rounded out the receiving corps. Kieve, aka KFC, while also fast and elusive, was more of a possession receiver: a lean, muscular, arm-tattooed six-footer who had great hands and was fearless over the middle. He ran a family painting business with his father, had a four-year-old son named Jamari, and had played at South Boston High School alongside Southie and offensive coordinator Leon "Fink" Finklea. Bottom line, these guys should have been giving the Buccaneers' defense fits. But the offense kept bogging down.

On defense, we suffered the same fate. While Insano, Pee Wee, Derrick, Aaron, Ace, and the rest of our solid defense—the pit bulls to the receivers' greyhounds—did manage to hold the potent Brockton offense and their scrambling Michael Vick clone quarterback in check, they still frequently got flagged for late hits, offsides, and other undisciplined penalties, all of which eventually handed the Buccaneers the game.

I watched alongside the other reserves and benchwarmers, most of whom, save for Elvis, were in their early 20s. Rome, short for Jerome, a rookie, gentle giant of an O-lineman, had just graduated school as an apprentice carpenter. Linebacker Gio Lopez, so called because of his middle name, Giovanni, was a property manager. His younger brother Lenny, also a linebacker, was a graphic design student. Soft-spoken Freddie Vicente, a safety/running back who lived in the Charlestown projects, was a data entry temp with John Hancock Insurance. A Head Start teacher named Sam Merejo exposed me to my first taste of football smack talk. When an enormous, large-gutted Buccaneer defensive lineman wearing number 99 jumped offside two plays in a row, Sam, who'd been harassing any Bucs' player who came within the slightest earshot of our sideline, cupped his hands around his mouth and yelled, "Yo, nine-nine, what's your hurry?! The center ain't snappin' *double cheeseburgers*!"

As the game marched on, I found myself seeing two diametrically opposed Panther teams. One was an athletic, sleek, fine-tuned, well-oiled Ferrari that roared up and down the field from 10-yard-line to 10-yard-line at will, smacking the Buccaneers in the mouth, taking the fight right out of them, and dominating the game in total yardage. *That* team was incredible to watch. *That* team was what I'd imagined semi-pro football should look like. I was amazed by the sheer speed of the game. Plays that probably looked slow to develop from the stands happened in the blink of an eye at field level—Southie zipping passes into the flat; Amos, our small but shifty running back, cutting outside on sweeps; Todd battering his way up the middle; Jeremy, Sam, and KFC blowing past frozen defensive backs; Insano, Derrick, and Pee Wee powering through the Bucs' offensive line. My new team seemed unstoppable.

But the *other* Panther team—the one that managed to make it to the Bucs' 10-yard line over and over and over, only to have the wheels fall off? That was a rusted-out Yugo *disguised as* a Ferrari. I don't know what it was, but whenever crunch time came, and we needed a crucial first down to keep the drive going, someone would do something stupid. Late hits. Offsides. Delays of game. Illegal formations. Holding. Mouthing off to the referees. That Panther team was undisciplined, selfish, mentally unsound, physically beaten down, lazy. The offense would sulk their way off the field, bitching, complaining, pointing fingers. We went into halftime tied at 6. After the half, we came out flat and never recovered.

The game-winning Buccaneer touchdown came with just a few minutes left on the clock on an interception return by a skinny, young-looking Bucs defensive back wearing number 23. Not that I enjoyed it, but there was certainly a sense of justice that I could appreciate. Number 23 had stoically endured cocky, interminable trash talk from our sidelines for four straight quarters. For whatever reason, Sam and our other benchwarmers had singled out this one guy and were just relentless, unleashing everything from mother and sister insults to barbs about his play. "Yo, two-three, you can't cover shit!" "Hey, two-three, you're afraid out there, I can see it, you're afraid!" "Two-three, you might as well just go home, you're not supposed to be playing with the men!" They rode him and rode him as our wide receivers beat him for big gain after big gain, time and again. But we could never turn those big gains into touchdowns. Number 23 bent but didn't break, and to his credit, he never let the incessant chatter from our sidelines get into his head. And when Southie let go a fluttery screen into the flat intended for Amos, who was swinging out of the backfield, 23 jumped the route, snared Southie's pass, and took it to the house for a 60-something-yard TD. Game over. On his way back to his own sideline, he made sure to hold the ball aloft for our now-silent sideline to see.

Final score: Brockton 13, Panthers 6.

As the seconds ticked down, all hell broke loose on our sidelines, thanks mostly to the pressure cooker tension that had been mounting with every stupid penalty, every offensive series that imploded so close to the end zone. Guys started screaming at each other, tossing blame around, finger-pointing. Defensive players screamed at the offense. Offensive players screamed at the defense. Everyone screamed at our offensive coordinators, Mark and Leon, for their apparent lack of creativity and inability to take advantage of our countless trips into the Buccaneer red zone. Mark and Leon fired back at anyone about anything.

It was chaos.

Then, for some reason, Donnie, the team's elder statesman and my would-be holder, and Cliff, a former player who'd joined the coaching staff for this, his first year out of uniform, were suddenly up in each other's face. As guys tried to pry them apart, Cliff took the conflict to the proverbial next level with a bitch-slap right across Donnie's cheek.

Donnie stared at Cliff, more shocked than angry. Cliff, waiting for Donnie's inevitable response, stared back. There was a brief moment of silence—a collective gasp and a wide-eyed sensation of *Yo, can you believe Cliff did Donnie like* that?! Donnie snapped: arms and fists flailing, eyes bulging, feet motoring and digging into the turf, bounding left and right, straining with everything he had to bull his way past the considerable bulk of Insano, Khary, and Mohammad, who'd stepped in as peacemakers and had formed a human tackling sled. Cliff was also being held back, albeit by only one smaller player. In my estimation, Cliff wasn't trying *that* hard to break free. He was no dummy: Cliff gave up about a 100 pounds to Donnie. It would have been like Michael Clark Duncan fighting Michael Jackson.

"I'll kill you, motherfucker!" Donnie wailed. "I'll *kill* you!"

The fans behind us watched in disgust and disappointment—except for my drunken hecklers, who jumped up and down and got each other into playful headlocks like an unruly crowd at a WWF steel cage death match. Packs of players pushed and shoved—defense versus offense, benchwarmers versus starters—stabbing fingers into each other's chest, tossing blame around, sulking and storming away, tossing helmets, kicking over water coolers, screaming obscenities and accusations at each other. And right in the middle of this skirmish, unbelievably, there were still guys complaining about a lack of playing time, even though most of them, from what I'd heard from the rebuttals, hadn't even been to practice that week. It was an absolute trainwreck.

Yes, after only four quarters of football, the team that just hours before in the locker room had been a family—praying together, joining hands, laughing, joking, cheering each other on, getting each other pumped up—and had been right in the game at halftime, was coming unhinged right before my eyes. Not wanting to be a part of it (okay, not wanting to get my ass inexplicably kicked), I just backed away—glad for the first time thus far that I was smaller and more inconspicuous than most—holding my Panther helmet against my chest, fearing that either (a) I'd be run over by one of the marauding scrums of players and engulfed by the chaos around me or (b) someone would snatch my helmet from me and use it as a weapon.

All jokes aside, I could only think, *I drove down from New Hampshire at 80 miles per hour for* this? *I bought 400 bucks' worth of stupid football equipment and inhaled toxic spray-paint fumes for* this? *I hoped to be a part of* this *bunch?*

It couldn't have been a worse start for me and the Panthers, many of whom were now threatening to quit outright or defect to other teams that didn't "diss them" and would "show them the respect they deserve" or "give them the run [playing time]" they wanted. After a halfhearted attempt by Coach Pitt, Reggie, and Delaney to restore order, and a half-assed team meeting in which we were admonished for our behavior and told to be at practice on Tuesday, everyone bolted, going their separate ways. Some stormed off to the locker room, others straight to their cars, speeding away with their uniforms—dirty cleats, helmets, and all—still on.

I silently headed back to the locker room, where I would just gather my stuff and get out as quickly and inconspicuously as possible, like a pale, thin, white ghost. *Poof! Number 63? What number 63? I didn't see any number 63.*

As I approached the runway under the stands, a large shadow appeared on the turf alongside me. I turned to see the bald-headed Reggie, his Letterman-esque gap-toothed grin in full bloom.

"So, you glad you came, Mark?" he asked, laughing and shaking his head in an *I'm too old for this shit* kind of way. Nothing seemed to faze Reggie.

Now, I'd seen sports-related outbursts before, both players and coaches: Latrell Sprewell strangling P. J. Carlessimo; Bobby Knight

chair-bowling; Kermit Washington sucker-punching Rudy Tomjano-
vich and almost putting his fist through his skull; the list goes on.
But while it's one thing to see such explosions on *SportsCenter* from
the safety of your couch, it's quite another to see them up close and
personal, in 3-D, on my own team, no less, between players who
were supposed to be teammates. Honestly, I didn't know what to
make of it.

"That was . . . interesting," I said. "Never seen a bench-clearing
brawl involving *one* bench."

"Welcome to the Panthers," he said with a laugh and ran ahead,
disappearing under the grandstands.

PRACTICE, PRACTICE, PRACTICE

FIRST INCORPORATED as a city in 1846 and annexed to Boston in 1868, Roxbury was originally named "Rocksbury" thanks to its hilly topography, known for its rich, arid farmland. In Colonial times, thanks to the same hills, it served as a strategic military outpost during the Revolutionary War. Over the decades it became a center of industry, with mills, tanneries, factories, and warehouses sprouting up along with tenements and row houses to house workers and their families. At around the turn of the century, the neighborhood was a diverse mix of German, Irish, and Jewish immigrants, and soon saw a huge influx of African Americans who'd journeyed north to escape the Jim Crow South. Later, with Dudley Square station serving as one end of the Boston Elevated Railway and part of the MBTA's Orange Line, people of all races and classes traveled back and forth to vibrant, bustling Roxbury to enjoy its hotels, silent-movie theaters, restaurants, department stores, and other hot spots of business and entertainment. Its jazz and dance clubs were frequented by the likes of Cab Calloway and Benny Goodman. "Boston Strongboy" John L. Sullivan, considered the first modern world heavyweight boxing champion, hailed from Roxbury. Petty thief and street hoodlum Malcolm Little spent some time in the neighborhood before converting to Islam during a prison stretch for armed robbery, during which he changed his name to Malcolm X. Roxbury-born Louis Eugene Walcott, inspired by Malcolm X, also joined the Nation of Islam, and ultimately changed his name to Louis Farrakhan and became the religious movement's leader. And, of course, let's not forget New Edition cofounder and 1980s pop/R&B star Bobby "Mr. Whitney Houston" Brown.

As was the case in most large cities, urban renewal in the '60s and '70s led to the neighborhood's decline. Today, despite a spurt of gentrification, along with Dorchester, Roxbury is one of the more hardened, gang-infested, crime-ridden parts of the city.

I drove on Columbus Avenue across Massachusetts Avenue, out of the "fashionable" part of the South End. In my mind, Mass Ave. had always been an informal 38th Parallel, quasi-demarcation line between "safe" and "unsafe" neighborhoods that I'd literally never crossed before the other night, despite living in Boston for nearly 15 years.

Practices were supposed to start at 6:00 P.M. sharp. I arrived a few minutes early, expecting to find everyone already there, waiting, stretching, salivating to put the debacle in Brockton behind them (er, us) and start preparing for game two, against no less than the defending EFL Super Bowl champion Middleboro Cobras. Instead, guys were sort of lounging around in the few spots of shade, or sitting in cars listening to music, or chatting on cell phones. I killed time the way I had before the Brockton game, checking voicemail messages I knew I didn't have, tying and retying my cleats, trying to look busy and in full prepractice preparation mode, et cetera. Even a full half hour later, guys were still basically just chilling out, many of them looking tired, bored, and even a little bit annoyed by having to be there in the first place. I knew this was a workingman's league and all, and guys had jobs, kids, wives, girlfriends, bosses, responsibilities. And maybe football practice was a pain in the ass, an obligation rather than enjoyment or a privilege. You might think that football would be a release from the strains and pressures of everyday life, something to look forward to. If that was the case, these guys didn't show it. As far as I could tell, we were looking at an 0–10 season.

We. Who did I think I was? I hadn't even so much as had a full conversation with anyone but Reggie yet, and even that was over the phone. I had no right to call myself part of a *we* yet. At that point, the Panthers were still very much a *they.*

After lacing up my cleats for the 38th time, I headed out to the practice field, carrying a brand-new Nike football I'd just bought at City Sports (after flipping the box over and over for several minutes to make sure it was regulation size; it would have been oddly appropriate had I shown up with a junior-size ball).

If not for the players dressed in football gear, you wouldn't have known that this portion of the park sandwiched between the two baseball diamonds was used for football at all. My first "practice"—those 10 or so tryout kickoffs—took place after dark, so while I had noticed that there were no goalposts anywhere near this field, it didn't really register until now. Clearly, a kicking game wasn't really on their radar. What the hell would I do at practices? Kick into the giraffe cages at the Franklin Park Zoo?

I sat down and started stretching out my creaky limbs, pretending that (ho, hum) this was just another football practice for me, and trying to look as relaxed as possible. There were a few guys nearby, two of them tossing a worn football back and forth, four or five standing in a circle, talking. I didn't say much to anyone. No one said much of anything to me, either. Not that they were *un*friendly—I got the occasional "hey, man" and "how ya doin'?" and chin nod—but it wasn't like my arrival was noteworthy. This was both good and bad: I wanted to blend in as much as possible, but I also wanted to at least start to get to know these guys and *not* feel like I was the new kid in school walking into the cafeteria at lunchtime, holding my tray of sloppy joe and wondering where the hell I was going to sit.

Suddenly I felt a slap on my back. Coach O'Neal. "How you doing, Mark?" he said as he passed by and headed out to the field, cigar clenched between his teeth, whistle around his neck.

"Hey, Coach," I said, but that's where the conversation ended. *No, you keep going, I'll catch up with you later.*

About 30 guys had now more or less assembled themselves in lines in front of Insano and the other captains—Mohammad, Khary, Todd, Southie—who were impatiently waiting for a few more guys to leave their cars, and the shade, and get out to the field for calisthenics and stretching. I walked out and inserted myself at the back corner of the far line.

"Let's go, y'all," Insano called out to the stragglers. For emphasis, he repeatedly struck the top of his helmet with his palm, like he'd done at the first practice I'd observed—*Whack! Whack! Whack!* "Time to get back to work!" Insano yelled, smacking the top of his helmet. "We gotta forget Brockton and get back to work!"

Captain Insano. Such a nickname implied a certain anger, rage, craziness, recklessness, aggressiveness, brashness, cockiness, none of which Darrell Jones displayed off the field. The off-field Darrell Jones, 24, was polite, respectful, but quick to laugh, with an endearing humility and honesty. Plus, as the third youngest of eight kids (four brothers, three sisters), he learned quickly that if you didn't control your emotions in a group and learn to channel the type of high energy and aggression necessary for success on the field when you were *off* the field, you could get yourself in trouble. "If you get too fired up, everyone else will come down on you," Darrell tells me. "My older brothers and sisters taught me pretty fast to be able to get fired up quickly, but to calm myself down quickly. I don't know what it is, just the way that I am. There's been times when I got mad or threw my helmet or something because we lost or a play didn't go well for me, but that only hurts the team, especially when you're the captain, because everyone else feeds off you. If you're not on top of your game, no one else is gonna be."

His skill was apparent early on. "We had tons of trophies for football, baseball, basketball, we played it all," he says, adding that all his brothers had played football, including an older one who played a couple of games with the Panthers in their inaugural season, and a younger brother who planned to join the team the following season as a nose tackle, being even bigger than Insano's six-foot-one and 245 pounds. Growing up in Roslindale in an athletic family, he was always the best football player in his neighborhood. At 13, he won defensive player of the year honors in a flag football league . . . a *19-and-under* flag football league. In high school, however, his path was blocked by older players until his junior year, when he got his first chance to start. But he didn't have a ton of extra time to devote to football practice. "I had to work," he says. "I needed money to get to and from school, pay for books, stuff like that, so I had to skip practice a lot to work." His father was a welder and his mother a halfway house social worker, so while not poor, the Joneses struggled to make ends meet. "Money was real tight growing up."

Then came senior year, and everything clicked . . . for a while, anyway. He was loving football, worked harder than ever before on conditioning, learning plays, formations, schemes. He started on offensive line and at middle linebacker. More important, he was starting to get some college interest. But it didn't last. Darrell had to miss practice time once again to work and make money for himself and his family. "I couldn't do it no more, I had to stop coming to practice. I still made all the games but the defensive coordinator sort of benched me, said I was only going to play in certain situations. So I didn't get many college looks. I was hurt by it because I was a senior, and this could be the end of my whole career, ever, so I was like, Gimme a chance to play, you know? But it wasn't happening."

Despite his lack of playing time, after graduation he went on to Curry College, a Division III independent liberal arts college in suburban Milton, Massachusetts. He only played one season for the Colonels, however, his freshman year.

"It was a good program, but it was real time-consuming, especially for a school that didn't offer scholarships," Insano says. "They were asking a lot: go to study hall, go to practice, go watch game film, go get treatment, get into the gym and work out. I did all that. But in the end I wasn't gettin' the respect I deserved."

Nowadays, whenever a professional athlete talks about respect (or lack thereof), it often comes across sounding like a whining, clichéd sound bite. If not for the mute button, these comments could sometimes render SportsCenter unwatchable. But when Darrell talks about not getting respect, it doesn't sound insincere or inaccurate. He was an underprivileged kid who realized that despite hard work and good attitude, he still wasn't being given the opportunity he deserved. Even teammates who were getting his playing time said he should have been playing in front of them. But for whatever reason, the coach didn't see it that way. "It might have been because I was injured—I dislocated my shoulder—so maybe he was just saving me for whatever reason, or maybe he just didn't like me? I don't know, but it was painful. It was just another case of someone doubting me, and no matter how much you believe in yourself, sooner or later you might start to listen to the doubters."

And what resulted was the biggest disappointment of all: he lost the love for football. Didn't want to ever play again. Stopped going to games. Couldn't watch it on TV. And the day before the last game of his freshman year, Darrell quit the team. A year later he left school entirely. "It was just too expensive," he says. "It was like thirty thousand a year my sophomore year. Financial aid did help me out, but it wasn't enough. So just like in high school, I had to keep a steady job, and my grades started slipping. So finally I just left."

For the next two years he worked at various hourly jobs and weighed his options. But then a cousin told him about a (now defunct) EFL semi-pro team, the Quincy Granite. After watching a few of their games, he felt that familiar urge to be out on the field mixing it up. He missed football more than he thought. But when he went to practice one night with the intention of joining the team, the Granite coach had other plans. "Before I even stepped on the field, he said, 'You're not going to play for this team unless you're a diamond in the rough . . . and I just don't think you are.' I thought it was wacked that he could make that judgment without even seeing me play. I knew I wouldn't get a shot, so I said, forget it, I'm going to go to this new team, the Roxbury Panthers, and see what I can do over there. It's a new franchise, maybe they could use me."

It was with the fledgling Panthers in 2002 that for the first time in his life, he felt he would be given a *real* opportunity to show his stuff. "It was an awakening. Everybody accepted me from day one. And now that I guess I'm a veteran, I try to make sure it's the same for other new guys. We accept new players the second they step on the field. Like with you. We didn't care that you'd never played football before, or where you came from or whatever. We saw you could kick that first night you came out, you could help us, and that was that. I always try to just treat people with the same respect I want to be treated with myself."

Joining the Panthers was a turning point. "I always believed I was a good football player. People said I'd never play in college, but I did. Only a year, and it was only [Division III], but I played. They said I wasn't good enough to play semi-pro, but I'm playing semi-pro. It's not the NFL, but it is semi-professional football, the best football for people who really love the game."

"Soon as he walked on the field we saw something in him, immediately," Coach Cliff says of Insano. "He was shocked when I said,
'You're gonna captain the defense.' He was like, 'Huh? I haven't been
on the team for a day yet!' We just seen it in him, ya know? Whatever
that 'it' is, we saw it in him."

Insano was now using that indescribable "it" to persuade the stragglers. "We all gotta work, we all got stuff to do, but we gotta be out
here on time!" Insano's having to cajole guys onto the field didn't
amuse Todd.

"We're oh-and-one, man, and that ain't good enough!" the fullback yelled, pumping his helmet in one hand for emphasis, his eyes
narrow slits of frustration. "We lost to an *expansion team*! Get your
asses over here and let's get to work! We got two weeks to get ready
for the champs, fellas. Let's use every minute of it!" Thanks to a
schedule quirk and an uneven number of teams in the EFL, we had
a bye in our second week. We wouldn't be facing the Cobras until
July 17.

As I placed my helmet on the ground beside me and started
stretching just to look like I had a warm-up regimen, I noticed a familiar face under the helmet in front of me. "Hey, Reggie," I said.

Reggie turned and greeted me with the same friendly, gap-
toothed grin he'd left me with after the Brockton game. "So you decided to come back," Reggie said, laughing through his black face
mask, which alerted me to the fact that everyone else had their helmets on. So I quickly put mine on, yanking it down over my ears and
uprooting a few innocent clumps of hair. No wonder so many football
players had crew cuts or were shaved bald. "Thought you'd change
your mind about playing with these thugs."

"That was pretty wild," I said.

He shrugged. "Par for the course with these little bastards. It ain't
the first time that's happened. Last year, in preseason, a coach and a
player got into an argument. They were in each other's faces, guys
pulled them apart, we thought it was over. And then the player starts
walking away, but then winds up, takes like four running steps, and
WHAM!, just cold-cocks the coach across the skull. Coach's eyes

rolled into the back of his head and he just dropped. I seriously thought he was dead. All hell broke loose." Reggie laughs. "It was like the Ultimate Fighting Championship. Some guys were on the coach's side, other guys were on the player's side, and they all started running to their cars to get their guns and I thought it was going to really jump off before everyone finally calmed down. It was crazy."

I nodded. *Guns? Assaults with helmets?*

Reggie watched two of the energetic younger guys goofing around, getting each other in headlocks, and shook his head. "I wish you could take my head and put it on their bodies," he said. "Some of these little bastards don't take this game seriously, don't know what they're wasting. It goes so fast. If you took my experience and their youth, you'd have a helluva player. But they'll learn soon enough. You think it'll last forever, but it never does."

Even though I was a rookie, my age, I assumed, excluded me from this "little bastard" group. I felt an immediate kinship with the old guard. I felt I'd probably have more in common with the coaches than with most of my new teammates. Coaches Pitt and O'Neal were in their early forties, and the recently "retired" Coach Cliff was 38. As far as I knew, I was the third-oldest active player on the team after Donnie (41) and Reggie (38). Delaney (36) was a year younger than I was. After that, the team was stocked with guys who were in diapers when I was getting my driver's license. Brandon, Jeremy, Southie, Insano, Big Paul, twin offensive linemen Jason and Anthony, Mohammad, my fellow sideline reserves during the Brockton game—all were in their early to mid-20s. Ace, Caleb, Pee Wee, and some others were right in the middle, in their early 30s.

Coach Pitt blew his whistle and ordered us to come over and take a knee. He glared at us, exhaled long and slow, gathering his final thoughts, and then spoke in low, measured tones.

"I'm embarrassed for you not just as players, but as men. People were watching. Women. Kids. Potential sponsors. And you acted like animals, like the thugs that people already *think* you are. Fighting. Using the n-word. The EFL needs fans, and you go and put on an embarrassing display like *that?* If you want to argue with coaches, fight with your teammates, fine. But do it somewhere else. You won't be missed. And if you think you can play that way against the Cobras, you're crazy. A veteran team like the Cobras will eat you alive if you don't start playing—and acting—like men."

Pitt sounded calm, but veins were bulging on his temples, on his thick neck. His fists were clenched. "Captain Insano, do you think we're capable of playing like men?"

"Yes, sir," Insano replied.

"What about you, Prince?"

Respected, well liked, Mohammad Bitahi was only 23 but carried himself like a 10-year veteran. A Northeastern University graduate who worked for a software company north of Boston, his family hailed from Morocco, and the guys often kidded him about being Moroccan royalty: riding camels, having harems, and living in castles. Hence his nickname, Prince. "Hell yes, Coach," he answered with conviction.

"Anyone here think we're *not* capable of playing like grown men?" Pitt asked.

"No, sir!" everyone replied in unison.

"What's that?" Pitt asked, cocking his head.

"No, sir!" Our voices—even I found myself chiming in—carried all the way over to a softball game on the adjacent diamond. The right fielder, holding a beer in one hand, momentarily turned and shaded his eyes to see what the commotion was all about.

"I want a full lap," he instructed. *"Both fields*, no shortcuts . . . and then, captains, line 'em up."

Most of the team quickly completed about a half-mile jog around the fields and gathered back where we'd started. Some of the "less conditioned" players, however—okay, the fat guys—still toiled a good hundred yards behind, jog-walking past drunken softball fans who taunted them, holding out beers and hot dogs like spectators offering cups of water at a marathon.

"Looks like the Klump Family 10k," a voice behind me cracked. I turned to see Ace, the lanky defensive end, standing next to his fellow D-lineman, Derek, broad-chested and muscular under a white tank top, doubled over laughing and stomping one foot, his hand on Ace's shoulder for support. I couldn't help but chuckle myself.

"Someone call nine-one-one," another player cracked. "Those big niggas gonna *explode*!"

Ignoring the laughter, Insano started clapping, smacking his helmet, urging the stragglers on. "Way to work, big fellas! Bring it home! Few more yards!" Still clapping, he turned to the rest of us, and his face said it all: start cheering or you will pay dearly. Wisely, the laughter trickled out and we cheered the big guys on until they stumbled across the imaginary finish line, panting and heaving, and collapsed into the grass.

We formed lines and the captains led us through a battery of stretches and jumping jacks, or "Panther jacks," as Khary called them.

"On your stomachs," Insano ordered when we finished our Panther jacks. We got into push-up position and he led us in a set of 20. And then another. At the end of the third set, he began pausing in mid-push-up, his body board-straight, thick arms bent at the elbow, shaved bald head protruding from his pads and moving from side to side, like a cobra, grinning, just waiting for the weak to drop.

"Hold it . . . hold it," he ordered, as guys grunted and exhaled in short little bursts under the strain. *"Hold it . . . not done yet."*

"Aw, this is some GI Joe boot camp *bull*shit," the guy beside me, a reserve defensive lineman nicknamed Sugar Bear, muttered.

"With them big ol' titties, Bear, you more like GI *Jane*," someone else chirped. The back corner broke out laughing like the bad kids in class, just as Insano mercifully ended the final set of push-ups and a fleet of torsos hit the ground with a dull *oomph*. Beads of sweat ran down my forehead into my eyes, a salty sting trying to burrow under my contact lenses. My arms shook and my elbows felt like they'd pop right out of my skin . . . but I hadn't stopped pushing. I did all of them. Barely.

Guys rolled over onto their backs, panting, removing their helmets. While some were clearly in great shape—Pee Wee and Derek looked like they tossed 50-pound free weights around like Frisbees, and receivers KFC, Sam, and Jeremy were lean, fit, Olympic sprinter types—the team as a whole clearly wasn't overly fit. I hoped Kelly was trained on defibrillator paddles.

"Keep those helmets on, gentlemen!" Pitt ordered. "This isn't field hockey. On your feet. Five lines across, facing me." Sprints now. He moved about five yards farther away after each set. Shuttle runs: 10 yards up, back; 15 yards up, back; 20 yards up, back. Soon, guys were doubled over, hands on knees, coughing up internal organs, but my wind was good thanks to running along the Charles all summer. I finished first or second in my group almost every time.

"Fourth quarter, gentlemen," Pitt called out. "You'll remember this when you need extra gas in the tank. We *will* be the best-conditioned team in this league. Count on it."

As I won another set and went to the back of my line, I heard voice call over to me.

"Yo, kicker!"

Startled, this being the first time anyone had really singled me out, I turned to see Todd, in his trademark royal blue practice pants, hands on his hips, panting, glaring at me. "Just kick! *Kicker.*" He spat "kicker" in his slight South Carolina accent as if it were a swear.

A bunch of guys looked over at me, waiting for my reaction. Was he just kidding? He wasn't laughing. *Just kick?* What Todd clearly meant was, *Stop being such a running hero and showing everyone up, and just fucking kick.* Breathing heavily, I said nothing and looked away.

I purposely finished last (or close to) on each remaining sprint. But I didn't feel good about it. An oddly competitive voice in my head chastised me for tanking. *Why should you dog it to make them look better?* Pitt finally blew his whistle, ending the *Full Metal Jacket* portion of the program. "Defense with me," he ordered. "Offense with Fink and Mark." Mark Harding was a former EFL player (he'd won an EFL title in the '90s with the Randolph Oilers) and ran the offense along with Fink. Off the field, Fink (who was also nicknamed "Cerebral" by a few of the guys for his offensive schemes) was ironically more concerned with defense: he was a federal law enforcement officer at the Federal Reserve Bank in downtown Boston. And we're not talking rent-a-cop here—Fink went through the same training as any other police officer or SWAT team member, and had official power of arrest for federal (but not city or state) offenses. At well over 200 pounds, he was heavier than he'd been in his playing days, but he still had a competitive spirit.

"No lying down, fellas," Fink barked, echoing Pitt. "On the hop!"

Guys broke off with their respective units. Me? I had no idea what to do. I *had* no unit. And there certainly wasn't any special-teams coach. So I grabbed my ball and went to the far baseball field that had a high backstop behind home plate that would at least make for *some* kind of target. Problem was, I didn't have a holder—human, mechanical, or otherwise—so, like MacGyver, I improvised. I found a crushed McDonald's soda cup, ripped it in half, crumpled and bent it into a half-moon shape, placed it just in front of the pitcher's mound, and leaned the ball against it. It wobbled in the wind, but stayed up. I had my holder.

As coaches' whistles chirped behind me and the sun dropped over the trees, I kicked my lone ball into the backstop, aiming for the high center section, pretending it was the center of actual football uprights. Each one slammed into the chain link fence with a loud metallic rattle, after which I'd jog over, pick it up, jog back, tee it up, and do it again. Five extra points from near the pitcher's mound (about 17

yards). Five from second base (about a 30-yard field goal, I guessti-
mated). Five from the short outfield (about a 40-yarder). I even
started having a little competition with myself: I couldn't move on to
the next set/new distance until I'd booted all five directly into the
top-middle section of the fence. If I hit only four, even if I hooked it a
foot left or pushed it a foot right, I'd have to start all over from the
same spot. I laughed, imagining what Celia would say about this utterly atypical display of anal-retentive discipline.

The extra points I hit easily—when the ball didn't topple over on
my approach thanks to its makeshift holder, that is—soft chips high
and straight. And it felt good. Moving back, however, my accuracy
waned. I hit only three of five from 30 yards. *Do it over,* that strange,
competitor's voice told me again. *You don't move on until you hit five
straight, you little Nancy boy.* Next set, four of five. Shit! Wind blew the
last one wide! *Stop bitching about the wind, Sally, and compensate for it
next time. Do another set.* Four of five. *Do another set.* Stop riding me.
Let's see *you* hit five in a row from 30. *I'm not the one who has to do it
in a game, you are, so stop your crying and do it.* Perhaps only to shut
this annoying voice up, I bore down and cranked five straight bombs
dead center. Take that, fucker! *Goody for you. Now move back 10 more
yards.* I did, and eventually, after a few shanks, hit five straight from
that distance, too. Yes! I pumped my fist after the last ball slammed
high into the fence and dropped back down to the dirt around home
plate. Then I turned around to make sure no one had seen me.

All said, I got in maybe eight sets of five (along with several sets
aborted by missed attempts). After about 45 minutes, as tired from
the endless ball-retrieval as the kicking itself, I finally headed back
over to the offensive drills, battered, scuffed ball tucked under one
arm. As I stretched, I watched Southie zip passes to Jeremy, KFC, and
Sam, and Amos slither between the tackles on running plays.

O'Neal sidled up alongside me, smoking a cigar. He nodded toward the far baseball field and the backstop. "I saw you getting in
some work over there. You got a good foot."

"Thanks," I replied. I decided not to tell him about the little contest I had going with my internal Lombardi. Didn't want him thinking I was, well, insane.

"Sorry you didn't get any play down in Brockton."

"That's okay. You guys have to see if I can actually kick first,
right?"

He nodded. "Pitt needs to be convinced, yeah. But I saw you

booting the shit out of the ball over there. I'm not worried. I played soccer, too, at UMass. I can tell when someone has a good foot, and you have a good foot. I'll work on Pitt."

Toward the end of full offense vs. defense drills, a scrum of players suddenly started pushing and shoving. A couple of guys were trying to pry Ace off one of the big twins (Jason or Anthony, I couldn't tell which). Ace had the twin's face mask clenched in a death grip and looked like he was trying to twist his head off. Mohammad and Insano finally wrenched Ace free and dragged him off to one side as the big twin, shorter but wider, laughed and walked away. The two captains counseled Ace even as he occasionally tried to break away from them and go back after the twin. Shades of Brockton all over again. "How come everyone *always* thinks I'm the only one startin' shit?!" Ace shouted. "Everyone always points the finger at me, I'm *always* the bad guy!"

"That's because trouble follows him everywhere," muttered Delaney, now standing beside me watching the scuffle. "Same thing every year. Guys are too forgiving, they believe his shit when he says he's gonna turn a new leaf, but he never does. No wonder we've never beaten teams like Middleboro or the Shamrocks. We can't even stop beating up on ourselves."

While the Cobras were a perennial EFL power, with championships in 1973, 1974, 1976, 1979, 1988, and 2003, the Marlboro Shamrocks were the league's true dynasty: 18 EFL titles, seven USFA national championships, minor league football's "team of the decade" for the 1990s, and holders of every EFL Super Bowl championship since 1991—11 straight—until the Cobras finally broke the amazing streak in 2003.

"We've never beaten Middleboro or Marlboro?" I asked.

Delaney shook his head as Ace threw his helmet, which bounded toward the parking lot and slammed up against a small, wooden fence. He stormed off after it, stripping off his jersey and shoulder pads and throwing them, too. Mohammad and Insano—reluctantly, it seemed—started after him.

"Let him go," Delaney called over to them. "If he wants to quit again, let him."

Whether we'd get our heads together in time for Middleboro was anyone's guess. But it didn't look good. If Marlboro was the New York Yankees of the EFL, we were the Tampa Bay Devil Rays.

TAKING ON THE CHAMPS

THE GOOD NEWS? Game Two was finally here, another chance to possibly get in and see what I could do. The bad news? It was against the defending EFL champion Middleboro Cobras.

At least it was our home opener, at English High School. Founded in 1821, English was the oldest public high school in the United States, and had produced such notable graduates as financier J. P. Morgan and actor Leonard "Mr. Spock" Nimoy. It was now home to 1,200 students from more than 40 countries. The field itself lay between busy Washington Street at one end zone and a parking lot and basketball courts at the other. With brand-new FieldTurf, grandstands running the length of our home sideline, and bright stadium lights, it was like Gillette Stadium compared to our dumpy Franklin Park practice field.

The game was at six. Coach Pitt said he wanted everyone there at 3:00 P.M. sharp. Yet, when I arrived on time, I was the only Panther there. Not a soul around. I briefly panicked. *Did I read the schedule wrong?* Anxious, I stretched a bit and watched a legion baseball game being played on an adjacent diamond. (This was my first real exposure to what Donnie and my other teammates called CPT, or "Colored People Time." Apparently Caucasian people tell time differently.)

After an hour or so, guys finally started rolling in. Rome. Kamiki. Sugar Bear. Each of them went out of his way to walk over and give me a hand-slap greeting. Soon the younger set of twins on the team, Chezley and Chelston, aka the Twinkies, also showed up. At 18, they were the youngest players on the team, having just graduated from West Roxbury High. The Puerto Rican contingent of Elvis, Lenny, and Gio rolled in soon afterward, chattering away and effortlessly jumping back and forth between English and Spanish. Then came Stanley, an outgoing young kid with distinctive reddish-brown hair who'd been named the special-teams captain. He wanted to be a cop and was planning on taking the Police Academy entrance exam either here, or in New York, where his cousin was in the NYPD; Jason and Anthony, the big twins, Jamaica Plain natives who lived right up the street, arrived. Walking toward the group side-by-side, broad chests naturally puffed out, I saw they brought with them the two pregame staples they apparently never went without: (1) their battered, duct-taped, paint-stained boom box, quite a throwback in this day and age of iPods; and (2) Jason's black pit bull, Bruno. Even when cranked up to 11, the box produced little more than ear-splitting static from what, I would quickly learn, was their *only* pregame music: former Soundgarden Chris Cornell's new band, Audioslave. Wouldn't have guessed they were Grunge guys.

"Damn, man, can you at least play some *real* music?" complained Coach Cliff, who'd just shown up and winced as the twins passed by. "Gimme some Lloyd Banks. Gimme some G-Unit or Fitty. We gotta crack some Cobra skulls today, baby, and this depressing Kurt Cobain rainy-ass Seattle Starbucks shit ain't gonna help!"

The twins walked right by in perfect stride, buried deep in their pregame trance, not even noticing Cliff's protests. Bruno, however, growled at Cliff, sizing him up as an appetizer.

If there was one thing Cliff Braithwaite loved more than football, it was music. Prior to a jail stint in the '90s for a domestic charge, he'd been living a fast life as a DJ, club emcee, and budding A&R guy for a local record label. Almost every night of the week he attended shows, schmoozed current and potential artists, and did whatever it took to move up the chain. Drugs, booze, women, guns—in his 20s, his life was something straight out of a rap video.

His jail time, while no vacation, turned out to be an oddly welcome break from the breakneck speed he'd been traveling. "I had a lot of time to think about how I was living my life, and it led me to gain a stronger belief in the Lord," he tells me. "Prison was a spiritual wake-up call for me. Even though I'm not big, dudes didn't mess with me too much on the inside. I was an O.G. from Humboldt [Avenue, a notorious stretch in Dorchester], and dudes also knew me from the music stuff. Plus," he adds, laughing, "I worked in the kitchen so guys would always try to get on my good side because I had the hook-up on snacks, drinks, and food." Without having to sweat some of the normal problems behind bars, Cliff was able to hang out in his cell and read the Bible, which ultimately helped him learn how to rein in the one thing that had always haunted him (such as at the end of the Brockton game): his temper. "I used my jail time to try to learn how to control my anger. I know I have a problem with my temper, and even though I didn't do what she [his former girlfriend] said I did, what got me locked up, I accepted that this was the Lord's way of telling me to slow down or else I was going to die young."

Even when he was living hard and fast, football was a love and a diversion for Cliff. He played Pop Warner as a kid growing up in both Dorchester and Newton; played at English High; and, despite being small even for a defensive back, had several tryouts with pro teams on both sides of the American-Canadian border. At age 22 he even tried out for a few NFL teams during the strike year of 1987. "They used to have scouts coming to EFL games, looking for scab players," he says. "A few noticed me making some plays. I tried out for the Patriots. I tried out for a few CFL teams, too, like the Ottawa Rough Riders." However, even though he was a good athlete, he wasn't much bigger than I was, maybe five-nine, 160 soaking wet—doable for a kicker, but not for a pro cornerback. "Every single tryout they'd tell me, 'Cliff, man, we love your skills, but any chance you can get bigger and come back next year?' My size just kept working against me. I eventually saw that the Lord had a different plan for me than a future in football."

Before finding a more spiritual path, however, Cliff's sexual exploits hadn't been exactly holy: he has 10 children with five different women—"That I know of," he adds, only half joking—five boys and five girls ranging from ages five to 18. "Some dudes are addicted to booze. Other guys are addicted to drugs," Cliff says. "Sex was my addiction. Women and sex." During his music heyday, he lived under the same roof with two of the babies' mothers and several of his children. "At the time, I thought I was cool, a real tough guy, sleeping with two chicks at once, all that bull-jive gangsta stuff," he says, shaking his head, the passing of time letting him reevaluate his wild youth. "I was making a lot of money working for the record label and dee-jaying, and was throwing money around left and right like a real playa. But now I realize it was just stupid, know what I'm sayin'? My priorities were messed up."

A little older and wiser, he now just wanted to be a good father, and worked part-time at a local church running the PA system during services. "I want to give my kids all the things I never had growing up. Ant [Anthony, his oldest] is a good student and a good football player, and I'd love for him to get a scholarship somewhere. If it's a football scholarship, great. But I'd be even happier with an academic scholarship. After all the shit I been through, my goal in life is clear now: I want Ant to be a better man than I ever was. With the Lord's blessing, he's gonna be a better man than me."

By five o'clock, only an hour until kickoff—I couldn't help but wonder whether I'd actually be doing the kicking off this time—most of the team had arrived. There had to have been at least 45 guys there, all in various stages of dress, scattered up and down our sideline. The English High locker rooms cost an extra 500 bucks, which Delaney didn't want to pay. Hence the sidelines were our de facto, au naturel locker room. Guys either came already dressed in their uniforms, or came dressed enough so that they wouldn't scare the women and children by stripping down right there in public. And bathrooms? There were none, unless you counted an electric generator hidden behind some trees and bushes near the tennis courts. It was just about the only private area anywhere near the field, and I couldn't help notice that more than a few guys had disappeared behind it from time to time and, afterward, emerged hitching up their belts. Having brought and already nearly emptied an entire bottle of Gatorade and eaten a chocolate–peanut butter PowerBar since I'd arrived, I was forced to make a trip behind the generator to release some nerve-fueled urine of my own.

As some guys jostled for position in line for Kelly to tape up their ankles and knees, others casually played catch, stretched, joked, or sat stoically listening to music on headphones. Sam, one of our stud receivers, sat on the turf and rolled some kind of log-shaped pad under each of his thighs, up and down, up and down, as if slowly tenderizing them.

Meanwhile, across the field, here came the Cobras. Like most EFL teams, they drove themselves to games (there were no team buses), and their vehicle of choice was evidently the oversized pickup truck—Ford F-250s, Chevy Tahoes, American small-town heavy metal for your average farm boy. Middleboro was about 35 miles south of Boston in the southeastern corner of the state, down toward the Cape, closer to Providence than Boston. Like our players, most of them already wore their football pants and carried their shoulder pads and helmets with pale, beefy arms that exploded from beneath tight, sleeveless undershirts. If I saw one giant, square, close-cropped head of granite, I saw 50. If I didn't know better, I might have thought it was the Mass state trooper all-star team. "That's one big white boy," Sugar Bear said, looking at the Cobra sideline. While they did have a few black players, they were indeed mostly big white boys of the corn-fed variety, each walking with the swagger of a champion.

About a half hour before game time, as I was wrapping athletic tape around my right cleat over my laces to flatten the kicking surface (a handy tip I'd read online), I heard someone calling my name.

"Mark, come here a second," said Coach Pitt, sitting on the bottom row of the grandstands above our bench area. Jogging over, I looked up at him. He didn't say anything for a moment—he just kept squeakily drawing on a Magic Marker board (diagramming defensive schemes?)—and I wondered for a moment if I'd been hallucinating.

"Do you have a tee?" he asked, briefly taking his eyes off his work and looking down at me.

"Yeah," I replied.

"Good. Not sure who's going to kick off tonight, but lemme see you and Khary each hit a few and we'll go with the hot hand."

Oh, shit. A kick-off for the kickoff.

Khary and I headed out to the 30, each with a ball. "You wanna go first?" I asked, secretly hoping he'd say yes, boot one clear over the far end zone, over the fence behind, and into the Orange Line T tracks, and instantly make my involvement in this kicking contest totally moot.

"You go ahead," Khary said.

Taking a deep breath, I teed up the ball and backed up. Unlike on field goals and extra points, I'd never really paid attention to how many steps back and to the side kickers typically took on kickoffs. I just had to wing it. *Here goes nothing.* I ran forward and let 'er tip. Unlike in Brockton, when I'd almost decapitated Pitt on a total shank, my first kick sailed right down the middle of the field to the 20-yard line, about 50 yards. Short by NFL standards, but not bad for my first try. Jeremy, who, along with playing receiver, returned punts and kick-offs, smoothly caught it, made a few faux juke moves, and threw a tight spiral back to me.

Khary's turn. He teed it up and hit it square with his toe. It, too, soared long and straight. Jeremy caught it around the 10-yard line, a good 10 yards past mine. I looked over and saw Coach Pitt watching us and saying something to O'Neal, who nodded, cigar in the corner of his mouth. Damn. When he got hold of one, Khary had a foot on him. This was over. I'd be a spectator. Again. Surprisingly, however, I booted my second kick to the 10, long and straight down the middle. It felt clean, crisp, solid. Meanwhile, Khary's second kick, showing the inconsistency of the toe style, sliced badly off to the right and bounced into our bench area. Not pretty. I was back in the game.

We went back and forth, with me hitting them straight, albeit on the shorter side, and Khary hitting some long ones, but mixing in some out-of-bounds shanks that would have been 15-yard penalties and given the Cobras great starting field position. This was not lost on Coach Pitt.

"Mark, aim one to the right side."

I nodded and booted one toward the right corner. It dropped into Jeremy's soft hands around the 20, which again didn't inspire confidence in my leg strength, but at least it was accurate. And a high kick wasn't all bad: it would allow our coverage team extra time to get downfield.

"Nice one, man," Khary said as he passed me on the way to tee up his fifth kick. He toed it pretty long and high, but it started hooking left and, once again, sailed out of bounds around the 20. Flag, 15 yards. My last kick, on Coach Pitt's instruction, I aimed toward the left corner, and it stayed in-bounds. That did it. Pitt walked over to us. "Okay, Mark, you'll kick off today. Do you punt?"

Holy God in Heaven above, no! "Um, I can if you need me to."

My answer did not inspire confidence in Pitt. "Khary, you punt."

"Cool." Khary shrugged, jogged back out to the field and began punting to Jeremy.

"Have you practiced extra points yet?" Pitt asked.

"Not yet."

"Donnie isn't here tonight. He's gotta work. So Jammer will hold. And I need Reggie on the O-line because we're shorthanded there, so Insano will be your snapper. Find those guys and get some PATs in."

Christ. In all the kickoff confusion, I'd forgotten about extra points and field goals. The only practice I'd had was with a friggin' McDonald's cup and a baseball-diamond backstop.

I rounded up Insano and Jammer and we set up for extra points. Insano snapped, Jammer got the ball down, and I, remembering how I'd done it at Franklin Park against the backstop, chipped my first-ever extra point high, straight up, and right down the middle. Mohammad, stretching nearby, yelled over, *"That's* how you hit it, Mark." We set up 10 more times, five of which I hit clean through the uprights. But the other five, what with Insano and Jammer not being the regular snap-hold team, were either botched snaps or fumbled holds. Not good. Thus began my first experience with kicker head games. I had enough to worry about without wondering whether the ball would be down for me, and I prayed Insano and Jammer would be on the ball come game time.

After all the talk, my football "career" was about to begin. For real this time. To celebrate, I jogged over to the bushes near the tennis courts, slipped behind the electric generator, and promptly vomited up green-yellow Gatorade and little chunks of chocolate–peanut butter PowerBar.

The referees blew their whistles and took the field.

"Not much else to say," Pitt told us as we gathered around him.

"That's the defending champ over there. They have what we haven't earned yet, and they know it. They don't respect us. No one respects us."

"Fuck 'em," someone in the pack muttered.

"No, not 'fuck 'em,'" Pitt continued. "We have to respect them. But we don't have to fear them. We fear no one. This is *our* house. And no one—*no one*—comes into our house and beats us in front of our fans. It's time to take care of business. Everyone find a teammate and bow your heads."

"Heavenly Father," O'Neal began as we put a hand on each other's shoulder pads, two anonymous, weighty mitts pushing into mine, "we ask for Your blessing as we prepare to take the field of battle. Watch over these players, and guide them to compete to the best of their ability, with honor, pride, and self-respect. Keep them safe and out of harm's way. We thank You for blessing us with this great game of football, which makes us better men, better fathers, sons, and brothers, and better members of our communities. Amen."

The captains returned from midfield to our tight circle, which opened and let them into the center. "They got the ball first," Insano told us, sweat already beading his forehead. "We're kicking off." Instantly, my liver squirmed out of its normal resting place and firmly lodged itself in my esophagus. We—I—would be kicking off. The Cobras would receive, and try to run it back down our throats with their big, square, crew-cut jarheads.

"Special teams, let's get it crackin'!" Ace shouted, his eyes already wild with excitement and adrenaline. "It's on you to set the tone. Get out there and bust someone in the mouth!"

Everyone belted out his agreement and raised an arm high and touched hands in the center.

"Whose house is it?" Khary asked.

"Our house!" everyone responded.

Khary leaned in, his voice raising a few octaves. "*WHOSE* house is it?!"

"OUR HOUSE!"

"WHOSE HOUSE IS IT?!"

"*OUR HOUSE!*"

"How y'all feel?!" Ace screamed.

"Aaa-iiight!"

"I said how y'all feel?!"

"Aaa—iiiiight!"

"DOGS?"

A low, barking *Woof!* exploded around me.

"DOGS?" Ace repeated.

"WOOF!"

"DOGS?!"

"WOOF!"

"Panthers on three," Insano yelled. "One . . . two . . . three."

"PANTHERS!" everyone boomed.

"Kickoff team," O'Neal called out to us. "Kickoff team."

My hands trembling, I tried and failed to snap my chinstrap. Again and again, the little bastard just kept slipping off. Thankfully, Reggie jogged up beside me, stopped me, and quickly buckled my strap. "Keep your head on a swivel, Mark. Guys like to take potshots at the kicker."

Great. I'll end up eating my meals through a straw for the rest of my life.

"Don't worry," Reggie continued, sensing my anxiety. "We got your back if anyone tries anything." Then he grinned and added, "But keep your head up anyway."

Reggie was officially the Devil. It was he who'd gotten me into this mess in the first place, asking me to try out. Damn him! And to make things worse, there was my new uniform number. An O-lineman, Johnny B., who'd missed the Brockton game, had returned and needed his jersey back, the infamous number 63. So Delaney had given me an even *bigger* one, if that was possible: number 70. It looked like I had a parachute tucked into my pants.

The kickoff coverage team was gathered at the 30: 10 guys, all of whom would soon be barreling downfield to hit anything that moved. A linesman handed me the game ball. I teed it up and tried to block out all the voices in my head begging me to tell the ref that this had all been a terrible mistake and I would like to go home now. I knew that Celia, along with her cousin Chip, and Holly and Ben, were in the stands watching me this very second, but I didn't dare look up. There was no turning back. Hundreds of people—teammates, opponents, fans, referees—now waited on me.

I walked back to the coverage team, huddled at the 30, and looked at them.

They looked at me.

I looked back at them, waiting for someone to say something. Do something.

Finally, Elvis came to my rescue. Elvis was the team's answer to

Notre Dame's famous football walk-on-turned-cult-hero, Rudy Ruetigger, an energetic, terminally upbeat guy who couldn't have been more than five-foot-seven and gave his all on every snap, practice or game.

"Okay, baby boy, here's what you do," he instructed. "You say 'Deep middle, deep middle' or wherever you're going to kick it, say it twice, and then say 'Ready?' and we'll all yell 'Break!' Then we'll spread out on either side of you—five to your left, five to your right. All you do then is raise your arm, yell 'Ready on the right, ready on the left!' and when you see we're all ready, you put your arm down, run up, and kick the holy shit out of that ball. We'll follow right behind you, bro."

"Okay." I nodded. The directions might as well have been in Swahili. I began Elvis's cadence. "Deep middle . . . deep middle . . ." and then I froze. One second, two seconds . . . *shit, what comes next?*

"Ready?" the merciful Elvis cut in.

"Right . . . ready?"

"Break!" they all shouted, clapping in unison and fanning out on either side of me.

I raised my right arm, as if testifying in court, and looked left.

"Ready on the left?"

"Ready!"

I looked right. "Ready on the right?"

"Ready!"

The whistle blew. I began my approach—a slow trot at first, then a gallop, then a full-on sprint, then a swing of the leg and—*contact!*—sent the ball flying, end over end down the middle of the field. A distant red-and-white shape fielded my kick around the 20 (*way too short, dammit!*) and followed his blockers to his left (my right) toward our sideline. Then, a second later, a distinctive plastic crash of pads and helmets as special teamers collided. From the stands it must have looked something out of *Braveheart*. Everything froze for a millisecond. *Good, he's down*, I thought. But then, there he was: white-and-red number 13, still moving, breaking out of a scrum, fending off a tackler with a stiff-arm and fighting for space outside. Holy Christ, if no one got to him soon, he'd be tightrope-walking down our sideline . . . right over my forehead. I headed toward him, trying to maintain the proper angle, even though I had no idea what the proper angle was. I'd watched lots of NFL action and seen the occasional kicker or punter forced into the unfortunate position of being the last line of defense, and always wondered how I'd react. Now I was going to find out.

I don't know whether it was adrenaline or fear or some primal survival instinct, but something foreign took over: something that told me I had to stop him no matter what. I picked up speed. If I just kept him angled toward our sideline, he might run out of room.

Ten yards away now. Five. One. I dove, head down, shoulder first, and braced myself for the impact . . . which never came. Why? Because number 13 had deftly cut back inside, and I missed him by a good three feet. I did manage, however, to tackle a large chunk of FieldTurf on our sideline. After a few awkward somersaults, I came to a rest tangled in several pairs of legs and lay on my back. Maybe if I just play dead, I thought, no one will notice. But before I could begin my possum act, Coach O'Neal appeared above me, reached down, grabbed my hand, and helped me up.

"Way to follow the play, Mark," he said, slapping my helmet.

"Huh?"

He pointed out to the field where Elvis and number 13 lay tangled on the turf. Turned out, number 13 choosing to cut back into the middle of the field instead of simply barreling over me was a bad move, because waiting for him there was the never-say-die Elvis, who had continued his pursuit and had a full head of steam going and blindsided him at midfield.

Elvis came bounding off the field along with the other special teamers, giving and receiving head butts and high fives, whooping and hollering, setting the tone for the day.

"Way to go, baby boy!" he shouted when he found me, grabbing either side of my helmet in both hands. "You slowed him down, made him hesitate so I could crack him!" Before I could even prepare myself, he head-butted me and jogged off to get some water. My first real football head butt! I had arrived.

On their opening possession, however, the Cobras showed why they were the defending champs. Three plays—screen pass to the tailback good for 20 yards, draw play right up the gut for 15, fade to the tight end in the corner of the end zone for the score. *Bam! Bam! Bam!* Just like that, before my helmet stopped vibrating from Elvis's head butt, they had kicked the extra point and taken a 7–0 lead. The stunned defense walked off the field, shaking their heads, kicking the turf, angrily unsnapping and yanking off their helmets and yelling at each other. Ace shoved Jammer, and Jammer gave it right back before guys stepped between them.

"D-block, down here with me, now!" Pitt yelled. Playbook in hand, he marched down to the far end of our sideline, strategically stopping in front of a section of the grandstands that didn't have as many fans. Pitt was a harsh guy at times, but he was a family man and didn't want any women or kids to hear him or his players cursing up a storm. Pitt went over assignments, looking each guy in the eye as he did so. *Caleb, cover so-and-so in the flat. Pee Wee, don't overpursue on the draw plays. Ace, Derek, bull-rush those tackles, they can't contain you.* Then, as if nothing had happened, they had their hands raised to the center of the circle and, on Insano's three-count, yelled, "D-BLOCK!" I guess you had to have a short memory in football.

Middleboro kicked off, a wobbly grounder that bounced *not* to Jeremy but directly to an up lineman. Unaccustomed to handling the ball with his meaty paws, he bobbled it on our own 40-yard line, where an opportunistic Cobra player swooped in, scooped it up, and ran it in for another touchdown. This time our special teams came stomping off the field, arguing, finger-pointing, two guys jawing at each other and shoving, something about filling the wrong lane. The Middleboro fans, dressed in red and white and taking up a full section of the stands behind our bench, cheered. Our own fans were silent. In about four minutes, we'd given up two touchdowns, and had more shoving matches than points scored.

"You can't play with the big boys, Boston!" one Cobra fan yelled in a raspy, cigarette-ravaged voice. "You don't belong on the same field! Different year, same story, Panthers!"

The Cobras kicked off again, and this time the speedy Jeremy fielded it at the 10 and darted out to the 39. After a no-gain running play on first down, Southie, on second and 10, faked a pitch outside to Amos, dropped back, and connected with Sam on a beautiful 50-something-yard bomb right up the gut of the Cobra secondary. Touchdown.

Our crowd exploded. Our bench surged off the sidelines, pumping their helmets, congratulating the guys as they trotted off the field. As I slapped helmets and cheered, it hit me: *Shit, I'm not just observing here, I have to kick an extra point!* I pulled on my helmet and ran over toward Coach Pitt, who was indeed holding up one finger. "Field goal team!" O'Neal yelled. "Field goal!"

Heart pounding, I jogged out onto the field, snapping my chinstrap. As my offensive line got into their stances, facing their Cobra counterparts, the ref blew the whistle. Insano, subbing for Reggie, bent over, gripped the ball on the PAT hash mark. Jammer knelt seven yards behind him. Standing over him, I toed a spot on the turf just to his left, where he placed his index finger. "Here?"

I nodded. *Your guess is as good as mine, man.*

I backed up two long strides, and then moved two shorter strides to my left. I looked up at the yellow uprights. The space between them suddenly looked much more narrow then I'd remembered. *Head down, watch the ball, but get under it, chip it,* I counseled myself. *This isn't soccer. You don't want a low line drive. Too low and those big bastards over there will block it. Do not get this blocked. Repeat, do* not *get this blocked. Oh, and do* not *hyperventilate.*

Just as I refocused on the hold spot, Insano snapped. Too low. It skimmed the turf, bounced off Jammer's hands, and skittered a few feet away.

Before I could even start my approach, Jammer yelled "FIRE, FIRE!," sprung up out of his holder's kneel and scooped up the errant ball, but was quickly gang-tackled by two Cobras. Whistles blew. I jogged off the field, disappointed that I hadn't gotten a shot. "My bad, Mark," Insano said as he passed by me, slapping the top of my helmet. "Bad snap, my bad. We'll get the next one down."

I took off my helmet and settled in on the sideline. I took a hit from a Gatorade squeeze bottle before realizing that, while we'd botched the extra point, we *had* just scored. Christ, I was up again!

"Kickoff team, kickoff team!" O'Neal yelled. Where was the tee? I frantically scanned the ground where I'd left it before and it was nowhere to be found. *Shit, where was the goddamn tee?!*

"Let's go, Panthers," the zebra-striped side judge urged. "You have a kicker or what?"

"He's coming," O'Neal said, holding up one finger. "Mark!"

Resnapping my helmet, I ran through the clumps of players on the sidelines. "Tee? Anyone have the tee? I need the tee!" Similar cries echoed throughout the guys on the sideline. Finally, Brandon spotted the tee under a bench. "Looking for this, Kick?" He grinned and tossed it. I sprinted out to the field.

But then something awful happened: I'd apparently forgotten how to kick a football. Maybe it was the panic of having to find the tee and hastily set up for the kickoff, but whatever it was, my concentration was nonexistent, and I rushed my approach. I caught a large chink of turf along with the ball, and sent a pathetic, low, wobbling line drive no more than 20 yards . . . and drilling the very first man on the Cobra kickoff team directly in the chest.

Momentarily stunned, the stocky special teamer dropped to the ground and curled up around the errant ball, like a mother bear protecting a cub. One of my teammates reached him and nonchalantly tagged him down.

Fuck! I wanted to tear my head off along with my helmet. I had just given the Cobras the ball on *our* 48-yard line. The defense would *not* be happy. I'd given Middleboro the shortest of short fields. Kickers were noticed only when screwing something up, and I'd just screwed up, big time.

"GodDAMMIT!" I swore, and slapped the side of my own helmet as I walked off the field, keeping my head down, not wanting to make eye contact with anyone. And that's when I learned my first lesson on being a teammate. Mohammad stopped me cold in my tracks and grabbed me by both shoulder pads, smiling widely. "Don't worry about it, Mark, chin up," he said, almost chuckling at how rough I was being on myself. "You'll hit the next one. Just have some fun out there!"

I nodded, appreciative, but still felt like gouging my own eyes out as I headed into the crowded pack of players on our sideline, ripped off my helmet, and squeezed some water into my mouth, over my head. Other guys went out of their way to come up to me with words of encouragement. "Settle down, Kick, gonna give yourself a friggin' heart attack," Brandon teased. "Good strategy, though—drill the guy in his ribs and knock him out of the game."

"Fuck off." I smiled and he laughed, walking away down the sideline.

Elvis, Jeremy, Amos, Insano, the big twins, Coach O'Neal—all of them and more either told me not to worry about it, or just reassuringly slapped my helmet or shoulder pads as they passed by, an unspoken absolution of my kicking sins. No one shunned me, or banished me to solitary confinement on the Island of Misfit Kickers, and I was feeling better . . . until I saw the massive, quiet, powerlifting defensive end, Pee Wee, approaching me through a parting sea of black jerseys and silver helmets. I almost choked on my last swig of water. He reminded me of ex-New England Patriots linebacker Vincent Brown, who starred for the team in the late '80s/early '90s. Often on the cover of muscle and fitness magazines in his playing days, Brown, nicknamed "The Undertaker," was so ripped head to toe that a teammate once famously quipped, "He's even got muscles *in his face*."

Pee Wee hadn't said more than two words to me since I'd joined the team. But then, he didn't talk much at all. A Dorchester native, I'd heard he'd never even played high school football due to some legal difficulties—namely, a stretch in Massachusetts Correctional Institution at Cedar Junction, formerly Walpole State Prison, one of the state's toughest maximum-security facilities. The details of his alleged crime were fuzzy. I heard something about gang involvement, maybe something drug- or gun-related. No one knew for sure, but there was plenty of speculation, and even little hints dropped by Pee Wee himself. "The first time I met Pee Wee, one of the first things he said was, 'My parole officer thought it would be a good idea if I play football,'" Kelly, the trainer, tells me. "He's a real mystery man."

I didn't feel right snooping around behind Pee Wee's back to get his story. I also didn't know Pee Wee well enough to ask him myself. I tried Donnie. While he didn't know the real story either, he did offer this insight: "Mark, there are two people that black folk don't talk to about personal stuff: the white man, and writers," he teased in his slight southern drawl, laughing. "And you're both. Good luck getting *that* cat to open up."

In any event, Pee Wee now stood a foot away, slightly stooped over, leaning his helmet toward me and holding out the unsnapped ends of his chinstrap.

"Kicker, can you get these?"

"Sure." I reached up to snap them, praying I wouldn't fumble around like I had with my own helmet. He stared right at me, expressionless, a little silver stud under his bottom lip glistening in the stadium lights. (Until that point, I didn't even know he had pupils, let alone a pierced lower lip.) Why he'd chosen *me* to help him I had no idea. But I sure as hell wasn't going to argue. After a few jittery false starts, I snapped each one on tightly.

"Thanks," he said. And that was that. He turned and started out to the field with the rest of the defense.

What the—?

Before I could start analyzing the odd little moment, he abruptly stopped and turned around. "Hey, Kicker, watch this—I'm gonna get the ball back for you." He didn't smile, didn't so much as smirk; he was dead serious. But through his face mask, I saw a barely perceptible glint of mischief in his eyes. I immediately pitied the Cobra quarterback.

On the very next possession, the quarterback faded back, checked off his first read, then his second—he was taking too long even by semi-pro standards—when Pee Wee, a silver and black blur, roared past an overmatched blocker and drilled the quarterback right between the numbers on his back, square between the shoulder blades. Whiplashed, the guy fumbled. *"Ball!"* our entire bench screamed.

As Pee Wee and the quarterback landed in a heap, Ace darted forward, scooped up the fumble, and galloped about 60 yards into the end zone, where several defenders soon caught up and piled on him. He returned to the sideline, holding the ball aloft, head-butting, high-fiving. Pee Wee followed a few feet behind, calmly unstrapping his helmet.

"Told ya," he said as he passed right by me, wearing a small grin. I laughed and slapped his helmet, and then headed out to kick the extra point. But again, I never even got the chance: Jammer bobbled Insano's snap, the Cobras smothered him. Disappointed, embarrassed—even though the flubs weren't technically my fault, I felt like everyone in the stands assumed I'd choked—I jogged to the sideline.

Pitt came toward me waving his clipboard. "What happened?!"

"We didn't get it off." I wasn't going to throw Jammer under the bus for his bobble; it was a team screw-up. "They had a good rush."

Before storming off, he paused and glared at me. "We'll need to make a damn extra point *sometime* this season."

Feeling like a chastised child, I grabbed the tee, set up, and kicked off again: high floater that number 13 fielded at the 20 and took back to their 40. They ran one play (an incomplete long pass to the end zone), and the clock ran out.

At the half: Cobras 14, Panthers 12.

For the final two quarters, it stayed neck and neck, lots of three-and-outs and stalled drives. They scored again halfway through the third to go up 21–12. We answered back toward the end of the same quarter. After a long run by Amos got us down to their two, Todd rammed it home to cut the lead to 21–18. Shockingly, however, Pitt decided to go for two again. Two points did us no good! An extra point would have made it 21–19, and we could have won with a late field goal if it came to that. But if we missed the two-point conversion, we'd be down by three and could only *tie* with a late field goal.

O'Neal, sensing my confusion, walked over. "Pitt wants the points, and I guess he thinks it'll be easier to get two than one." I nodded. I wasn't going to start questioning his decisions, but even I, with zero coaching experience, knew you took the point here and set yourself up for the win. Then again, my kicking unit had done nothing yet to gain his confidence. Catch-22. For the first time that night I looked up into the stands and found Celia. She waved. I shook my head and made a disgusted face. She scrunched her face. *What's wrong?* I shook my head again.

The two-pointer, a Southie naked bootleg, came up a yard short. We were still down by three. On the ensuing kickoff, I at least made up for my earlier shank and booted a long, high floater down to the 15-yard line, where our coverage team wrapped the returner up. Relief flooded over me; I'd done my small part to help the field-position battle. Maybe I'd soon get a shot to tie this thing if we couldn't find the end zone? The thought, while exciting, more than anything made me want to throw up again. I'd have to work on my less-than-steel nerves.

D-block clamped down on the potent Cobra offense that next drive and those that followed, stopping them time and again on big third- or fourth-down plays. Pee Wee, Insano, Ace, Derek, Caleb, Jammer, and the guys were flying all over the place and making hits. Our offense got close a few times, but came up short of the red zone on all occasions, out of field goal range (at least in Pitt's estimation, though I thought I'd have a shot) and forcing the busy Khary to punt. Back and forth we went, the proverbial slugfest, until the middle of the fourth quarter. That's when Southie led us on an impressive drive from our own 12 down to their 20—a mix of run and pass plays that kept the tiring Middleboro defense totally off balance and ate up huge chunks of the clock. With an escalating buzz, everyone there sensed it: the upstart Panthers were driving to knock off the defending EFL champs!

Third and short now. If we got this first down, it was over. No way they'd keep us out of their end zone. We'd eat up more clock, ram it home, go up by a couple of points, and force them to drive for a tying field goal or winning touchdown with only a few ticks left on the clock and no time-outs. "Panther football, y'all!" Elvis and the other special teamers cheered, waving their arms and pumping their helmets above their heads to amp up the crowd. "Get it up for your Panthers!" And that's when an overeager offensive lineman stuck a bowie knife into our momentum: a false start, knocking us back 10 yards. Now, instead of third and short from the 20, we faced third and 11 from the 30. We ran a draw play that the alert Cobras sniffed out, containing Amos after only four yards. The Panther crowd hushed; the smaller Cobra crowd, clad in red and white, rose to its feet and cheered on its defense.

Fourth and seven from the 26. Clock running, almost two minutes left. Southie called time-out, our last. He jogged over to Pitt, Mark, and Fink on the sidelines for a conference.

Snapping on my helmet, I lingered nearby and watched. This was one of the situations that all kickers dreamed of, or so I imagined: a shot to hit a game-tying or -winning field goal with time running out. This was what the position was all about, being a difference-maker, the X factor. But this was no measly kickoff (and I'd been average at best in that department so far): snap from the 26, hold on the 33, this would be a 43-yarder . . . for the tie . . . against the champs . . . in front of a live crowd . . . including my wife and best friends. Was I remotely mentally and physically prepared to be the Panthers' X factor? I had to be. If I didn't step up now, I never would. I had to at least give my coaches and teammates *the impression* that a game-tying 43-yard field goal was something I'd done a hundred times before. A chip shot. *Might as well put the points on the board now, fellas.*

I headed up the sideline toward Pitt, Southie, and the other coaches. I watched them converse and, seconds later, my heart sank as I saw Southie nod, buckle his chinstrap, and head back out to the huddle. Pitt was going to go for it on fourth and seven. My chance to be a hero would have to wait. Deflated, I unbuckled my helmet and drifted back into the pack of players standing on the sideline. Clapping, banging our helmets, we eagerly awaited the crucial fourth down.

"Let's go, O!" Insano yelled, standing alongside the rest of D-block, who were on their feet cheering their offensive counterparts. Southie took the snap, three-step drop, faked a screen pass to Amos in the right flat, then tucked the ball under one arm and took off on a bootleg around the left end. He reached the line of scrimmage, gained a yard, two yards, five yards, and . . . was met by two Cobra defenders who knocked him out of bounds at the 15—two yards short of the first-down marker. The Cobra fans stood up and whooped. Our fans groaned. Cobra ball on downs. Game, for all intents and purposes, over.

While some teams would have just called three basic running plays to eat up the rest of the clock and not rub in the win, the champs went for the throat. On third and long after an incomplete pass and a stuffed sweep, they called a draw play, freezing most of D-block in their tracks. Their quarterback lofted a perfect spiral down the left sideline. It floated over Keon's diving, outstretched hand and landed on the finger-tips of the receiver on the 20-yard line, who cradled it in and waltzed into the end zone as the whistle blew.

Final score: Cobras 27, Panthers 18.

Dozens of grown men who'd just beaten each other's brains out for two hours now gathered at midfield for a postgame prayer. Red, white, black, silver uniforms intermingled on the blue-and-white English High logo. Coach O'Neal asked everyone to take a knee and touch the shoulder or grab a nearby hand. I rested my right hand on the left shoulder pad of the Cobra next to me, only to realize it was the stocky guy whom I'd hit squarely in the chest with my second (and utterly dismal) kickoff. I didn't bring it up.

"Almighty Father," O'Neal began, "thank You for guiding and pro-tecting these men as they competed against one another this evening. Thank You for showing these men that if they can take the lumps and succeed out here on these playing fields, then they can succeed in anything else they want to do. Just putting on a uniform doesn't make someone a football player. Being a football player is something that has to be earned. And tonight, Lord, thank You for allowing these men to earn it. We may be enemies between the lines, but we're all friends and brothers off the field, united by our love of this game and our desire to be better men. You might get knocked down every now and then, and you might not want to get back up, but the true mea-sure of a man is how quickly he gets back up and keeps fighting. Thank You for watching over us so that we can go home healthy and strong to our families and our communities. Amen."

Amen, everyone responded.

Yes, we were disappointed, pissed off, frustrated about losing our home opener, dropping us to 0–2 on the season. But all wasn't lost. Our attitude and performance was a complete photo negative of the display two weeks prior, at Brockton. We never gave up. And Pitt commended us for it.

"I'm proud of you guys," he said as we remained at midfield after the Cobras had dispersed, most guys stripped down to sweat-covered T-shirts. Even I looked like I'd just gone swimming, thanks to the hu-midity of the evening and the intensity of the game. "We lost the game, but we won a lot of battles out there, and tonight was a victory in many ways. You guys pulled a 180, night and day from Brockton.

It's a long season, and this was a step in the right direction. I'll see you at practice Tuesday night. We'll get right back to work and build on tonight. Bring it in around your captains."

We clumped together and raised our hands to the middle. "Team on three, team on three," Insano said. "One . . . two . . . three."

" . . . *TEAM!*"

"Be safe this weekend, gentlemen," Pitt added.

Be safe. Those last two words stuck with me. Unlike most of these guys, I was heading back into quite possibly the safest part of Boston. No one was ever told to "be safe" when heading up to the State House, or down Charles Street. But my teammates? Many would be going home to places that, especially on a hot summer night, saw their share of random violence.

Celia, Ben, Holly, and Chip were waiting for me near our sideline, all wearing sympathetic smiles. "That was *awesome*," said Chip, a huge sports fan, high-fiving me. "When I heard 'semi-pro' I thought the players would kinda, you know, suck. But that was a great game. Right down to the wire."

"I thought they were going to bring you in for that kick at the end," Celia added. "I was going to be sick. Were you nervous?"

"Yeah, but excited, too." I shrugged, conveniently not mentioning that I'd puked before the game myself.

Just then, the big twins Jason and Anthony passed by with Bruno the pit bull, toting the battered boom box, Chris Cornell silenced for the evening. I introduced everyone. "Your man did great tonight, didn't he?" Anthony asked Celia as he put his arm around me and shook me, my spine rattling. "After that second kickoff, I told him to forget it, keep his head up. Look at him. I can tell he's still upset about it. Take him out for ice cream, cheer him up."

As we headed toward the car, the neighborhood around English High was still electric, hopping, humming with postgame electricity. The barbecue was still fired up. Half-dressed players from both teams were gathered behind cars and pickups in the parking lot, trunks were open, tailgates flipped down, offering easy access to coolers.

I thought about staying for a bit. I didn't want to just hightail it outta there, partly because I wanted to continue some semblance of bonding with my new teammates, and partly because never before had icy beer bottles looked so damned appealing. And had it been just me and Celia, we might've stayed. But we had Ben, Holly, and Chip with us, and I didn't want to make them all just hang around.

But I liked what I was starting here. I liked how it felt to have access to a vibrant new community and experience the thrill of playing real football. So much so that when we returned to Beacon Hill 20 minutes later, it was a letdown. The beers we had at my local bar just didn't taste as good as, I imagined, the ones in those coolers must have tasted.

WHITE PANTHER

WHEN THE WINLESS Panthers and I con-
vened at Franklin Park the following Tuesday, practice began with
some bad news. Sam, the Head Start teacher and sideline trash-talker
extraordinaire, was out for the season. During the Cobra game, on
the very first kickoff coverage, he had landed awkwardly on the turf,
caught his cleat, and torn his ACL. He'd wanted to keep playing but
Kelly, fiddling with his knee for only a moment, immediately understood the extent of the damage. Against his protests, he was done.
But there he was at practice, on crutches, bulky Ace bandage on the
knee, receiving hand slaps and shoulder bumps of condolence.

Then there was Joe, a starting outside linebacker. He'd played
football since he was eight and was now working toward a criminol-
ogy degree part-time at Northeastern. He had to call it quits due to
recurring knee troubles. I didn't fear the same wear and tear as a line-

backer, but the news made me think about my own balky left knee. I had about 15 years on Joe, and, back in high school, I tore a ligament in a moped accident—as embarrassing as it is to admit that I rode a moped in the first place. It still ached sometimes after exercising, and it made a weird clicking/crunching sound when I walked. I'd also sprained my ankles umpteen times over the years—usually during athletics, but once by actually tripping on a Nerf basketball in my office, a calamity that, on the embarrassment scale, easily trumps the moped. And I cracked a rib in college during a violent, midair disagreement with an exceedingly stubborn soccer goalpost. If a kid as young as Joe could break down, what chance did I have?

Another thing about Joe's departure: I was now the only white guy on the team. And I wasn't the only one who noticed. As I sat in the grass wrapping my right cleat with athletic tape (which was not only necessary for more accurate kicking but had also quickly become a superstitious necessity), Coach O'Neal walked up beside me, unlit cigar in hand.

"I know, I should quit," he said. "But next to a good woman, there's nothing better than a good cigar. And the smoke keeps the bugs away. If I have to catch a little lung cancer in exchange for not being eaten alive by one of these mutant, ghetto mosquitoes, so be it." He exhaled a thin stream, lifting his chin to blow away smoke from me.

Mike O'Neal, 43, had a playful, dry wit, and liked being out here among the "young bucks," as he called the players when he wasn't calling them "crack whores." A distant cousin of both NBA superstar Shaquille O'Neal and former Red Sox pitcher Dennis "Oil Can" Boyd, O'Neal was a combination of brains and brawn. He'd graduated from the University of Massachusetts in the mid-80s and went on to Howard University to pursue a master's degree in analytical psychology. He was only 18 credits short of that degree when his mother got sick and he had to move back to Boston to take care of her. "It was disappointing, but family comes first," he says of the foregone conclusion that was his decision to leave school.

About six-foot-two with a trim 215 pound build, O'Neal was a fine athlete in his day. He played soccer at UMass, and quarterback in high school, the semi-pros, and in several flag football and park leagues. He even landed a tryout with the then Houston Oilers (now Tennessee Titans) during the NFL strike year of 1987, and could still sling the football when he wanted to. The only thing about him that looked his age were his eyes: despite their mischievous sparkle and his handsome features, O'Neal had red-rimmed, tired, slightly basset hound eyes, a product of his having to work long, crazy hours as a manager of a local CVS store, as well as working a second job at an auto mechanic's. Nothing against CVS managers or mechanics, both good, honest work, but it disappointed me to hear of a guy who almost had a master's degree making an hourly wage loading and unloading boxes of nail polish remover and Trojans. That said, O'Neal *had* put his academic training to use as the founder of a nonprofit organization called Fathers, Inc., which counseled mostly inner-city men, ex-cons and current convicts, on being better fathers, better men. And he was a writer, too, having contributed an essay to a 1997 anthology titled *Black Men Speaking.* Edited by National Book Award winner Charles Johnson, the volume examines whether black men—due to institutional racism, a crumbling educational system, economics, and gang activity—are an endangered species. In other words, there was far more to O'Neal than cigars and playful jokes.

O'Neal, Cliff, and Coach Pitt met in the early '90s while playing in a local flag football league. Cliff had drifted off on occasion—his jail time, for one—but O'Neal and Pitt had remained close.

"Murph says you grew up in Wellesley?" he asked me.

I nodded. "Yeah. Lived there until I was about 17, then we moved outside of Hartford."

"I'm from Needham," he said, adding that his family had moved north from Trenton, New Jersey's tough Stuyvesant Avenue neighborhood. "We were the first black family in our neighborhood, and they signed a petition to keep us out. When I walked down the street, people would stop what they were doing and stare and point at me, like I was Sasquatch." He shook his head and laughed—one of those infectious chuckles. "This wasn't that long ago, either; this was the early '70s in the Boston 'burbs. It's not like we're talking 1950s Mississippi."

"Hate to say it, but that's just foreign to me," I said. "I mean, this is literally the first time I've really ever put myself in a position where I'm the clear, obvious outsider. I know it's not the same thing, but—"

"You know what, Mark?" O'Neal interrupted. "You could move into a black neighborhood tomorrow and no one would probably give you any trouble. Anyone who's ever been through the kind of discrimination that black people have had to endure would never want to make someone else feel like that. Sure, if you were an asshole or if you barged in and thought you were better than everyone else, you wouldn't exactly be welcome. But the guys here"—he gestured with his cigar at the players now lining up for calisthenics—"they can tell you're a stand-up guy. We don't see you as just some white guy—I mean, we can see you're white, but we just see you as a football player.

"That's what we should call you: the White Panther," he joked.

"I like it," I nodded, smiling. "Makes me sound more vicious and powerful than I am."

My status as the token White Panther didn't last for long, however. The first new arrival was Jason, a 31-year-old Florida native. Jason rolled into practice one night on a souped-up "rice burner," as a Harley rider would derisively call it, his Kawasaki motorcycle. A cross between former NFL cornerback Jason Sehorn and—I use the next comparison as complimentarily as possible—one of the Backstreet Boys, Jason was every bit the Florida boy: tan, fit, good-looking, wearing wraparound sunglasses, a tight white tank top, and sporting a barbed-wire tattoo that wrapped around his sizable right bicep (the ink of choice among white football players everywhere). But he wasn't just a brainless, weight-lifting pretty boy—he was a doctor who had recently moved to Boston with his girlfriend for a pediatric internship at prestigious Children's Hospital. From the first few snaps, everyone could tell that, while a little raw, he was clearly a very good athlete who immediately held his own in defensive drills: good speed, soft hands—surgical training, perhaps?—and an innate sense of where the ball was going to be. Jason was a graduate of the University of Florida, where he'd tried out for the team as a walk-on and, after not making it, played flag football. So when he moved north he started looking into flag leagues. "I eventually came across the Panthers' site and figured I'd give the real thing a try," he tells me. "I'd never played real football before, but figured I could handle it." Clearly confident but not cocky, everyone immediately liked Jason and, of course, started calling him "Doc."

The second NWGOTB—New White Guy on the Block—was Jeff. His first night out, while most guys wore shorts and T-shirts to combat the humidity, here came Jeff clad in full pads, mouth guard, pants, eye black, the works. I'm surprised he didn't start doing solo shuttle runs to warm up like Jim Carrey in *The Cable Guy*.

"Hey, bro," he said to me as I stretched out, "you the quarterback?"

"Uh, no." Quarterback? I had to laugh. "I'm the kicker."

"I'm Jeff," he said, extending his hand.

I reached up. "Hey, Jeff. Mark."

"Hey, Mahk," Jeff said with a thick Boston accent. "The twins told me to find Coach Pittman or Delaney. They around?"

I scanned the field. Neither had arrived yet. "Nope. Delaney usually drives a tan work van. And you can't miss Pitt. He'll be the guy with no neck making us run until we puke."

Jeff grinned sickly. "Cool."

I learned that Jason and Anthony had met Jeff at the Drinking Fountain, a bar across the street from English High. A Jamaica Plain native, Jeff was a deliveryman for a local used-car dealership, and was the youngest of five boys in a tightly knit, blue-collar family. "I learned to take a beating from an early age," he says. "Might be why I love football so much. After the brawls me and my brothers got into, a little football contact didn't scare me." He played offensive lineman at English and did some long snapping. After watching him bound around slapping helmets and eagerly cheering on virtual strangers during his first practice, we could tell he was one of those guys who just liked being out there with the guys, running around, getting some hits in. He was the Caucasian Elvis.

He was joining an 0–2 squad. Meanwhile, both Brockton and Middleboro had won their first two games. We'd have to get our act together if we were going to keep pace with these two league leaders. Also looming on the schedule were the venerable Marlboro Shamrocks.

Whenever the subject of Marlboro came up, Panther players and coaches shrugged it off and pretended that our next game was the only one that mattered. It was an old sports cliché, the "one game at a time" axiom. But there was a good reason coaches and athletes beat that one to death in press conferences and interviews: in any sport, that was the way you *had to* approach a full season. Whether it was a 10-game semi-pro schedule, a 16-game NFL campaign, or a 162-game baseball marathon, you just couldn't get ahead of yourself and overlook a perceived lesser opponent who might sneak up and bite you in the ass. And right now, the Charlestown Townies were that opponent. They were also 0–2, and we knew we had better-skilled players and should beat them easily, especially at home. Still, very dangerous. The proverbial "trap game."

The team's veterans had already been talking about the impending visit from the mighty Shamrocks in August. They clearly had re-spect for the EFL dynasty Marlboro had built over the decades. "That's what I'm trying to do here in Boston," Delaney told me. "I want to establish that kind of winning tradition, that veteran players can pass down to younger guys, year after year. I want to bring a little football respect back to Boston and eventually make people fear play-ing us."

But this season, while there was respect, there wasn't any fear. We were the youngest team in the league, which was a double-edged sword as far as Delaney was concerned. "Me, Cliff, Reggie, Donnie, Pitt, all the older guys understand what Marlboro is. But these young dudes don't know and they don't care. A lot of them aren't scared of anything or anyone—or at least they pretend not to be—because that's what you have to do on the street, act tough, pretend that you ain't scared of nothing. Problem is, that means the young guys don't know how to just walk away when trouble comes up. We got a lot of straight-up knuckleheads on the team, too, kids who think that if you back down, or turn the other cheek without getting into a fight, then you ain't a man. Some guys have *too much* pride. What they gotta un-derstand is that teams like Marlboro or Middleboro, they've earned respect. But some of these young guys, they think that being tough, or having a gun, or getting in a fight earns them respect. It doesn't. *Winning* earns you respect. How you carry yourself on and off the field earns you respect."

That week leading up to the Charlestown game, I had my most pro-ductive practices yet. Both Reggie and Donnie were there both nights and, for the first time, I got to work with my official long snapper and holder. No disrespect to Insano or Jammer, but it was night and day from before. On every snap, Reggie fired tight spirals back to Donnie's outstretched, waiting hands. And in one swift mo-tion, Donnie caught each snap, placed the ball exactly where I'd put my toe, spun it laces out, and had it waiting at the perfect angle for me. Over and over again we hit extra points, field goals, all high and down the middle, right into my favorite chain-link backstop. Clock-work. I was on fire. I was more ready than ever before. I didn't want to feel cocky, but my small part of the Panther attack was locked and loaded. I couldn't tell you how important it was to me to know that my holder and snapper were veterans like Murph and Donnie. I was good to go for that Saturday's game against the crosstown Townies, salivating to contribute. I had faith in my still-new teammates, but it nevertheless remained to be seen whether we'd finally get into the win column in 2004.

A WIN IN SIGHT

ENGLISH HIGH. An hour before the Charlestown game. I was stretching on the sidelines when Delaney approached. "Hey Mark—catch," he said, and tossed me a clumped-up black jersey. I unfolded it to reveal a beautiful, single-digit number: 6. "Used to be Ace's number," he informed me. "But Ace said it was cool with him if you wore it . . . plus, it was getting too small for him after all the washings."

I found Ace a few minutes later.

"Thanks for the new number, man," I said. "I was starting to feel like a jackass in the O-lineman's uniform."

"Just don't make it look bad," he joked. "A lot of good plays been made in that jersey."

Ace was certainly an enigma, almost as much as Pee Wee. Even those who knew him best agreed that he could be a tad . . . mercurial. "One day you love him; the next day he gets on your damn nerves," Reggie explains. "He can be the most humble guy one day, and a straight asshole the next. He's actually a good kid, and deep in his heart he really loves football. He's a good player, plays hard, but only plays hard when he wants to, and he'll tell you himself, his biggest problem is that he doesn't listen very well." Turns out, Ace didn't *see* very well, either.

That's because he was legally blind.

Ace—his real name was Aaron Smith, but he'd had the nickname for as long as he could remember—was born in 1974 with an optical condition called retinoschisis, or RS. It's a disease of nerve tissue in the eye that causes a splitting of the eye into two layers that, in turn, causes a slow, progressive loss of vision. It affects peripheral vision and deteriorates central vision, reducing it to anywhere from 20/30 to 20/200, depending on the severity. Ace's was on the severe end: 20/200. In fact, as a child and teenager, his mother, having been told that Ace would likely be completely blind by the time he reached adulthood, wanted to prepare him early. She sent him to the legendary Perkins School for the Blind, the 175-year-old school on the tranquil banks of the Charles River in Watertown, whose most famous student was an Alabama girl who'd lost both her sight and hearing by the time she was 19 months old, and whose tutor, Anne Sullivan, brought her to Perkins in 1888 when she was 6 years old. Her name? Helen Keller.

At Perkins, Ace learned to count money by feel, read Braille, and do all the other things necessary for life as a visually impaired adult. "I can still read Braille," he tells me, imitating running his fingers over an invisible piece of paper, like Stevie Wonder tickling the ivories. "But I'm a little rusty. Been a while, but I could do it if I had to."

One thing he was told he'd *never* do, however, was play football. Even moderate contact to the head or face could cause instant, permanent damage—he was forbidden from so much as diving headfirst into a swimming pool—and doctors warned that while RS would probably eventually cause blindness, a violent contact sport such as football could speed up that process and make permanent blindness a certainty. That, Ace says, is exactly why he loves the game so much. "That's why I'm always out here yelling and screaming and getting all jacked up. Because they told me I'd never, *ever* play football because of my eyes. They said I couldn't even dive headfirst into a pool because *even that* was too much contact. I can't drive, can't do a lot of other stuff, but they'd never stop me from playing football. I think that's why I sometimes get in trouble out here and act up: because the game means so much to me and I just get, you know, overly emotional about it sometimes. But I'm the engine on this team. Yeah, an engine might overheat from time to time, but it keeps the car runnin'."

But how can "the engine" keep running if it can't see? "Long as I can see the ball, I'm fine. I play on instinct, mostly. I can see—it's not like I'm full-on Ray Charles out there—but I can't see distances too good, so I just look for the holes closest to me and plug those, hit whoever's coming through. But I can't see to the sideline to know what down it is, so I usually have to ask someone in the huddle, or the refs."

While his mother was preparing him for a possible life without sight, his father was passing down the love of football. His dad, Marion Jones, played briefly in the NFL for the Kansas City Chiefs and Atlanta Falcons before bad knees and other injuries prematurely ended his career. Moving home to Dorchester, Marion started coaching Pop Warner and soon became well known around town simply as "Coach Jones." At one point, he even coached the Mattapan Patriots, featuring a young player by the name of Reggie Murphy. "Dudes I don't even know still see me on the street and say, 'Yo, you're Coach Jones's boy!'" Ace tells me with a mix of pride and exasperation. "I'm like, I'm a grown-ass man but I'll *still* always just be 'Coach Jones's boy' to a lot of people."

Ace certainly had his share of inherent physical ailments to overcome, but many of his other problems were of his own doing. "I ain't never sold crack, and I ain't never robbed anyone, but if you got a beef with me, I'm gonna fight. I'm a fighter, that's my biggest problem." Fighting, he admits, had landed him in and out of jail since his early teens—after one particularly ugly altercation, state troopers even cuffed him and dragged him right out of a high school classroom. But off-field troubles aside, Ace's heart was in the right place with regard to football, and for all his occasional bluster and controversy, he did keep everyone loose, and appreciated what football brought to his life. "You have somewhere to focus your energy, instead of focusing out here on the street where there is nothing but death or going to jail. On the football field, you know you don't have to act like someone you're not, you're just you and everyone will re-spect you for that."

I couldn't help but think that Ace loved football more than any-one else on the team. After all, he was the only player literally willing to go blind to keep playing. And the Panthers? While many players used football to stay on the straight and narrow, for Ace, the team was his North Star. "I got two families," he says, rubbing the tattoo on his right shoulder, three aces of spades, symbolic not only of his nickname, but also of his three children, whose names all begin with the letter *A*. "I got the family I was raised with, and the family I play football with."

Just before we launched into pregame calisthenics, I stretched my new (and far more kicker-friendly) number 6 jersey over my pads, lifted the whole ensemble over my head, and poked my head and arms through. Tucking and stretching, I adjusted the 6 so it was cen-tered, and hitched my belt. I was instantly proud of number 6. I wanted to do right by it. I wanted to earn it.

Charlestown, in their red, white, and blue uniforms, kicked off and we took control quickly. On the second play, Southie faked a handoff to Todd and hit Jeremy on a pretty fly pattern for the first score of the game. Panthers 6, Townies 0.

I trotted out to my spot for the extra point feeling more confi-dent than ever. The new number helped, weird as that sounds. Mainly, however, it was because both Reggie and Donnie were finally there, the first time I'd had my official snapper and holder out there together.

As the linemen on both sides dug in, I told myself to just pretend I was at Franklin Park. *Nothing to it. Right off the McDonald's cup and up into the middle of the fence.* Reggie got off a crisp snap. Donnie snatched the ball, placed, spun. I lunged forward and hit it dead-on perfect, straight, up high, higher—but apparently not high enough, because a meddling Charlestown player managed to wedge between our tackles, leap, reach up with one big paw, and . . . *THWAP!* My heart plunged as I heard the horrifying sound of leather meeting skin.

But I must have really gotten some power behind it because, de-spite the deflection, the ball still managed to flutter upward, drunkenly veer left, and clank against the upright. It then hovered in midair, cruelly taunting me, deciding whether to career right (and drop safely inside), or left (and seal my fate as an unreliable choke artist). I heard a voice taunting me from my past. *Way to choke, you little fuckin' pussy.*

But the kicking gods must have been looking out for me. The ball mercifully chose to career right. The ref lifted both arms. *It's good!*

Ugly though it was, it was the most glorious point in football history as far as I was concerned. I slapped Donnie's helmet. Mohammad walked back and softly head-butted me. I high-fived Reggie (he was no longer the Devil).

Panthers 7, Townies 0.

I jogged back to the sideline to grab the kickoff tee, but it was nowhere to be found. Like before Middleboro, Khary and I both practiced kickoffs in warm-ups. "Anyone seen the tee?" I asked, lifting up sweatshirts and gym bags, thinking it might have gotten accidentally buried underneath since warm-ups. A few guys turned around, shook their heads. "The orange tee? Anyone seen it?"

I'd hit a few good ones, a few bad ones; Khary, too, but not enough to make Pitt change his mind and take away my kickoff duties. Or so I thought.

"Khary's already got it," Reggie finally answered. I looked out to the field and saw Khary teeing up the ball, readying for our first kickoff of the game, Elvis and the special teamers waiting for him a few yards back. And that's when O'Neal, for the second time in three games, put his arm around me and relayed a coach's decision. "Mark, Pitt wants Khary to kick off today. So you can just concentrate on extra points and field goals. All right?"

"All right," I replied. In other words, Pitt saw that my first extra point was almost a disaster and decided that I had enough on my plate. That, or my 10-yard kickoff into the Middleboro guy's solar plexus the previous game hadn't exactly won me points. In any event, I'd officially had one of my job responsibilities taken away after only two games. *Nice work, super foot. Nice work.*

But after a momentary battle with wounded male pride, I realized I didn't mind being benched for kickoffs. Khary could really give it a ride when he got that toe into it, and I'd rather our defense have the best field position possible. Whatever was best for the team. Pitt made the right call: I *did* need to concentrate on extra points and field goals. That was where I was needed most.

We scored twice more in the game, once in the second quarter on an Amos 25-yard scamper, and the third on a Southie-to-KFC pass, a leaping, twisting catch in the corner of the end zone, his number 88 making him look like acrobatic former Steeler Lynn Swann. Each time afterward, with that first successful PAT finally under my belt, I drilled those next two extra points, one of them clear over the fence behind the end zone, over Washington Street, and into the parking lot of a gas station. I was in a rhythm now. But just as a kicker couldn't dwell on past failures, he also couldn't get too pleased about successes. A kicker could become a goat in seconds. Just ask Scott Norwood, who, despite a *very* good career with the Buffalo Bills, will only be remembered for two words: wide right, his Super Bowl XXV-losing miss against the New York Giants.

After each PAT, however, my teammates celebrated like I'd just kicked a 50-yard game-winner. I received so many head butts and helmet slaps I'd thought I'd need a CAT scan afterward. Coach O'Neal was always there waiting for me, with a huge grin and big high-five. "There's my soccer player!" he exclaimed, slapping the 6 on my back. "Hey, Pitt, we're not leaving points on the field *this* year, baby." Coach Pitt looked our way momentarily, but then went back to his clipboard. Football lifers just don't get too jazzed up about one silly extra point.

But it wasn't all wine and roses on the sideline that night. After one particularly ugly three-and-out series (two badly overthrown incomplete passes and a stuffed draw play that lost five yards), a frustrated Southie stormed off the field, angrily unsnapping his helmet . . . and he just kept on walking, past Pitt, past Fink and Coach Mark, and headed all the way down to the very end of the sideline. I thought he was just going to keep walking to his car, get in, and drive away, uniform and all. But he didn't.

Instead, he sat down hard on a metal bench next to one of the water coolers, yanked his helmet off with both hands, and slammed it on the ground. But that wasn't enough. He reached up into his jersey, unhooked his shoulder pads, yanked them off, too, and slammed them against the cement wall behind him. He then sat there alone, sullen, expressionless, just staring ahead into space in a sweat-soaked gray undershirt as the spectators behind him looked down, pointing, shrugging, wondering just what the hell had happened.

I admit, I didn't really know Southie very well. On the mellow side, but friendly and well liked, he was in his early 20s, worked for the Boston Department of Transportation as a meter man, and, as his nickname implied, went to South Boston High, where he had starred at cornerback on the same team as KFC and Fink (who played quarterback). He was a little aloof, sure—sometimes he'd skip sprints or run his own side drills during practice—but most good athletes could be aloof, especially quarterbacks. Still, anyone could tell from the blank expression he now wore that, for whatever reason, he'd just mentally shut it down.

Fink finally went over and sat down beside his high school and college buddy (the two had attended Hudson Valley Community College in Troy, New York). They conferred alone on the bench—or, I should say, Fink conferred, and Southie stared off into space, not even looking at him. Occasionally Southie would break out of his trance and gesture animatedly toward the field with evident frustration.

"Who cares?" Reggie answered with a shrug when I asked him what the problem was. "Some of these little bastards can't take a little criticism, I guess. Hey, if your skin's too thin, you don't belong on a football field. This isn't recess."

"What criticism?" I asked, looking over at Fink and Southie.

"After that last series," Reggie explained, "a few guys told him he's holding the ball too long instead of getting rid of it. But he *is* holding it too long. Chuck it away, man, don't keep taking sacks. It's killin' us."

Finally, Southie cooled down. Fink must have talked him off the ledge. The quarterback retrieved his helmet, shoulder pads, jersey, and got suited up again. The next series he was right back on the field, driving us down into Townie territory as the third quarter ended. But the drive stalled as the fourth quarter began. We now had the ball on the Charlestown 33, fourth and three.

Pitt had always gone for it on fourth down. Never having had a kicker, that was his MO. But now, being fairly deep in Charlestown territory, I guess he figured that a punt from Khary wouldn't do much good, so why not go for the field goal? I'd already hit three extra points—crushed two of them—so maybe he finally thought that I just might be able to kick after all. Or maybe O'Neal urged him to give me a shot. I started stretching out, loosening up just in case by some bizarre stretch of the imagination Pitt ever decided to—

"Field goal!" he suddenly yelled, holding up three fingers. "Field goal team!"

Taken aback, I strapped on my helmet and ran out onto the field with Reggie and Donnie. A stiff wind blew in our faces. It hadn't been a problem on extra points, but would be a bitch to kick against on what would be—holy toeless Tom Dempsey!—a 50-yard field goal attempt from the left hash mark, which was a more difficult spot for a right-footed kicker.

Instead of concentrating on setting up for the kick, I found myself obsessing over Pitt's motivation. Why *this* kick? Why *now*? We'd had three fourth-down situations earlier in the game deeper in Townie territory that would have made for shorter field goals, all from the center hash mark, and each time he'd chosen to go for the first down instead. If he wasn't into giving me a shot from 30 yards, why try a friggin' 50-yarder . . . into the wind . . . from the left hash mark? Was he just testing my leg? Was he trying to embarrass me?

The offensive line got set. Reggie hunched over the ball. Donnie turned to me.

"You ready?"

I nodded. I was thinking about the wind too much. And Pitt. And the distance. And the snap. And the hold. And the freakishly big-handed Townie defenders. But I couldn't help it; this was not only the first *field goal* I'd ever attempted, it also was easily the longest, far surpassing any distance I'd covered in practice. I'll admit it: I was intimidated, psyching myself out.

Donnie signaled for the snap . . . but it never came. Three seconds passed, then five. Then there were whistles and yellow flags. The O and D lines straightened up. And that's when it hit me: Pitt had never intended to have me kick—he was just trying to draw the Townie defense offside. Alas, I was only a decoy, and Charlestown didn't bite. Khary would punt.

Donnie stood up and sympathetically slapped the top of my helmet, also figuring that we were done, and we started back to our sideline when we saw Pitt holding up three fingers.

"Field goal! Get your asses back out there," Coach O'Neal yelled, smiling. For the love of God, *now* Pitt was going to go for it?! He wasn't going to give me a shot from 50, but now that we'd received a five-yard delay-of-game penalty, he felt perfectly okay throwing me out there for a 55-yarder? Add in the extra degree of difficulty for the left hash mark and, screw it, let's just call it 95 yards! What kind of head games was Pitt playing with me here?

"Just a chip shot, Kick!" I heard Brandon call from the sidelines, clearly joking. And then Elvis. "You got this one, baby!"

"Nice and easy, Mark," Donnie said as he crouched down beside me. The referees blew their whistles, windmilled their arms, time was running. I delicately touched the turf with my toe, the hold spot, where Donnie placed his index finger. I backed up two steps, side-stepped two.

"You ready?"

Again I nodded.

Reggie fired a tight, low spiral. I stepped forward, planted, brought my right leg through the kicking zone with as much power and speed as humanly possible. The linemen converged with grunts, growls, aggression. I connected, arms out, head down, right leg swing-ing up near my left ear, balancing on my left foot. If they had semi-pro football trading cards, this might have been mine.

It felt good. Real good. I nailed it. Donnie and I looked up simul-taneously and watched the ball flying high, long, heading straight to-ward the middle of the uprights. *Holy shit,* I thought, *I've just kicked a 55-yard field goal into the wind from the left hash mark! Screw college ball! Screw Arena League! Bring on the NFL!*

But then something happened. I'm not sure what exactly, but here's my best guess: an exotic butterfly living deep in the Amazon rain forest had flapped its wings sometime around Christmas 2003, setting off floods in Portugal; typhoons in Thailand; sandstorms in the Sahara; melting ice caps in the Arctic; volcanic explosions in Hawaii—all of which finally culminated in a relatively weak but highly unwelcome gust of wind here in Boston, summer 2004.

I grimaced as the stiffening breeze indeed blew my once-straight kick left . . . left some more . . . and *still* farther left, until the emascu-lated ball seemed to hit an invisible midair barrier and dropped like a cartoon anvil a good 10 yards left of the uprights, landing in the mid-dle of the end zone. Still a helluva kick, if you ask me, but well short of the crossbar. The crowd, who had stood and gasped at contact, now sat back down and groaned.

"You hit it good, Mark," Donnie said, standing up. "We don't get that delay of game, that thing's good."

"Yeah." I now hated the wind—and exotic butterflies—with every fiber of my being. Our O-line walked off the field past me, guys of-fering up "nice tries" and "almosts." Even one of the Townie players, who'd swooped in from the left and tried in vain to block the kick, gave me props as he brushed some black rubber FieldTurf granules off his pants. "Nice boot, kicker."

The "penalty knocking us back five yards" excuse, I surprisingly concluded, was no consolation. The old Mark would have shrugged, maybe offered up a "whatever," and forgotten all about it. But the new, football-playing Mark? He was angry. He wanted to make that kick. He wanted to make *every* kick, 50-yarders or extra points. It'd only been a couple of weeks, but thanks to simply being around these guys, and this game, something foreign was growing inside me, a strange new mental toughness I'd never really felt before. And, while I knew that had I made that kick, I should have been playing at Gillette Stadium, not at English High, it was still annoying as hell. Not disappointing, but annoying. I'd failed in far more important sports situations in my life—a missed breakaway my freshman year at F&M that would have given us an upset win over our archrival Elizabethtown came to mind—and didn't bat an eye. *Whatever.* I never really thought about it again (until now, that is). But this? The failure wasn't 30 seconds old and it already gnawed at me. I knew I'd be up all night playing and replaying it in my head.

"Thought you had that one, baby boy!" the terminally positive Elvis said as I reached the sideline, grabbing my helmet in both hands and shaking my head. "If you ever make a kick that long, you gotta do the airplane."

"What's the airplane?" I asked, unsnapping my helmet.

As Gio and Lenny (never far away from Elvis) and I watched with amusement, Elvis tilted his body, spread his arms out to his sides, and ran around in a little circle, like a pro soccer player after scoring a goal. "*Goooooooooooooaaaaaaaaaaaaaaaalllllllllllll!*" Gio yelled, cupping both hands to his mouth as Elvis swooped around like a Cessna gone wild. The game wasn't over yet, but the atmosphere was loose. While I was no doubt disappointed not to have made my first field goal try ever, I could take some solace in the fact that the conditions *were* against me, and that, if not for the penalty pushing us back, we go up 24–12 (Charlestown had scored two inconsequential TDs, missing a PAT and a two-point try). All in all, it wasn't a total loss. My form was good. Best of all, I think, I'd instilled some more confidence in my teammates that, if ever called upon again, I could hit a long one.

A few guys slapped me on the shoulder pads or my butt as I walked toward the stands to get some water. Insano, Jeremy, Brandon, Coach O'Neal. Filling my paper cup, I briefly looked up into the stands to where Celia, Ben, Holly, and Chip were sitting, but didn't want to be one of those players who was more concerned with what's

going on behind him than in front of him on the field. We were going
to win, but the game wasn't over yet.

As I dumped one cup of water over my head and wiped it off my
forehead, Pitt passed by, but then stopped and turned toward me. I
looked at him. It was as if Jason's pit bull, Bruno, was now walking on
his hind legs, carrying a laminated playbook and wearing a tight white
polo shirt. Even so, I thought for sure that finally he was going to actually have something positive to say to me—nice kick against the
wind, you hit it good, something like that, anything.

Instead he looked right at me, his eyes all business. "Wish you
stretched out some more before that kick," he said, letting that sink in
before adding, "Next time, stay loose on the sideline instead of just
standing around." He turned and headed back through the packs of
players over to his defense, who waited farther down the sideline for
some last instructions before heading back out onto the field.

What the hell did he mean, he *wished I would have stretched
out*?! All I *did* on the sidelines during games was stretch, jog in place,
limber up, kick invisible balls. I was more than stretched out, goddammit! And, if not for his stupid delay-of-game penalty, that field
goal's good from 50, I'm being carried off the field, and he's singing
a whole different tune! What was Pitt's *problem*? Was he just a sour
guy? Did he not like kickers? Did he not like white guys from the
'burbs? Or did he just not like *me* in particular? He had, after all, grimaced at me and called me "rich boy" on the first night we met.
Everyone else had been so cool to me, players and coaches alike, not
treating me any differently than anyone else. But Pitt-bull? He just
wasn't buying me, on any level, personal, athletic, you name it.
Maybe this was a battle I'd just never win. Maybe Pitt just wouldn't
ever give a shit that he now had a kicker who—I know this is a radi-
cal concept—*might actually be able to kick*! If so, why even keep playing? Why keep running my ass off at practice and doing push-ups
and trying to prove that I belong if the one guy who had any real say
in my fate, the coach, was against me?

For the final few minutes, I remained a few feet removed from
the other players at the far end of our sideline, on one knee, gripping
the face mask of my upturned helmet and using it for balance. Our
defense held the Townies to four meaningless yards on their final series. The clock expired.

Panthers 21, Charlestown 12. We were officially in the win column.

Both teams gathered at midfield to shake hands and take a knee for the postgame prayer. There was a lot of crossbreeding, if you will, between the Panthers and the Townies. Not only were we the only two teams within Boston proper, but also several of our players had once played for Charlestown: Reggie, Donnie, Delaney, Cliff (who had technically retired but still suited up for practices), Jim "Jimbo" Murphy, a 24-year semi-pro veteran—24 years!—who had just started coming to our practices after defecting from the Townies. A stocky, neckless, barrel-chested, lifelong Charlestown townie through and through, Jimbo was a union truck driver for the local movie industry, but easily could have been on-screen playing the role of Irish Mob Enforcer #2. He started playing football in the now defunct Boston Park League, and had played for almost every team in the EFL over his quarter century of semi-pro action: Middleboro, Marlboro, Charlestown, Randolph, Quincy, and now Boston. He and Reggie were especially tight and went way back. "Reggie's my brutha from anutha mutha," Jimbo said of his fellow Murphy, and immediately, almost from the second he got to his first practice and found out I was the kicker, started calling me "Supah Toe." Or, translated from the thick Boston accent: Super Toe.

As always, Coach O'Neal, after telling us each to find a hand or a shoulder of the guy next to us, led the postgame prayer, but this time the guy next to me took my hand. Under any other circumstances this would have seemed profoundly bizarre—rarely in other walks of life—say, on a subway or at work—did another grown man randomly take your hand, especially when his was calloused and bruised and sweaty. But this was just further proof that the world of semi-pro football was radically different from any other world I'd ever visited. In fact, the guy who took my hand just happened to be the same player who'd almost blocked my first extra point, a stout, freckle-faced Irish guy of about 30. He looked over at me and shook his head. "Almost had ya on that first kick, ya lucky bastid," he whispered with a thick Boston accent, grinning. "You kicked it too friggin' hahd. Almost took my fingahs off." He wiggled his index and middle fingers as proof that they still worked.

"I almost had a heart attack," I replied. "You timed that jump nicely, man."

He shook his head. "Nah, white Irish boys can't jump, bro. You just kicked it a little too low. Gotta get under it a little more next time."

I nodded, promising myself that it would be the last time I ever gave someone a chance to get his hands on a kick of mine. Extra points should be gimmes.

"Dear Lord," O'Neal finally began, his head bowed, eyes closed, "we thank You for watching over us on the field tonight . . ." and he went into his standard postgame thoughts about brotherhood and football making us better men and all of us being enemies on the field but respected combatants off of it. Some of my teammates, I saw, started smiling to themselves. O'Neal was known to be loquacious, to say the least, especially when he got on a roll during his prayers.

"Simply putting on a uniform doesn't guarantee you respect," O'Neal continued, to everyone's growing amusement. "One has to *earn* respect—respect of his peers, his opponents, his teammates, and You, Lord. Tonight I think we earned each other's respect, and fought as brothers striving for a common goal: to be better players and better men. In the game of football—"

"—Ahhh-MEN!" Ace interrupted, rolling his eyes and smiling. "Coach, the Lord wants you to wrap it up." O'Neal conceded.

The whole group laughed, stood up, shook hands one last time. Former teammates gave each other shoulder bumps, caught up, promised to meet for a beer. There was a "dysfunctional yet tight-knit family" feeling in the EFL. Brothers fight, cousins argue, but they're still part of the same gene pool.

So there it was: we had officially reached one-third of the team's victory total from the previous season, when they went 3–7. Personally, I hadn't made any more progress with Pitt, even though I'd hit three extra points (well, two and a half, considering my first one barely squeaked through). As a team, we hadn't made much progress either. Sure, we'd beaten an undermanned, less-talented Townie squad, but there were still a lot of stupid on-field gaffes and mental errors, many of them involving the big twins Jason and Anthony, who were flagged on countless occasions for everything from holding to unsportsmanlike conduct. They were nice as could be off the field, the proverbial big teddy bears. But on the field they had a hard time controlling their tempers, costing us valuable penalty yards that a better team than Charlestown would have taken advantage of.

This wasn't lost on Pitt. After O'Neal's prayer, he left without saying much of anything, except this: "We won. But I'm not happy. I'm not happy at all. Tuesday, 6:00 P.M. sharp."

God help us.

IN GOOD HANDS

I FELT VERY SECURE with Donnie as my holder. Mostly because he was a 16-year EFL veteran and always put the ball in perfect position, laces out, tiled just so. But partly because he carried a gun.

He did so legally: Donnie was a private investigator.

"My office is my car," he says of his two comfortable used luxury models, a Jaguar and a Mercedes. Donnie traveled in better style than anyone except maybe Caleb, the private school teacher, who drove a sleek Infiniti sedan, or Jimbo, who drove a brand new Jaguar (I guess the union gig paid pretty well). "Some days, I can sit out front of some guy's house for five hours waiting for something to happen, like watching paint dry," Donnie says. "Other days, I'm out there five minutes and boom, suddenly a guy's out of his house and you're chasing him all over town."

A Portsmouth, Virginia, native with a smooth demeanor and seeming perpetual Cheshire cat smile, Donnie was born in the mid-60s—"Right about when they were taking down the 'No Coloreds' and 'Whites Only' signs," he says. The second-oldest of four children, he spent the early part of his life in the tough Lincoln Park section of the bustling port city. Like nearly everyone else in Portsmouth, his father was a navy man, so Donnie's upbringing, between his father's military discipline and his mother's devout Catholicism, was strict. "They always told us kids, 'If Momma don't see you [doing something bad], God does,'" he says with a laugh. But he still has a great admiration for how his father ran his household. "I respected the hell outta that cat. Like James Brown said, 'Papa don't take no mess.' He worked two, three jobs to support us. He was always a worker. I learned so much from him."

When not working, however, Donnie's father would take him to local high school football games, where he'd explain the rules and break down the action on the field. (One of their Friday Night pilgrimages was to see the legendary 1971 Virginia state championship game between T. C. Williams High and Andrew Lewis High at Victory Stadium in Roanoke—later re-created for the climax of *Remember the Titans*.)

A talented wide receiver at Manor High School, Donnie, then a slim 130 pounds, led the city with a 16.5-yards-per-catch average as a senior despite missing three games with a knee injury. But as graduation neared, college wasn't even a consideration. "Where I grew up, the thought process was, You get your diploma, then you get a job," he says. "There was never talk of college." Portsmouth was—and still is—home to the oldest and largest naval shipyard in the country. After graduating from high school in 1981 and working at McDonald's for a year, Donnie followed in his father's (and older brother's) footsteps and joined the navy's delayed-entry program.

For job training, he chose aviation structural mechanic—"To this day, I can't change the oil in my car, but I can tear apart and rebuild an F-16," he jokes—and was eventually sent to boot camp outside of Chicago, followed by stints in Tennessee, Jacksonville, and eventually Japan, all in nine months. Pretty whirlwind for a 21-year-old kid who'd never left Virginia before. While he still relishes his navy experience, he can't help but feel that he was tricked somewhat by the delayed-entry program. "I had no idea that even though I'd sworn the oath and all that, I wasn't officially in the navy yet. I still could have gone to college."

And he could have played college football. Before Donnie's service officially began, his cousin, a talented local high school player, was offered a full scholarship to James Madison University, and told the JMU coach about Donnie. The coach knew of the speedy, if undersized, receiver from Portsmouth—think Deion Branch—and offered Donnie a chance to attend JMU, where he would have played with future Cowboys' and 49ers' star Charles Haley. However, thinking he had officially enlisted in the navy and would be arrested if he didn't show up after that six-month delay, he turned the offer down and soon found himself halfway around the globe, at Kadena Air Force Base, Okinawa, Japan.

While he still regrets never having a chance to go to college, Donnie says his navy experience was unforgettable—partly for the travel, partly for the women who accompanied said travel. You name it, the young, single, good-looking Donnie and his pals did it, burning a swath of romantic destruction through Europe and Asia that would make General Sherman blush. "Our philosophy whenever we went to another country," he recalls with a grin, "was this: To hell with the Eiffel Tower, forget the Great Wall—I'm banging one of your chicks first. *Then* we'll go sightseeing." Once, while stationed in Italy, he even had a chance to hook up with a beautiful young Miss Ohio, who was on a goodwill world tour with her fellow Miss America hopefuls. While the women were visiting the ship, Donnie, never the wallflower, started chatting them up, in particular Miss Ohio, the most gorgeous of them all. Taken in by his southern charm, Miss Ohio invited Donnie and his friends to meet them at a club later that evening. But he ended up blowing her off because he wasn't 100 percent certain that he could "seal the deal" with her, as it were, and already had more of a "sure thing" waiting for him elsewhere in town. It was a decision he'd always regret: Miss Ohio's name was Halle Berry.

"Who would have gotten the better of *that* deal—Donnie Williams, fat semi-pro football player, or Halle Berry, Academy Award–winning actress?" he laughs, ruefully shaking his head.

But such renegade behavior during his navy days didn't come without its pitfalls. Donnie had been in countless brawls, and had had knives pulled on him more times than he could count. That danger, however, was nothing compared to what was waiting for him back in the States one early Saturday morning several years later. Donnie, then 31 and just having been honorably discharged, was

married and living in Tallahassee with two young daughters and a
third housemate—his youngest brother, Troy, 20.

That morning, he and Troy had a church league basketball game,
but because his wife was sick and needed some rest, he agreed to
drop his daughters at his sister-in-law's. Near her house, a car was inexplicably parked in the middle of the intersection, completely
blocking their path. Two men sat in the front seat, not moving the
car. Donnie gave a quick toot of the horn. Nothing. He honked
again, longer this time. Nothing. Finally, seeing that the men weren't
budging, he maneuvered his Chevy Impala around their car, inching
to its left and squeezing his way through the intersection. As they
passed, Troy yelled at them to "get their damn car out of the street,"
and he and the driver then exchanged some more words. Nothing
too bad, as far as Donnie was concerned. "Troy and the guy talked a
little smack to each other and we just kept going," he says. "I thought
it was over."

Far from it.

After bringing his daughters into the house, Donnie and Troy
briefly stopped in the front yard to chat with neighbors and were
about to head to the basketball game when he heard the screeching
of tires.

"Donnie," Troy yelled, pointing out to the street, "they're coming
back around!"

Donnie turned to see the two men from the other car now running at them, one carrying a shotgun, the other holding a pistol and
looping back around another nearby house, presumably to cut him
and Troy off and corner them. After that, Donnie says, "It was something straight out of *Miami Vice*."

He and Troy sprinted to the Impala, where Donnie planned to
just back out of the driveway as fast as humanly possible and speed
off. That's when they heard the first shots.

"I'll never forget that sound," Donnie recalls. "It was like BAM!
BAM! BAM! Loudest thing I ever heard. Dude thought it was Dodge
City." The man shot out Donnie's front tire and back window. This,
Donnie says, changed everything. "I was just trying to get the hell
outta there and diffuse the situation, but when he started shootin',
that's when the evil in me kicked in. I knew then he wasn't just trying
to scare us; he was trying to kill us, and my survival instinct kicked in.
It was kill or be killed." Fortunately, Donnie, who by then had begun
his private investigation career and was working as an investigator for

the public defender's office, had a legal .9-millimeter pistol and a
.380 Magnum in the car. ("Plus," he jokes, "this was Florida. Everyone
and his mother had guns.")

Over the exploding of glass and booming rifle reports, and now
"filled with a rage I'd never felt before," Donnie stepped out of the
car, aimed the .9-millimeter, and began to fire at the oncoming rifleman, who immediately began retreating. "I had just gotten out of the
navy," Donnie says, "and you might not believe it looking at me now,
but I was in *great* shape. This dude was a big ol' fat guy, so I was going
to just run him down and kill him, right then and there. He's running
away and I'm about to take him out, got his fat ass lined up . . . and
that's when my gun jams. I was screwed."

Out on his own and holding a useless weapon, Donnie realized
that the second gunman was circling around ahead of him and would
soon be joining his rifle-toting buddy. So he ran like hell back to the
car. There, he saw what would later become a sight to laugh about,
but at the time didn't exactly tickle his ribs. "I dive into the front
seat, and see Troy, curled up, saying, 'Oh, my God, Oh, my God, Donnie, you saved my life, you saved my life.' If he wasn't my brother, I
would have killed him *myself*! I gave him the other gun so he'd actually come out and help me, not sit there in the car muttering like
Rain Man! *He was the one who got us into this mess in the first place*!"

Ignoring the shredded tire, Donnie peeled away as the two men
fired a few final shots, and he and Troy sputtered to a gas station several blocks away. There, he looked at his watch and turned to his
shaking, sweating brother.

"We only got five minutes until the game," he said, perfectly
calm, as if they *hadn't* just been in an O.K. Corral–style shoot-out. "I
think we can still make it."

Troy gawked at his older brother. "We almost just died and you're
still worried about the *basketball game*?!"

"My attitude was, Nothing we can do about it now," Donnie tells
me, laughing at his own bravado. "We might as well go play some basketball."

But the sound of sirens ruined that plan. "I didn't know Tallahassee had that many policemen in the entire force," Donnie marvels.
The cops surrounded the car, ordered the Williams brothers out,
hands over heads, on their knees, flat on their stomachs. The worst
part for Donnie, however, wasn't the fact that they were being arrested; ever the ladies' man, he saw that a local sorority was having a

car wash across the street, and the scantily clad, suds-covered young ladies had of course stopped to watch the live episode of *Cops* unfolding in front of them. "The cops were making me look bad in front of the honeys!" Donnie laments.

Despite maintaining that they were only defending themselves, Donnie and Troy were thrown in jail by the skeptical police, in separate cells. Donnie was not only handcuffed, but was also chained to a wall with plastic bags on his hands to protect any evidence of gunpowder residue. "Manson got treated better," he jokes. "They had me locked up there like Hannibal Lecter."

All charges against the Williams brothers were eventually dropped. It turned out that the two other men were known skinheads, and had been involved in a number of other local shootings and robberies. Also, a policeman who was nearby at the time of the shooting had heard the first shots and, being well trained, recognized them as rifle shots, not .9-millimeter pistol fire. Hence Donnie was exonerated under Florida's No Retreat Law, which provides that "a person need not retreat from an attack, may 'stand his ground' and use deadly force if he reasonably believes he or another person is threatened by death or serious physical injury."

When all was said and done, the skinheads, despite their shady record, got only four days in jail and two years' probation. They concocted a story for the judge, claiming that two black men had robbed their house earlier that morning, so they were upset at black people in general, and even though they knew Donnie and Troy weren't the two black men who'd allegedly robbed them, they just started firing at the first two they saw.

"And the judge bought it," Donnie says. "If it'd been me, a black man in the South shooting at two white guys, I would have gotten a helluva lot more than four days, that's for damn sure."

In any case, it was great to know Donnie was cool under pressure, to say the least. I mean, once you've been shot at by skinheads, a last-second field goal probably doesn't seem all that scary.

While I'd never be fool enough to claim that our punishment at practice on the Tuesday after our shaky Charlestown win was anywhere

near as harsh as a life-or-death shoot-out with skinheads, it sure as
hell wasn't pleasant.

    After we did our normal calisthenics and two long laps of both
baseball fields under the scorching early August sun, Pitt added a
painful new twist to our regimen: a sadistic routine called "rollovers."
Pitt held a football out in front of a line of us as we crouched down
on all fours, hands planted into the turf, feet digging and running behind us. When Pitt moved the ball to either the left or the right, in
unison we'd drop and roll in that direction, reset ourselves on all
fours, feet still digging furiously until he moved the ball again, after
which we'd drop and roll in that direction—dig dig dig, *roll left*, dig
dig dig, *roll right*, dig dig dig!—over and over and over. Sometimes
he'd fake the ball to the left and then move it right, causing a Panther
pileup, some guys falling for the fake. "Watch the ball, dammit!" Pitt
yelled whenever he fooled someone. "Move on the ball! That is why
we got all those stupid offsides and false starts last weekend, because
you guys were not *KEEPING YOUR EYE ON THE DAMN BALL!*"
Pitt was in rare form.

    I did every drill that night. Took the same punishment as my
teammates. When darkness came, we finished up with a good half
hour of sprints.

    "Fourth quarter!" Pitt yelled, watching us run back and forth, his
arms crossed at his chest as, next to him, an orange-red cigar tip
glowed in front of his trusted lieutenant, O'Neal.

    "Run, you crack whores," O'Neal joked, taunting us. My lungs felt
like they were covered in barbed wire, but I couldn't help but
laugh—the laugh of a delirious mental patient who has no idea what
century it is.

    "I told you we're going to be the best-conditioned team in this
league, gentlemen," Pitt called out. "That means mentally as well as
physically. If you can't get the mental part together, we'll just keep
hammering on the physical part. It's up to you."

    When he finally blew his whistle, it was past nine o'clock. We'd
been out there for three hours. Driving home, feeling like every
joint, muscle, and tendon was on the verge of snapping like a
frayed rubber band, I realized we still had a long way to go if we
were going to be considered a serious contender for the EFL title.
Middleboro and Brockton were both 3–0, clearly the class of the
league. And even though we were about to play a team, the Middlesex Mayhem, that wasn't considered one of the best in the EFL,

we couldn't take anyone for granted. We hadn't earned that right yet.

That Saturday I drove up Interstate 93 almost to the border of Massachusetts and New Hampshire to UMASS–Lowell, home of the Middlesex Mayhem. Their record was solid—2–2, not having had their bye week yet—but they'd beaten the two doormats of the league, Randolph and Rhode Island. It was hard to gauge what kind of team we'd be dealing with. Along the way I tried to visualize my extra points and field goals sailing through the uprights high and straight.

In warm-ups, I was on fire. Everything I kicked was a straight, booming shot, many of them garnering applause and cheers from my teammates. "Oh, yeeeeah, Adam Vina-*tizzy*!" Ace yelled, all six-two of him leaning down and head-butting me. Shouts of *Hell, yeah!* and *Dial it up, fellas, dial it up!* echoed throughout our end zone. Every single player there was energized, jumping around, banging shoulder pads, focused, yet loose, laughing, enjoying himself. Except one.

Pee Wee spent most of the pregame all by himself at the far end of our sideline, sitting on the turf, calmly stretching, looking past the field and over the top of the stands with a million-mile stare. Occasionally Kelly would walk down and sit with him. While at first it looked like she was just doing her trainer thing, pushing on his back, stretching his legs, and helping him work out some of the kinks from the car ride, it soon became apparent that she was consoling him. His head hung low. Every now and then he would say something, a brief word or two, and she would nod.

"What's going on with Pee Wee?" I asked Donnie as we gathered on our sideline to watch the coin toss.

"His brother got shot last night," Donnie responded. His tone was matter-of-fact—not unkind or unsympathetic, but just the tone of someone for whom a shooting wasn't the most foreign concept in the world. Donnie had been shot at more than once in his life.

"Jesus. What happened?"

"Not sure. Just heard he got shot."

"Is he okay?"

Donnie shrugged and wiped away a bead of sweat with his fore-arm. "He's in the hospital. But they don't know if he's gonna make it."

Wow. This was one of those moments that slapped me across the face and reminded me that while we all had football in common—the same jerseys, the same helmets, the same team name—our lives couldn't have been more different. Just like that, someone was shot. And here his brother was, the very next night, about to play a foot-ball game. Would I have been able to come out and play football if my brother or sister got shot? No chance. I'd be in a state of shock, or too outraged. Maybe Pee Wee just needed something to take his mind off of it? Maybe he wanted to make the opponent pay for what hap-pened? Of all sports besides maybe boxing, football was the ideal arena for purging any anger or frustration. I looked down at Pee Wee and Kelly. He was still just staring off into space as she gently rolled out his neck, both hands on either side of his head. His eyes were closed, like a cat having its head rubbed, yet his chiseled face was as stoic as ever, pure granite. I then looked over at the Mayhem sideline and immediately had another quarterback to pity.

The captains won the toss and guys jumped on Insano, Moham-mad, Todd, and Khary as they returned from midfield. We packed in tightly and raised our hands high into the center, touching a shoulder, a helmet.

"Nothin' else to say, y'all," Insano said, head down, voice calm and even. "Let's just get it crackin' from the start and never look back. Team on three, team on three, one, two, three—"

"TEAM!"

Only a chain-link fence and a sloping grass embankment sepa-rated our sideline from the highway. Cars occasionally honked as they passed by, some of them filled with girls who whooped and hollered at the sight of men in tight uniform pants. "The females are out tonight, fellas!" one player announced, waving at a passing car.

The pregame excitement didn't carry over to the first quarter. Despite Pitt's hard-line approach that week about mental toughness, we were still killing ourselves with dumb penalties, and after some impressive drives, we were still scoreless after one quarter. It didn't help that the refs were practically shredding their rotator cuffs throwing flags on us, mostly against Jason and Anthony up front, who, from my vantage point as I paced the sidelines and stretched out, were most often just reacting to some extracurricular chippiness by the aptly named Mayhem. One time, seconds after a play was whistled dead, one of their linebackers took a two-step run and shoved Jason into the pile of players on the ground. Jason stood up, turned, and shoved the linebacker right back. And only then did the flags fly . . . on Jason. For the first time that season, I began to suspect a slight bias against the team from the 'hood. "They're talking just as much shit as we are, Coach!" Anthony explained to a glaring Pitt as he walked off the field after another unsportsmanlike-conduct penalty had killed a potential scoring drive.

"Just shut up and ignore them," Pitt pleaded. "Can we do that for once?"

Late in the second quarter, on a third and seven from the Mayhem 49-yard line, Southie dropped back, pump-faked to Sam on the right, and then hit a streaking Jeremy on a perfectly timed, high-arcing bomb down the left sideline, hitting Jeremy in stride. Some of the defensive players, along with me and my sideline crew of Elvis, Lenny, Gio, Rome, et al., momentarily escorted Jeremy down our sideline, cheering him on. But he didn't need our help; he switched on that gear that only the elite athletes possess and pulled away from the flailing D-back—a Ferrari outrunning a Ford Taurus—and galloped untouched into the end zone. We mobbed him when he came off the field, still holding the ball. Panthers 6, Mayhem 0. The rout was on.

As I was about to head out with the kicking team for the extra point, I heard a collective groan: several yellow flags littered the field. A scrum of Panthers and Mayhem players was still pushing and shoving back at the line of scrimmage, a chaotic mess of black, silver, red, white, and blue, with the zebras trying in vain to pry everyone apart. Jason was kneeling on the turf with both hands under his mask, holding his face, yelling in pain. A Mayhem player was suddenly shoved backward out of the scrum onto his ass. He got up and started to charge back in but was restrained by his teammates. It was a train wreck.

"What happened?" Pitt called over to the side judge. "Mr. Referee, what was the original penalty out there?"

"False start and unsportsmanlike conduct on black . . . *again*," the side judge answered, with what I detected as a hint of a smirk in his voice. "That pretty touchdown's coming back, Coach."

"Unsportsmanlike on who? For what? What number?"

"Sixty-eight *and* 69. Hitting after the play." The big twins again.

"Who called that?"

"I did," the ref, a red-faced little fireplug of a man, answered defiantly. "Number 69 hit the opponent below the waist after the play."

"How can you make that call from all the way across the field? There were 20 guys standing between you and the play!"

"Unsportsmanlike, Coach. Your guys have been doing it all game."

There was another collective groan on our sideline, and a few angry curses. Ace slammed his helmet to the ground.

"Naw, ref," Donnie complained, his Virginia twang turning the single syllable *ref* into the two-syllable *ray-uf*. "That ain't right. You gotta call it both ways now."

The ref stood stoically nearby, ignoring the reaction, arms crossed at his chest. Pitt, fuming, walked right past him onto the field and called the big twins over. I thought he might go Woody Hayes on them and smack them upside the head, or grab both of their face masks, and crack their helmets together like Moe schooling Shemp and Larry. Instead he gathered himself and coolly asked, "What happened?"

"Their guy jumped into the neutral zone, then poked my brother in the eye after the play, Coach, on purpose, and right in front of the ref!" Anthony explained, his voice high and full of frustration. Jason stood next to him, nodding, still holding his hand up to his eye and wincing. "He's been doing that shit all game, chop-blocking, head-slapping, and the refs just lettin' it go! They're gettin' away with murder out there, Coach. We gotta fight back at some point! And they jumped offside, we didn't false start!"

Pitt sighed. I'm sure visions of the implosion at Brockton swam through his head. O'Neal chimed in and told Coach Pitt that he'd been keeping track of penalties. "Nine against us, Mike, and only two against them, and both just five-yarders for delay of game, nothing for unsportsmanlike or anything. I'd say that's a bit 'skewed,'" he added, rolling his eyes.

Pitt glowered, hands on his hips. Part of him was clearly frustrated by the one-sided officiating; it was pretty horrific. The other half of him, however, knew that this wasn't the first time the big twins had lost their heads and gotten personal fouls. It was that fine line of, Does trouble find the Panthers, or do the Panthers find trouble? Probably both. But if we'd been up 21–0, like we should have been at that point, none of those nine penalties would have mattered. As it stood, the game was tied and we'd just lost some serious momentum.

"All right, line it back up, get on out there," Pitt said, resigned, waving his playbook and shooing the offensive players who'd gathered near the sidelines during the brief delay. Jeremy could only laugh as he flipped the ball back to the ref. As the rest of the offense headed back out to the field, the side judge dropped an atom bomb—another bright yellow flag at Pitt's feet.

"Bench misconduct," he called over to the ref, blowing his whistle and pointing at our sideline.

Pitt just stared at him. While I'd seen him angry before and I had no doubt that he had the strength to forcibly remove someone's head from his body, I honestly never thought he'd actually do it. Until now. *Here we go,* I thought. *We'll be watching this on the evening news later.*

Instead he just smiled. An amused, wide, honest-to-goodness smile. I didn't even know he had teeth. "Tell me this is a joke," he said to the side judge.

"He told you to stay off the field, Coach," the ref, jogging over to defend his crew member, said.

"No, he didn't," Pitt said with a laugh. "He knew I was just going out to talk to my players. And how could you hear what he said to me, anyway? You were as far away from us as he was from the original play!"

The ref shook his head, went back out to the field, and walked off an additional 15 yards for the bench unsportsmanlike, on top of Anthony's 15-yarder for going after the guy who had eye-gouged Jason. Instead of being up 7–0, it was now third down and 37 for the first down.

"File a complaint with the league if you want, Coach," the side judge said as Pitt still pleaded his case. "Till then, get your players under control."

"You're just making this shit up as you go along, aren't you, ref? Is this your first *fucking* game?" I looked around to see what angry man had said that, and realized, to my shock, that it had been me. Everyone on the sideline looked at me, eyebrows raised, amused.

"Whoa, kicker's gettin' riled up," Brandon said, chuckling. "Look out!"

The side judge spun around and glared in my direction. O'Neal quickly slid in front of me like a Secret Service agent taking a bullet for the president. "We don't need you getting ejected," he whispered out of the corner of his mouth. "That's a one-game suspension in this league."

"This is *bull*shit!" Ace yelled behind me.

"Has it ever been this bad?" I asked.

"What, the refs?" He shrugged, frustration with a hint of resignation. "Let's just say the refs in this league ain't big fans of the team
from the 'hood. Lots of 'em live in these cow towns we play against,
so who do you think they're gonna give the calls to: the bruthas
from Boston, or the dudes they play cards with at the Elks club
every Tuesday?"

"Why don't you think they can just be impartial?"

He looked at me for a moment, somewhat incredulous, as if the
answer was obvious. He then held his forearm a few inches from my
face and pinched a hunk of his brown skin between his thumb and
index finger, pulling it up. "'Cause of this, Vina-tizzy."

"Because I'm white?" I kidded. "Those *bastards*."

He stared down at me again. A couple of other guys turned and
looked at me, too: Caleb, Insano, Jammer, Brandon. *Shit*. Had I chosen
the wrong time to be a funny guy?

Ace stared a moment longer and then broke a big grin and shook
his head. Mike and another young reserve named Malik, standing
nearby, also laughed. "Yup, the refs hate white kickers," Ace said with
a laugh. "Someone hide Vina-tizzy, he's gettin' us killed out there!"

Pitt, on the other hand, was still incensed. We were still tied with
a team we should have been running off the field, albeit a solid veteran one. And he had simply had enough of the stupid penalties, the
selfish, untimely fouls.

"Everyone bring it in!" he yelled. "Now!" We all gathered around
him, heads down, looking like children about to be scolded by their
father, although some guys, as was often the case, were either too
riled up or too prideful to be scolded, and didn't know when to
shut the hell up and listen. And, as always, there was ample finger-
pointing.

"Niggas on offense gotta start doin' they jobs out there," Ace
complained to no one, to everyone, just venting in general in his deep,
gravelly voice. "We doin' ours. You do yours and get some points up
on that motherfuckin' scoreboard."

"Ace, you always talkin' shit and *doin'* shit," Big Paul shot back,
laughing at Ace's hypocrisy. "You got more penalties than tackles."
This brought out a few chuckles, despite the tension, and Ace started
toward Paul. Paul, 23, lived down the street from our Franklin Park
practice field, on Blue Hill Avenue, and was a bouncer at an Irish pub

in the Back Bay named Clery's. Six-eight, 350, he always looked like he'd just woken up—bushy, unkempt Afro, sleepy eyes, lumbering steps—but could spring when he had to. Plus, being a bouncer at a pub in the trendy Back Bay, he'd no doubt dealt with unruly sorts before, but drunken stockbrokers, lawyers, and ad guys were probably a little less intimidating than a riled-up Ace.

Paul stood his ground, ready for Ace, but Insano grabbed Ace's shoulder pads and held him back. Then everyone started chiming in at once, total chaos.

"The refs suck!"

"You twins gotta stop holdin' on every single play!"

"Follow your blocks, Amos, stop dancing around back there!"

"I been open all game, get me the damn ball!"

"*All of you* shut the fuck up!" Mohammad finally boomed, glaring at everyone. "Coach is the only one talking here!"

The complaints trickled out. Pitt was silent for a moment. "This is bull crap," he finally said, his voice calmer now, a case study in controlled fury. "You know it. I know it. We should be running this team off the field. They can't hang with us, and we're keeping them in it. Just like Brockton, just like Middleboro, just like we almost did against Charlestown, we're shooting ourselves in the foot. When are you going to start acting like men?"

No one answered.

"You want the league's respect, you want your opponent's respect, you have to go out there and take it. No one's gonna give it to you. Especially us. Everyone already thinks we're out-of-control thugs, and then we go out and prove them right. This is disgusting. Get your heads together, or don't bother coming back next week! And I won't be back. I have better things to do with my time!"

He started walking off, but then turned and added, "And if I hear one more of you using the n-word, I'm gonna run you until you drop dead, you hear me?" For the older guys like Pitt, Reggie, and Donnie, the word "nigga" had a far different impact than it did to the younger guys. "These young dudes use 'nigga' way too much, you know, 'My nigga' and all that," Reggie says. "To them, saying 'nigga' is like saying 'Smith.'" For Donnie, the word evokes unpleasant memories. "When I was a kid, I was called 'nigger' a lot and, trust me, it was not a term of endearment. The first time was at a navy base pool. I was about eight years old and this little white girl—couldn't have been more than four—was playing in a puddle, and she looked up at me and totally out of the blue says, 'My mommy and daddy told me not to play with niggers.' I didn't even know what to say," he laughs, still not believing it. "I was like, First of all, little girl, I don't want to play with you, either; and, second, how will your mommy and daddy feel about this 'nigger' drowning you in that puddle you're playing in?"

Pitt's message was received loud and clear. Southie threw a quick slant to Sam on third and 37 and Sam, shedding two would-be tacklers, turned an eight- or nine-yard gain into a 43-yarder. Our bench went nuts. On the next play Amos took a draw play down to the Mayhem eight. Two plays and we were right back into scoring position. But to their credit, they clamped down and stopped two straight run plays and an attempted fade pass to KFC in the corner of the end zone.

My heart kicking into overdrive, I did some quick math: eight-yard line, plus seven yards on the snap back to Donnie, plus 10 yards for the end zone . . . this would be a 25-yarder. A chip shot. Little more than an extra point. If Pitt didn't throw me out there for *this* one, he'd never use me. I might as well have just undressed right then and there and driven home.

"Field goal," Pitt called out, walking down the sideline. "Field goal team, get on out there! Field goal . . ." But I already had my helmet strapped on and was trotting out even before he finished the sentence, as were Reggie and Donnie.

I set up on the 15-yard line, Donnie kneeling down beside me. Mohammad jogged past me on his way to the O-line. "You got this one, baby," he said, biffing my helmet with his palm as he passed.

The lines set. I set the spot with my right foot beside Donnie, backed up two paces, stepped two to the side, and looked at him.

"You ready?" Donnie asked.

I nodded and banged my right toe against the turf, a new Nomar Garciaparra-esque tick I'd started relying on to pack my foot as tightly into my cleat as possible.

Donnie turned to Reggie, who snapped. Donnie caught, held, spun. I stepped forward.

And I nailed it.

The ball flew not only through the uprights and over the track beyond, but also over another fence and down a hill beyond that. There it was: my first field goal ever! Relief flooded over me, through my veins. I had actually contributed more than a measly extra point!

A little kid in a Mayhem sweatshirt sprinted after the ball, tripped, got back up, and kept up the pursuit of the bounding foot-ball, perhaps thinking it was a stray souvenir, like at Fenway.

It was only 25 yards, but I *just crushed it*. Thing would have been good from *45*. I heard cheers from our side. Donnie stood up, and I slapped his helmet. "Nice hold, man." I waited and high-fived the linemen as they walked past me.

Panthers 3, Mayhem zip. Back on the sideline, even Pitt seemed to notice my contribution, finally. "Nice work, Mark," he said, glanc-ing up briefly from his playsheets and giving me a quick nod as I passed by him. Not exactly a bear hug, but I'd take it.

Those three little points seemed to reenergize everyone. And they reaffirmed the understated importance of a good kicking game. If I'd missed, we might have stayed deflated, scoreless, pissed off. Ahead now, however, we immediately forgot the shady officiating and, on the first Mayhem play from scrimmage, Caleb unleashed a perfectly timed hit on a Mayhem receiver, jarring the ball loose on their 30-yard line, where Insano recovered. On our first play, with the May-hem perhaps thinking we'd go conservative, run, and eat some clock before ending the first half with another field goal, Southie faked a pitch to Amos, set, and delicately lofted a pass to the corner of the end zone, where Jeremy made a one-handed, *SportsCenter*-worthy grab, with two men draped all over him, no less (shocker: no flag). I calmly drilled the extra point.

It was 10–0 at the half.

And still 10–0 late into the fourth quarter. Once again, we'd pulled our Jekyll and Hyde act, penalties killing touchdown drives, and knocking us out of field goal range on several occasions. We were letting the Mayhem hang around. They even got a safety when Southie and Amos collided on a handoff in our end zone. Amos fell on it before they could recover, but they were on the board. They now had hope. Panthers 10, Mayhem 2. A late touchdown and a two-point conversion would tie the game.

"There goes the shutout, D-block," Pitt said nonchalantly as the defense headed back onto the field. "Gonna let the win slip away, too?"

According to Khary, the answer was no. On the Mayhem's second play, Khary stepped in front of their tight end, snatched the intended pass, and ran it all the way back to their six-yard line before being knocked out of bounds. Two plays later, Southie handed off to Todd, who bulled his way into the end zone behind Donnie, who'd been put in at his old position, offensive line, after Jason injured an ankle on the previous series. Panthers 16, Mayhem 2.

Extra point. Reggie snapped, Donnie placed it down. I stepped forward and was about to swing my leg when, out of nowhere, Donnie pulled a Lucy-and-Charlie Brown: He grabbed the ball, stood up, and bolted back across my path to our left, heading toward the end zone as I stood mute and confused, reduced to a spectator.

A Mayhem special teamer immediately darted outside to meet him, as if he *knew* Donnie would run for it. They collided head-on—plastic, flesh, bone, violence—and crumpled to the ground short of the end zone.

The play was whistled dead. But Donnie and the guy didn't care. Fists flying, legs kicking, they rolled around, flipping and flopping over and over like two drunken sea turtles trying to mate. Whistles. Shoving. Chaos. Flags. Separation. Curses. Still incensed, Donnie yanked off his helmet and threw it toward our sideline and stormed off the field as the few scattered Mayhem fans, maybe 50 total, booed lustily from their side of the field. The 20 or so family and friends on our sidelines cheered him. Donnie was one of the most likable guys on the team, but he was volatile, man. If his temper got the better of him, look out. And we couldn't afford to have him kicked out of games. Like O'Neal said, a one-game suspension would follow an ejection, and we had the legendary Marlboro Shamrocks at home the following week. I didn't want to have to play against the EFL dynasty without my holder. I *needed him* taking those snaps from Reggie.

No such luck: Donnie was indeed ejected. Just a stupid play with so little time left. The Mayhem player, beet red and still swearing all the way over to his sideline, ripped off his jersey and shoulder pads and angrily tossed them at his bench. In their first fair call of the night, the refs had given him his walking papers, too.

Donnie, calm as ever despite the hurricane he'd been just 30 seconds prior—I pictured him in the front seat of his bullet-ridden Chevy Impala calmly telling Troy that he still wanted to play basketball—explained himself. "That was personal, Mark. Sorry 'bout that. That dude punched me in the stomach a couple plays earlier, and we had a beef last year, too. I remembered his number. If we needed that extra point, believe me, I never would have done that. But that was personal. I needed to hit that dude. And I told him after we scored to get ready, because I'm gonna be running that ball and if he had any balls he'd try to come get me." Donnie grinned. "I got in some good punches."

I couldn't help but laugh, but the worry instantly set in. "But you'll get suspended now for the next game, right?"

"Yeah, I might have to sit out a game. The long arm of the EFL law doesn't like me too much." He smiled sheepishly.

Khary kicked off. Middlesex ran three inconsequential plays and, on fourth and forever, launched a Hail Mary that Brandon picked off, ending the game.

Panthers 16, Mayhem 2. We were now 2–2 on the season.

It was an ugly win if there ever was one. And Pitt let us know it.

"I don't even know what to say at this point," he said as we gathered on our sideline after O'Neal's standard midfield, postgame prayer, and after exchanging a few "good games" with the Mayhem players. "We almost lost tonight to a team we should have *killed*. We *should have* lost. I wish *we had* lost. Maybe then you'd stop playing like a bunch of cocky, flashy street thugs. And from now on, anyone who uses the n-word drops and gives me 50 push-ups.

"And anyone who bitches about the refs is off the team. You, of anyone in this league, should be used to not being treated fairly by this point in your lives. No one's going to hand you a goddamn thing in life. But it's always someone else's fault with you guys. The refs, your teammates, the police, your boss, whoever. I'm sick of always hearing you guys pass the blame, and not step up like men and accept your responsibility. " He stared at everyone, long and hard.

"We're two and two. We're .500. And a win's a win. But we're going backward. I don't even know if it's worth my time to come out here two, three, four nights a week and keep wasting my time with this bullcrap. If you want to turn things around, you come out and prove it next week. Frankly, I'm sick of wasting my time on you. Life's too short."

As I drove back down I-93 a little while later, listening to the last few innings of a depressing Red Sox loss to the lowly Detroit Tigers, I had no idea how true Pitt's last three words were.

JENRY GONZALEZ

IT WAS ABOUT 7:25 P.M. Sunday night, two days after our second win of the year, when people heard the firecrackers. That's what they sounded like, anyway—firecrackers, just three quick pops. No one saw where they came from. But in seconds it was all too clear where one of them had gone.

One minute, Jenry Gonzalez of Roxbury—just one of more than 80 seven-to-15-year-olds at Carter Field near Northeastern University trying out for the South End Titans, a new Pop Warner football team—was running drills and playing with his friends; the next minute, he was lying on his back looking up at the cloudless, early evening summer sky, gasping for air, possibly bleeding to death. He had been hit by a stray bullet fired by an unknown assailant running alongside an adjacent basketball court, that had been intended for a young man fleeing on a bicycle. The man on the bike had thoughtlessly ridden toward the young football players (luring the gunman in the process), many of whom, on their coaches' instructions, tried to run and hide behind a nearby storage shed. Jenry, 11, didn't make it to the shed. The small-caliber bullet entered his back, slashing his left ventricle, ripping a piece of his lower lung, and exited his chest. *

The intended victim was a reputed gang member from the Lenox Street housing project, the gunman a member of the rival 1850 gang. Lenox Street and 1850 (the address of one of the Grant Manor apartments on Washington Street) had been embroiled in a long-standing turf war in the South End. Jenry was its latest victim. He lay in critical condition at Boston Medical Center. Meanwhile, witnesses, despite there being more than 150 people at the field that day, were reluctant to come forward. Gang reprisals were a sad fact of Boston's inner city.

One of the Pop Warner coaches on the field that night? Mike Pittman.

"I was the first one to reach that little boy," he told us before practice that following Tuesday, his voice a subdued mixture of sad, confused, and enraged. "I knelt beside him, put pressure on the wound until help came." He held up both of his hands for all of us to see, his eyes watering. "I had this little boy's blood all over me, and the first thing I thought of was you guys. All I could think as this little boy tried just to breathe was how you're wasting your talent out here. And wasting your time. And wasting *my* time. Here's this kid, just trying to do something he loves—play football—and just like that, for no good reason, he's lying on the ground in front of me, *dying*."

He looked out across Franklin Park toward White Stadium and beyond, where scraps of burnt orange sun hung in the sky, peeking out in thin slivers through growing clouds, stubbornly refusing to concede to dusk. "And I thought of you guys, the supposed adults, the supposed *men*." Pitt sighed. "You bitch, moan, complain, point fingers at each other. You have no idea how lucky you are to be able to play this game." He stopped, collected himself, and looked around at each one of us, taking his time, his eyes clear and focused, before summing it up perfectly. "You have no idea how much you take for granted. And it makes me sick."

Everyone was dead silent. Guys looked down at their feet, at the sky, at Pitt, at each other.

*Some details on the Gonzalez shooting are from "Silence" by Neil Swidey, *The Boston Globe Sunday Magazine*, February 26, 2006.

"Damn," Ace winced, perhaps thinking of his own kids. "He gonna be all right?"

"He's in critical condition last I heard," Pitt answered. "I'm going to see him tonight. As for right now, it's up to you guys whether you deserve to play this game any longer.

"Me? I don't think you do."

O'Neal was fond of saying that football is like a religion, Coach Pitt was a minister, and his ministry was this team. If that was the case, then Pitt never preached the truth more than that night. He'd often talked of selflessness, team play, and urged everyone to check their egos and attitudes at the door for the good of the team, or else they'd be gone. He was a throwback to a time when you respected your elders, listened instead of talked, and sacrificed individual gain for the good of the group. His proudest moment as a player? He was about 14, playing in junior high. He made a big hit, forced a fumble, and one of his teammates picked the ball up and ran it in for a touchdown. That's the kind of player he wanted. And that's the kind of player that, it was now finally dawning on him, the Panthers simply didn't have.

Pitt spoke straight from the heart. For the first time he seemed human, vulnerable. I realized that I, like my teammates, albeit in a quieter way, was also being selfish by thinking that Pitt was even spending one second trying to devise Machiavellian ways in which to discourage me, "keep me down," or prevent me from improving as a kicker and contributing to the team's success. He was no maniacal genius bent on breaking me; he was just a man who hurt like any other.

I'd never seen guys working harder than they did at that practice. Something just seemed to click inside every player there, to a man, from the most respected star to the newest walk-on special teamer. Drills were crisper. Honest, heartfelt encouragement was dispensed more freely. Sprints were run harder, with more determination, all the way across the finish line every single time, without anyone—even the slowest, fattest, most out-of-shape linemen or fourth-stringer—giving up. And when the sprints were over, Insano and Mohammad asked if anyone was up for running more, even though it was well after dark and everyone was tired, dirty, hungry, thirsty, dreading the aches and pains with which he'd wake the following morning before starting yet another long workday. But no one complained. A few guys got into their cars and repositioned them to face the field. As moths and mosquitoes danced in the headlights, silhouettes large and

small, young and old ran back and forth, the cry of *"Panthers!"* starting every new line of sprinters and echoing across otherwise empty
Franklin Park.

I never held back once. And Todd, who had once chastised me for
running too hard, hooted and cheered whenever I finished first, good-
naturedly teasing the position players. "The *kicker's* kickin' all your
asses!" If I hadn't actually had this thought prior, I did now: I would
do whatever I needed to help us achieve our goal as a team: win the
EFL title. Call me corny, call me melodramatic, but I'll always remember that early August Tuesday night as the moment when the
Panthers went from being just a football team to being a family.

Pee Wee's brother didn't die. Neither did Jenry Gonzalez.

TAKING ON A DYNASTY

THE MARLBORO SHAMROCKS and their
EFL legacy strutted into English High on August 8, a humid Saturday
evening. Like the New York Yankees, who had hypnotized opposing
teams with their pinstripes and won 26 World Series titles, the Shamrocks brandished their green and white uniforms and the lucky four-
leaf clover on their silver helmets, a logo as instantly recognizable in
semi-pro circles as the Green Bay Packers' "G" was in the NFL. We
should have been intimidated. We weren't.

As Delaney said, with such a young team, most of the Panthers
didn't know or care about the Shamrocks' legacy. They had no idea
how good Marlboro had always been, and certainly didn't care that
the Shamrocks were having a down year by their standards. They'd
started off with convincing wins over Randolph and Charlestown.
But something was missing; they simply weren't the Shamrocks of

old. According to their team website, the downturn was due to "the loss of many of their experienced players due to retirement, and a general apathy and lack of commitment on the part of the players that were left. Few people showed up for practices and too few showed up to play on game day. There were even times the Shams might not even have enough people to play games, and a few of the guys were forced to play both ways because of no bench support." The dynasty was crumbling.

While this may have been true, looking across the field during pregame warm-ups, all I saw were those uniforms, and the clovers, and knew we had a fight ahead. Their roster, unlike most EFL teams, was still filled in large part with players who had college experience: Boston College, UConn, Hofstra, Northeastern, Gettysburg, UMass, URI, Villanova, Alabama State. Not Texas or USC, but compared to our team—mostly kids with nothing but high school experience—they were blue-chippers.

"They're coming off a loss, and looking over there you can tell they don't have as many guys as they usually have," O'Neal told us as we gathered on our sideline prior to the kickoff. "But don't get cocky. Don't you think for a second that we can just throw our uniforms out there and we'll win it. They're still the Shamrocks." Donnie boiled it down into an ominous, down-home, southern conclusion: "Ain't nothing more dangerous than a wounded dog, fellas."

But Pitt had the last word: "Win tonight, gentlemen, and you'll send a message to the rest of the league that the Boston Panthers are a team to be reckoned with. Right now, we're a mystery. No one knows what to make of us. We don't even know.

"But maybe that's good. We can use that to our advantage if we're smart. It's up to you. I just hope you choose to go on out there and show the league, and show these home fans, what they can expect from the Panthers for the rest of this season."

Insano then ordered us all to get our hands up into the center. "Focus on three, focus on three, one, two, three . . . !"

"*FOCUS!*"

We kicked off. On their very first possession, Marlboro marched down the field and scored on a short rushing touchdown run to go up 7–0. D-block slumped off the field, angry, beaten, unable to solve the veteran Shamrocks' confusing, spread offense.

"They ain't shit!" Ace complained, angrily yanking off his helmet, a blue bandanna stretched tightly around his scalp. "They slow and old, and we lettin' 'em do what they want to us. This is *our house*! No one comes in here and does that to us in our house!"

On our first series, Southie and the receivers struck right back. Running a string of tight patterns and nicely timed throws, they marched right back down into Marlboro territory. I snapped on my helmet and kept stretching.

"Get ready for a field goal, Kick," Brandon said, passing by.

"Screw that," I said. "We're getting in. I'll take extra points all day."

On third and three from the Shamrock 10, Southie lofted a pass into the left corner of the end zone, where Sam, who had turned the Marlboro corner into a human pretzel at the line of scrimmage with a quick fake inside, then back out, effortlessly caught it. Our bench erupted, helmets held high in the air. Reggie, Donnie (who hadn't been suspended yet, pending a review of the altercation at Middlesex), and I hit the extra point. High, straight, clean: 7–7.

The Shamrocks, however, took the subsequent kickoff back about 60 yards, barreling right through our flailing coverage team. One pass play later, they went up 14–7. The mercurial Panther team I'd seen so far that season might have packed it in. But we didn't. With the defense and reserves standing and cheering on the O, the line opened a succession of big holes for Amos and Todd as we smash-mouthed our way downfield, catching the Shamrocks in deep pass protection, a sign of respect for our vertical game. As the second quarter wound down, we were in control, poised, almost businesslike, run after run, until Amos tied it up on a short burst up the middle. We went into the half 14–14.

After a quiet, collected halftime spent sitting on the tennis courts next to the field, drinking water, eating orange slices, listening to the coaches, and making adjustments, we calmly started the second half . . . calm, but with a sense of purpose. The time to turn around the season was now. It was funny: even at 14–14 against one of the nation's most successful teams, I never once thought we were going to lose that game.

They kicked off to start the second half and pinned us back on our own 10. Southie took us on a nice drive out to midfield, but we eventually stalled. D-block then held them to only four yards on their next series, forcing them to punt. And this is when we broke the game open.

Jeremy flexed his fingers and danced lightly from foot to foot as he waited for the ball. You could almost see the pistons in his legs getting ready to fire, and when he fielded the low line drive on our seven, it was as if everyone but he had shifted into slow motion. He burst ahead, cut outside around our 20, and was gone, as our home fans went batty behind us, spurred on by Elvis madly waving a white towel over his head.

Panthers 21, Shamrocks 14. We went back and forth to end the third quarter, and began the fourth with a long, clock-devouring drive that ended with a juking, dancing Amos TD run, putting us up 28–14. My extra points were afterthoughts at this point. Robotic. Autopilot. No crazy celebrating afterward; just a calm head butt and some high-fives for my linemen. Business as usual.

And 28–14 is how it ended. Oddly, knocking off the EFL legends was a bit anticlimactic. There was no Gatorade shower for Pitt, no roars of victory, strutting, or smack-talking. It was the most businesslike I'd seen us all year. The offense was efficient, unpredictable, flashy at times, workmanlike at others. The defense was spectacular. A beleaguered unit that had allowed a league-worst 24.6 points per game in 2003 had clamped down and, through the first five games, had given up only about 13 per game, including holding the Shamrocks to 10 fewer than their season average.

"The league will fear us now," a confident Coach Pitt told us as we huddled after O'Neal's prayer. "We're not going to sneak up on anyone anymore. How you handle this is up to you."

But even more memorable than the win over the once-mighty Shamrocks were three significant moments during our next game.

MAYHEM

THE FOLLOWING SATURDAY, the Middle-
sex Mayhem, whom we'd barely beaten two weeks prior, traveled
down to English High on a hot mid-August night. The stands were
only half filled but were lively. Delaney had booked a local marching
band and drill team, who strutted, danced, and twirled at midfield.
The barbecue was fired up, the hickory-sweet smoke wafting down
our sideline, a smell I'd quickly begun to associate with nothing but
home games at English. And I had a personal cheering section that
night, too. While Celia, Ben, Holly, and Chip had attended each of
our home games, my parents and my in-laws and their kids finally
made the pilgrimage to see what their insane son/son-in-law/brother-
in-law/uncle had gotten himself into. The kicker's fan club totaled
about nine people.

From the moment my cheering section arrived during pregame

warm-ups, above all other voices I could hear my four-year-old niece, Emma, screaming my name like a lunatic in a preschool stream of consciousness. *"GO MARK GO GO MARK KICK KICK GO MARK YAY YAY MARK!!"* It didn't matter whether I was lining up for a kick or getting a drink of water; she was just letting loose. It was all I could do not to burst out laughing right there on the sidelines. I'm not even sure she knew what a football game was, but she was glad to be there, reveling in her new freedom to scream as loud as she wanted without getting in trouble.

Emma certainly had lots to cheer about early on. We scored on our first drive, a Southie pass to KFC, who'd run a beautiful post pattern, leaving the beleaguered corner tangled in his own legs. The first one to greet KFC on the sideline was his four-year-old son Jamari, who, along with Todd's Brady jersey-wearing stepson, was happily serving as a water boy, lugging squeeze bottles in a rack big enough for him to curl up and sleep in. "Good catch, Daddy!" Jamari squealed, holding the rack with both hands. "Want some water?" KFC took a bottle from his son and after squirting some in his mouth, playfully squeezed a shot onto Jamari's head.

Up 6–0, we set up for the extra point but added two new twists. First, Donnie was wearing fur-covered cleats. You heard me: *Fur. Covered. Cleats.* Things would have made Joe Namath blush. And second, Reggie, for the first time all year, got off a horrible snap.

The ball sailed a good two feet over Donnie's head. For a moment, time stood absolutely, terrifyingly still. I think my heart stopped beating. And then it hit me: *Good God, that's a live ball!* which was followed by an even more horrifying realization: *Good God, it's my job to chase it down!*

My pulse returned and accelerated into fifth gear, pounding like a Gatling gun, echoing in my helmet. I turned and sprinted after the stray snap, which had landed past the 20 and bounced clumsily downfield, zigzagging left, right, end over end. Out of the corner of my eye I could see a blue and white blur pursuing me, like a monster in a nightmare where you're trying to escape, but can't, because you're wearing lead-soled deep-sea diving boots and you're in a swamp of molasses. I could now hear the thundering footsteps and, worse, the bloodthirsty breathing of the thing closing in on me as I, in turn, closed in on the ball, which had mercifully stopped rolling. If I didn't get there first, the water buffalo (or whatever hoofed beast was trailing me) would scoop it up and return it for a touchdown.

About five feet away now, I had a choice: attempt to snatch the ball up and do something constructive and/or heroic with it, like run or pass; or just fall on it in the fetal position and hope that (a) I didn't squeal like a little girl or (b) the Mayhem player didn't fall on top of me and crush my internal organs into a pulpy mush. At the very last second, oddly still hearing Emma's tiny falsetto voice—"*GO MARK YAY GO GO RUN MARK YAY!!*"—I had a horrible vision of hairy little Garo Yepremian trying to pick up an errant snap and throw a pass in the Super Bowl. That sealed it: I would just fall on the ball and pray. I dove and landed on the ball with a sound I'd never made before—something along the lines of *oofurghoffarghlurf*—and felt the ball try to burrow through my jersey, my stomach, and finally nestle snugly near my liver. I then curled into a strategic, heroic fetal position, protecting the ball and bracing myself for the inevitable impact.

For a moment I wondered if the Mayhem player had stopped when he saw the Steinway piano fall from the sky and land on top of me. But then I realized that the piano that landed on me *was* the Mayhem player. He led with his shoulder, clearly trying to jar the ball loose. No dice. They'd have to pry that damn thing from my cold, dead hands.

Whistles blew. I opened my eyes—yes, I'd also closed my eyes in manly fashion—and saw not one, but two Mayhem players lying on top of me. They peeled themselves off me, where I saw black socks sticking out of two French poodles. Donnie. He helped me up.

"Way to cover up, Mark," he said. "That was the right thing to do."

"Way to go, Kick," Brandon said as I walked off the field, unsnapping my helmet. "Nothing good happens when kickers try to be heroes."

"Don't worry, no chance of that," I joked.

O'Neal, meanwhile, was laughing his ass off. "Did you hear what we were yelling?"

"No." I grinned. Jesus, I could only imagine. "What?"

"*Run Forrest, Ruuuuunnnn!*" he shouted in a mock southern accent. Everyone around us cracked up.

As always, Elvis was pumping me up. "Way to use your head, baby boy! And don't worry about anyone hitting you out there. You know we got your back, right?"

"Yeah." I nodded. But apparently this was a more serious topic than I'd realized.

"I mean it, man," Elvis said. "You don't know this, but we talk about it all the time. We're all protecting you this year. If anyone ever cheap-shots you, every Panther on this team would have that guy's number for the rest of the game, and anyone messing with you would leave the field on his back. We're a family, we got each other's backs."

Family was everything to Elvis Figueroa. Elvis, 33, was a native of the South End's Cathedral housing projects who grew up in a strict Catholic household. "My parents were strict. I got to know my father's leather belt," he tells me with a grin, recalling days when corporal punishment was accepted by society. "But I wasn't a troublemaker. I learned early on that in a place like Cathedral, if you ran with the wrong crowd, it wouldn't lead to anything good. I was a homebody. After school, I'd come right home and hang out with my family. I didn't want to run with my friends, because I knew it was trouble. Most of the guys I was friends with growing up are either dead or in prison."

Elvis attended Boston High, a work-study high school where students would work part-time jobs in the morning and attend class at night, or vice versa. After graduating in 1989, he went on to be a jack-of-all-trades: appliance deliveryman and installer; pickup truck operator; property manager; janitor; self-taught car repairman. Today Elvis is a cable technician for Comcast. And while work and football keep him busy, the center of his universe is his one-year-old son, Gian. "If I had five bucks left to my name, and was going to starve, but Gian wanted to buy something with that five bucks, I'd give it to him. I love him to death."

Luckily, Elvis didn't have to stray far from his real family whenever he went to practice or games with his football family: Gian's mother, whom he's been with for 14 years, is Gio and Lenny's sister. "Those two are like my own brothers more than brothers-in-law," he says.

My first football hit under my belt, I was more confident than ever as the first half wound down into the final minute. We scored again on a beautiful, 80-something-yard punt return by Jeremy, who fielded the ball at our 18, took it toward our sideline, and, seeing his path blocked there by the Mayhem coverage team, reversed direction, ran clear across to the other sideline, juked, found daylight, and never looked back. I hit the extra point to put us up 13–0. And on their succeeding possession, after they'd driven down to our 25, a pass deflected off the shoulder of a Mayhem receiver and flew right to Caleb, who brought it back to our 30 with 20 seconds left. The sideline laughed as Caleb, one of the team's more low-key players—a mild-mannered prep school math teacher without an ounce of self-aggrandizing showmanship—launched into a spastic, stomping celebration "dance" that was about as artistic as a man on fire trying to put himself out.

We had no time-outs left. I thought for sure that Pitt would just order Southie to take a knee and run out the clock. But he didn't. He ordered the no-huddle offense. Amazingly, he was going to try to get us into field goal range. *Good God, is Pitt actually gaining some confidence in me?*

Out of the shotgun, Southie scrambled right and hit Jeremy about 10 yards upfield, underneath the Mayhem's deep prevent coverage, and he took it about eight more yards to the Mayhem 48 before running out of bounds, stopping the clock. Eighteen-yard gain. First down, 14 seconds left. Shotgun. This time the first read was Sam, who sprinted off the line, faked a deep post pattern, then slammed on the brakes and busted outside, where Southie's pass was waiting. Catch, out of bounds, 17-yard gain, first down at the Mayhem 31. Eight seconds left.

"Field goal, Mike?" O'Neal asked Coach Pitt. I stood nearby, stretching my right quad. Pitt didn't even react. "Mike?"

"I heard you," Pitt said. He looked up at the clock. He considered his options: (1) We could stand pat and attempt a field goal from the Mayhem 31, which would be a 48-yarder; (2) we could run one more quick pass play and get me closer, but that would require a third clock-stopping sideline pattern, which Middlesex would expect and could just as easily pick Southie off and bring it back to the house for a momentum-changing score heading into halftime; or (3) Pitt could fold his cards, take a knee despite the valiant effort, and preserve our lead. Pitt wasn't afraid of anyone or anything, but so far he hadn't been a risk taker, either. I knew he'd take a knee, hands down.

Knowing the play clock was winding down, Southie ran over to the sideline, palms upturned. "What are we doing, Coach?"

"You loose?" Pitt asked me without turning around.

"Yes, sir," I nodded and shook out my right leg. O'Neal looked at me and grinned, as if to say, *Finally.*

"White fifteen right slant on two," he instructed Southie, who nodded and sprinted back to the loosely huddled Panthers, who quickly fanned out and lined up. Southie handled the shotgun and fired a quick right slant to Sam, who tightrope-walked our sideline before going out of bounds at the 26. *Man*, that was close! Did he catch it? More important, did he catch it in bounds? Holding each other back, careful not to fall onto the field and risk a too-many-men penalty but wanting to see the ref's call, our bench collectively leaned forward . . . and exploded with a rousing cheer when he pulled both hands into his chest as if doing an invisible pull-up.

"Field goal!" Pitt yelled, walking down the sideline. "Field goal!"

The play took five seconds off the clock. Three left. The ref put the ball back on the right hash mark—better than kicking from the left hash mark for a right-footed kicker, but it still added an extra degree of difficulty, especially with the wind that had been picking up a bit and, sadly, blowing into my face.

Reggie and the line set up on the 26. Donnie knelt down on the Mayhem 33. The lines got set. "No chance, kicker!" a Mayhem player taunted, jumping up and down in front of Reggie, madly waving his arms. "No *fuckin'* chance!"

"You ready?" Donnie asked.

I nodded, trying not to think about the distance, which was 43 yards. *Forty-three yards. Did I mention that it was 43 yards? Shut up, stop thinking about it! Nothing but a long extra point. A really, reeeeeallly long extra point.*

I exhaled, ignoring my thoughts as best I could. Reggie snapped. Donnie caught, held, spun. Suddenly the entire field went pitch black, except for a bright path leading to Donnie's index finger, and the ball . . . and to those fur cleats. Although it was only a millisecond of recognition, seeing those ridiculous, beautiful fur cleats siphoned all doubt and fear right out of me, calming my frayed nerves, assuring me that while football was war (and all those other clichés), it was also fun, a game, something for a 41-year-old former navy man to goof on, something to keep him young. Stifling the inappropriate urge to smile, I let loose with everything I had. It felt more perfect than any kick I'd made yet that season, practice or game—crisp, clean, with barely *any* feeling of my foot even hitting the ball.

"It's good!" I heard O'Neal yell from the sideline, even though the ball was barely a second off my foot. But he was right. The kind little pigskin somersaulted through the night in a high arc and split those two beautiful, proud yellow uprights. Each of the refs underneath, standing on either side of the crossbar, waited for the ball to land, and then walked out into the end zone, arms raised straight up.

Good! Panthers 16, Mayhem zip.

"Yes!" I yelled, pumping one fist, as Donnie, Reggie, and the line mobbed me. Seconds later, the guys spilled off the sideline to join the fray: O'Neal, Brandon, Insano, Ace, all the defensive guys. Through the chaos, I saw the Mayhem player who'd tried to distract me, walking toward his sideline, shaking his head. *Damn*, it felt good shutting him up!

"Ohh, yeah, Adam Vina-*tizzy* in the house!" Ace said as he jogged past me, slammed my right shoulder pad, and headed down to our end zone.

"Way to nail it, Mahk," said Jeff, giving me a crisp high-five and whacking my helmet with his meaty hand. "What was that, a 50-yahda?"

"Forty-three."

"Forty-three friggin' yahds, nice!" Jeff exclaimed and jogged in his spotless uniform down to the end zone, passing Ace on the way, whose shoulder pads he also excitedly bashed with one balled-up fist.

"Way to go, baby boy!" I turned to see Elvis running toward me. Before I could defend myself, he wrapped both arms around my waist and lifted me up, spun me around, and dropped me back down. "You hit one *that* long, you gotta do the airplane, man!"

"Shit, I forgot to," I said, but was glad I hadn't. I didn't want to risk taunting the other team into trying to kill me in the second half. "Next time," I promised Elvis, smiling as he got me into a headlock and practically dragged me down to the end zone, where we gathered for halftime.

I received more congratulations while we rested. Pitt nodded at me. "Glad you stretched out before that one, Mark." He then did something that I never thought he was even physically capable of: he winked. O'Neal, who'd been present when Pitt had admonished me for allegedly not stretching out before missing that 50-something-yarder a few weeks back, just laughed. We were up 16–0 and every-one was feeling great. Except, suddenly, Ace.

"You didn't follow my block, yo!" he screamed at Jeremy, who didn't even seem to be listening. "Why am I bustin' my ass to block when you ain't even gonna follow me?!" Everyone turned in unison, thinking the same thing: *What in God's name is Ace railing about now?*

Jeremy, who just happened to take the punt return in question back for an 80-yard touchdown, just shook his head and rolled his eyes, as did most of the other guys sitting nearby. We were up 16–zip, for God's sake. Why would Ace choose to fly off the handle and bitch about something so inconsequential as Jeremy shifting direction on a punt that *he returned for a touchdown?!*

"Oh, I got it, the superstar don't have to answer for hisself?" Ace was now standing over Jeremy. It was amazing: 99 percent of the time Ace was one of the most well-liked guys on the team, keeping every-one loose, joking, being the "engine" he was. But that other 1 percent, when a dark cloud enveloped him . . . look out, you just never knew what would happen.

"Ace, man, in case you didn't notice, we're winnin'!" Todd yelled over, laughing but dead serious. "Why you gotta be beefin' like that?"

Ace just shook his head, clearly offended by some perceived slight on Jeremy's part, and looked like he was about to jump Jeremy right then and there, until he was finally ushered off to the side and talked down by his three biggest supporters on the team, Khary, In-sano, and Mohammad, who always seemed to be the ones pulling him away from some on- or off-field altercation. They formed a wall around him and occasionally biffed his helmet as he straddled the line between wildly gesticulating anger and conciliatory nodding.

"Someone's always bitching about something on this team," Reg-gie muttered, shaking his head. "Sick of these bastards."

Despite the bizarre halftime turmoil, we scored right away in the third quarter. After Jeremy returned the kickoff to the Mayhem 48, Southie and the O engineered a nice drive ending with Todd banging up the middle on a one-yard plunge.

The extra point, however, set off a disturbing chain of events. At-tempting to block my kick, a Mayhem player flew in from the side, half falling, half diving. I got under it nicely, though, and booted the ball just over his outstretched hands, straight up and through for a

23–0 lead. But the play unfortunately didn't end there. The guy's momentum—not that he made any grand effort to slow down—carried him right into Donnie's knees, knocking him backward just as he was standing out of his holder's crouch. It was a total cheap shot, and Donnie rolled over a few times on the turf in obvious pain.

"Whoa, late hit!" I yelled over to the zebra nearest me, throwing my arms up in disgust. "You gotta be kidding me. No flag there?" The ref just shook his head.

Still lying on the turf, Donnie called over to the same referee. "C'mon now, ref, that was a chickenshit play right there!" To which the ref responded by walking away. And that's when the Mayhem player, strutting past Donnie and looking down at him, added a whole new level of ugliness to my semi-pro experience.

"Get up, you lazy niggah," he muttered under his breath in a chowder-thick Boston accent, softly enough to prove that he was indeed a gutless prick, but loud enough so that a couple of us could hear him.

Donnie's eyes instantly widened, then went red, then pitch black. As if electrocuted, he leaped off the ground and charged. The Mayhem player backed up a few paces but held his balled fists at his sides, ready to throw down. Luckily, at the last second, Reggie, who'd also heard the slur—"I know Donnie, and I knew he was going to lose it, not that I blame him," he'd tell me later—deftly stepped between the two men and held Donnie back, which was no easy feat. (Luckily, I hadn't had to block my rotund holder's path; it would have looked like Warren Sapp steamrolling Kerri Strug.)

The Mayhem guy, smart enough to realize he'd opened a Pandora's box but stupid enough not to grin as he walked away, slinked around the grappling Panthers and headed back to his sideline. Without any plan of action, I followed, clapping mock applause in his direction.

"Way to go, tough guy!"

The Mayhem player stopped, turned, pointed at his chest, and did his best DeNiro-in-*Taxi Driver* impression.

"Talkin' to me?"

I was seething. "Fucking redneck," I said.

"Don't get your panties in a bunch, *kicker*," he said with a chuckle. Maybe it was the way he said "kicker," as if it were the verbal equivalent of catching crabs from a dirty motel mattress. Maybe it was the fact that he'd just dropped an n-bomb on Donnie. Whatever it was, I was suddenly channeling a personality I'd never quite possessed before. On the contrary, it—whoever this street-tough, no-nonsense, fearless psychopath was—possessed me. I could feel the heat rising in my face. My teeth were gnashing. I was breathing faster than a woman in the latter stages of childbirth. I was seeing the proverbial red, feeling downright irrational. This was how it must feel just seconds before you snap and take out an entire McDonald's with an Uzi.

"Can't control the 'roid rage or something?" I asked him.

Grinning, relishing the prospect of pounding a skinny, yappy little kicker into a pulpy mush, he took a few steps toward me. I had a momentary thought of, "Oh, shit, what have I gotten myself into?" But, truth be told, I didn't care; if I was going to get into my first football fight, and likely get my ass handed to me, this was a reason to do it. Not that Donnie needed me to fight his fights for him.

"You got something to say, you fuckin' pussy?" He was a few feet from me now, teeth wolflike and crooked, probably from using them to open Smirnoff Ice bottles at Nazi Youth rallies, his chest puffed out alpha-male style. I braced myself, fists clenched, ready for . . . I had no idea what. But just as I was about to learn what it felt like to swallow your own teeth, a bigger Mayhem player intervened, horse-collaring his teammate and yanking him back toward their sideline.

"Get over there," he growled at his guy, more annoyed than angry, and then just stared at me—only for a second or two, but long enough to make his message clear: *Just walk away, kicker.*

The red draining from my vision, I returned to reality and realized that I'd better do as he said. And that was that. What seemed like a five-minute standoff had taken about 10 seconds, but that was long enough. Almost hyperventilating, I headed back over to our sideline.

Donnie was still justifiably pissed, but he was laughing, too, staring across the field at the Mayhem player, and nodding enthusiastically, speaking to anyone within earshot. "Oh, yeah, I got his number. I better get his mama's address, too, to send her an apology card for what I'm gonna do to her little boy. Let's see if he's man enough to walk through that stupid Kumbaya line at the end of the game. Let's see how tough he is then."

Donnie never walked the postgame handshake line. "I don't want no part of that Kumbaya line bullshit. I grew up playing football in the '70s, when teams were supposed to hate each other, and weren't all touchy-feely like they are today. Why would I want to hug a guy who just tried to kill me? No, thanks." This time, however, he was clearly going to make an exception. He spent the rest of the game watching the Mayhem player whose uniform number he'd clearly filed away into his "To Be Continued" folder, like a lion eyeing a wounded gazelle on the Serengeti.

Speaking of the rest of the game, with a comfortable lead, Pitt decided to give the subs some playing time. And while Elvis, Lenny, Gio, Rome, and the others finally got to get some hits and make some plays, the Mayhem slowly inched back into the game. There was one particularly scary moment. Elvis, chasing a Mayhem receiver who'd just caught a slant pass across the middle, was leveled in his tracks by a second receiver, who was just waiting for him, almost salivating to deliver a blindside (and totally legal) block. *Whack!*, the guy lowered his shoulder and buried it right between the 5 and the 7 of Elvis's jersey. Elvis dropped on the spot as if he'd been shot by a sniper.

"Oooooooooh!" the fans groaned behind us, half horrified, half impressed.

Not wanting to appear as if the hit had any effect, Elvis popped up immediately—fans and players alike cheered—but something was clearly wrong: his helmet was almost turned around backward, and, like a newborn fawn, he took a few wobbly steps and headed back toward the sideline . . . the Mayhem sideline.

Despite themselves, our guys just about died laughing, holding on to each other to keep from falling over. Gio and Lenny ran after Elvis and steered him back to the right sideline. Kelly immediately ushered him to the bench, yanked off his helmet, knelt in front of him, and started shining a penlight in his eyes, moving it back and forth slowly, as O'Neal and some other players gathered around him.

"What day is it?" she asked, scrutinizing his ocular reaction to the light.

"Saturday," Elvis answered.

"Where are you?"

"English High. Football game."

"What's your name?" Kelly asked.

Elvis paused, stared groggily back at her for one second, two, five, and then grinned. "I am . . . *Batman*," he responded, quoting a popular Snickers commercial where a quarterback gets sacked absolutely loopy and forgets his identity. As everyone nearby exploded, Kelly shook her head, and, grinning slightly herself, clicked off her pen and stood up.

"Well, Batman, you could have a slight concussion. You're done for tonight." From then on, Elvis wasn't "E" or any other nickname: he was officially Batman.

While it was fun and games on the sideline, on the field things were not as entertaining. The Mayhem scored three—*three*—unanswered touchdowns on our reserves. Luckily, however, we blocked the extra point after the first, and they failed on the next two two-point conversions, so with the clock winding down, we still led 23–18. Pitt put the first-string defense back in to prevent them from driving for the winning score. It finally came down to a crucial fourth and inches to keep the drive alive. As the crowd and sideline chanted "Deeeeeeeeeeeeeeee-bloccccccccccccccccccck!," the Mayhem quarterback took the snap and tried a sneak, but Insano met him head-on at the line and knocked him back two yards. Game over.

It wasn't pretty, but we were now 4–2 on the year. Four straight wins, too.

As both teams lined up for the handshake, Donnie bided his time in the back of the pack, slyly waiting for his man. "Good game . . . game . . . game . . . nice job . . . good game . . . good game," came the monotonous grunts as we slapped hands. Guys who knew each other or had played together briefly stalled the line to hug or chat. But Donnie moved forward, on the prowl. Then, finally, he spied his nemesis, bringing up the rear of the line . . . *and still wearing his helmet!* Clearly he was hoping to slip through the line undetected. No such luck. When they met, Donnie paused, as if he were just going to shake the guy's hand, and then, just as the guy was about to pass behind him, he pounced. Donnie grabbed the guy's face mask and whipped his head back and forth.

"What you got to say now, huh?!" Donnie shrieked. *"Go on, big man, what you got to say now?!"*

The smaller man flailed and slapped at Donnie's hands and arms, as if fighting off a bear. I watched with sick amusement and thought Donnie was going to pull the guy's head clean off. Finally, players from both teams pulled their man away. Donnie stormed off toward our sideline, wanting no part of the postgame prayer; the Mayhem player was pushed away by several of his own teammates until he shot-putted his helmet toward the parking lot and followed after it, huffing, fuming, swearing.

Despite the bad blood and the altercation in the line, both teams finally gathered at midfield for O'Neal's prayer. Before he started, however, the Mayhem captain, raised his hand. "Excuse me, Coach, I'd like to say something if that's okay." O'Neal nodded.

"I'd like to apologize to the Panthers and everyone here today on behalf of the entire Mayhem organization for the actions of our player," he said in a solemn but firm tone. "We don't tolerate that kind of behavior on this team, and trust me, we'll take care of him on our own. We're all out here for the same reason: because we love playing this game. And there's no place for shit like—sorry, Coach, for *stuff* like that. I just ask that you let him leave in one piece tonight, and trust that we'll take care of him internally."

Everyone nodded, and a few guys clapped. O'Neal said his prayer, and the teams dispersed. Game over. Four straight wins, this latest being the most satisfying thanks to the 43-yard field goal. I felt like, finally, I'd done something to help us win.

"I was so nervous every time you walked out onto the field, I could barely watch," my mother said. "Even when you were playing [hockey] goalie, I never really worried about you getting hurt. But seeing you out there with all those huge players, I was petrified the whole game."

"Kickers don't get hit," I reassured her . . . or maybe just myself, I wasn't sure.

"Hey, we're all heading over to the Drinking Fountain for some beers, and Delaney's getting some wings and stuff," Jason said after I'd introduced him and Anthony (and Bruno) to my parents and in-laws. Off to one side, Elvis, whose family was from Puerto Rico, chatted and laughed in rapid-fire Spanish with Celia's mom's husband, Hugo, who also grew up there.

"You guys coming?" Jason didn't just mean me and Celia, he meant all of us: parents, sisters, kids, everyone. Before I could answer, Celia, who sensed that tonight, more than any other, was my night to bond with my teammates, chimed in. "You guys go ahead," she said to me and the big twins. "I have to take everyone else home."

After saying good-bye to everyone for a few minutes, I headed over alone to the Drinking Fountain. It was your typical nondescript, down-and-dirty neighborhood bar. Keno screens. Two pool tables in back. A few tabletop, 25-cent trivia consoles. Bathrooms in which you probably wouldn't want to actually touch anything. A flock of salty regulars straight out of "grizzled barfly" central casting. In other words, a great place.

As my eyes briefly adjusted to the darkness, for a moment I didn't see any of my teammates. A few of the regulars sitting at the bar holding keno tickets turned around and stared at me, neither welcoming nor intimidating, just . . . staring, disinterested. ZZ Top's "Sharp Dressed Men" wheezed out of the jukebox. Shit. Was I in the wrong place? Had the twins told me the Drinking Fountain as a practical joke? Would this be the night that I would from then on refer to as "Mark Gets His Head Jammed into a Flushing Toilet by Bikers" night?

Just as I was about to turn around and leave, I heard someone call out to me. "Mark!" I took a few steps in, squinted to see further down the bar, and saw Reggie waving me over, surrounded by Todd, Delaney, Insano, Reggie, Donnie, Mohammad, Pee Wee, Elvis, Khary, Cliff, and several other Panthers sitting on stools, holding Heinekens, sodas, and mixed drinks.

"Just kick it!" Todd yelled out as I approached, grinning a happy, jack-o'-lantern grin under some slightly tinted sunglasses. He was one of the few guys who could get away with wearing sunglasses indoors.

"Remember the first time you yelled that at me?" I asked him.

He nodded. "Stop runnin' and just kick . . . *Kicker,*" he joked, harkening back to those early sprints when I'd accidentally enraged him by—of all things—sprinting. Someone thrust a Heineken into my hand, the frosty green glass cooling down my palms that, I realized, had been as sweaty as a teenage girl's at her first school dance.

"Vina-*tizzy!*" It was Ace. Standing behind me, he grabbed my shoulders masseure-style and shook me. "Fifty yards, baby!"

"Forty-three," I corrected him. "But we can say 50."

Everyone raised his drink, a cacophony of clinking glass, and toasted our victory and my long field goal. Like I had imagined all those weeks ago after our first home game, the beer here in this dingy little bar in Jamaica Plain—even though it was the same as the Heineken served in bars on Beacon Hill—tasted sweeter and more satisfying than any beer I'd ever had.

The beers continued to taste that way over the next few hours. Jeff arrived, freshly showered, his hair slicked and clean, and that deliriously happy "We're going to tear it up tonight!" look on his face. Clearly at home in his neighborhood pub, he waltzed behind the bar, chatted up the grizzled veteran bartenders, and began buying beers for everyone. "Mahk, whatcha drinkin'?" he asked, and then handed me a Bud Light before I could answer.

"Hey, fellas, get 'em up: to the best friggin' kickah in the league!" Jeff toasted enthusiastically, then leaned over the bar and slammed my bottle with such vigor I thought he'd smash them both, leaving us with nothing but shattered long-necks and bloody palms.

"Thanks, man." I was by no means the best kicker in the league yet, but I liked hearing it.

"Ah, screw that, you're money out there," Jeff said. "Hey, Murph, what are you drinkin'?" and with that he was off again, playing a wild-eyed, fun-loving Santa Claus delivering beer to all the good little football players. Speaking of gifts, Delaney soon appeared with two deep aluminum trays of wings from a nearby barbecue joint. Everyone dug in with reckless abandon, piling the sauce-slathered goodies on paper plates until they sagged in the middle and threatened to burst right through. Beer. Wings. Another win under our belts. New friends. Didn't get much better than that.

While I chatted with Sam (the Head Start teacher who, despite his season-ending knee injury against the Cobras, still came to games and hung out afterward) and some of the younger dudes, I spent most of the night talking to the older guys: Delaney, Donnie, Reggie, and Coach O'Neal, who'd arrived a little while after our first toast.

"Yeah, he was a bit skeptical at first," O'Neal confirmed when I asked him about Pitt's initial reaction to me. "Even heading into the Charlestown game, he asked me, 'Do you think this guy can kick?'" O'Neal laughed. "I was like, 'Mike, I played soccer, I've watched him kicking against that damn backstop every practice like a savant—trust me, he can kick.'

"You gotta remember," Coach continued, "Pitt's never really had a kicker before, so he had to warm up to the idea and get used to having an extra option besides punting or going for two. But I think that 43-yarder tonight made your point better than anything I could tell him."

"Be honest now," I prodded him, grinning, "that first night I came out, Pitt thought I was Little Lord Fauntleroy, didn't he?"

"Whaddya mean?"

"You know—just a soft, rich boy from Beacon Hill."

"Anyone seeing that piece-of-shit Honda you sometimes drive would know you're not a trust fund baby," he kidded, and then shrugged. "Maybe. I don't know. I can't speak for Pitt, but he was skeptical, yeah. He comes off as a hard-ass, but he's a good man. Been a great friend to me. I think he's starting to realize what he's got in you. No one really knows where you came from, but we're glad you're here."

"Awww, O'Neal," I teased. "That's sweet."

He laughed. "Hey, that doesn't mean you're not just a dirty crack whore, just like all the other crack whores on this team." The two of us just about fell over laughing.

Donnie, who was listening nearby, chimed in. "I don't know what you two clowns are talking about, and I don't know what Scandinavian woods Murph found you in either, Mark. But I'm glad he did."

"Hey, Mahk, what are you drinkin'?!" Jeff again. Man, he was just a *machine*! He grinned the toothy smile of the happily buzzed, three frosty beer bottles clenched in each meaty fist: he looked like the St. Pauli Girl's drunk, chubbier older brother. I took one of the Bud Lights, and we clinked bottles for the umpteenth time that night.

"We need more guys like you on this team," I told Jeff.

He raised his eyebrows at me. "Nah, I'm just a mudder. I get down and dirty, but I'm no athlete."

"No, seriously," I said, pointing my bottle at him. "There can never be too many guys like you on a football team." Maybe I was just feeling extreme goodwill toward the unofficial emcee of the evening, but I meant it: he was the epitome of selfless. He practiced long snapping every night just in case Reggie was out; he played offensive line; he always volunteered for special teams, kickoff, and punt coverage, aka "the bomb squad," that unglamorous yet vital band of football brothers; his enthusiasm was boundless, always counting off the loudest during stretches, trying to run the fastest at practice, always the first (along with the big twins, to give credit) to start the chants of "Deeeee-bloccccccck!" whenever we needed a big defensive stop.

"Thanks, man," he replied. "I love playing this game. I may not be the best guy out here, and I'm not in the best shape, but I'll keep trying to run you over until I beat you, and I'll break my back to help this team win. These guys"—he motioned with his beer around the bar—"I haven't known some of them for real long, but they're like my family now, you know? I'd throw myself in front of a bus for any one of 'em."

"Hey, Coach," he yelled over to O'Neal, "that beer is *dangerously* low, my friend! You need anotha!" And he was off again.

I sat down next to Reggie. He was the Panther I knew best. He'd been my unlikely recruiter. However, I realized I didn't know *that* much about him. He smiled at me, the gap-toothed grin I'd come to look forward to every practice and game. "What's up, big Mark?"

"Don't mean to pry, but is there a story behind that missing tooth?" I asked.

"Oh, yeah," he said, sipping his beer. "Pretty good one, too."

Reggie was little more than an infant when his parents divorced in 1969, and was seven years old when his mother, Pearl, remarried Wilbert "Stoney" Ellis, a Louisiana native, in 1974. Over his childhood, Reggie and his six brothers and sisters moved from a two-family home in Dorchester (after it burned down), to the projects in Dorchester near Franklin Field, to Jamaica Plain, to Mattapan. While the family was never well off by any means, they weren't poor either, a rarity for some of the neighborhoods he lived in, where many families barely squeaked by. "I had a good life. We were comfortable," Reggie says. "But it wasn't so much because we had money, it was because of the way we were brought up. My mother and Stoney worked hard, and she raised us to never need anything. If we said, 'All the other kids have the brand-new leather Dr. J Converse basketball shoes,' she'd tell us that we might want them, but we didn't *need* them. So we'd get the canvas Chuck Taylors instead."

Reggie's mother worked as both an accountant and, later, a bus driver for the MBTA (she currently works for the Boston Housing Authority). Stoney worked at the General Dynamics shipyard in Quincy until he got laid off, and then, like Pearl, began working at the MBTA. So Reggie never had to wonder where his next meal was coming from, even though there were eight mouths to feed.

Stoney, Reggie says, raised him and taught him and his siblings a lot about life—"He was a good guy, you know? Just a good guy." Stoney was also the one chiefly responsible for instilling a love of sports into his stepchildren, especially baseball, which ran in his family: Stoney's cousin was major league pitcher Dock Ellis, perhaps best known for allegedly having pitched a 1970 no-hitter against the San Diego Padres while on LSD. Reggie excelled at football from a young age, playing for the Pop Warner Mattapan Patriots (at one point coached by Ace's dad, Coach Jones) and, later, at Hyde Park High. He was a good, if sporadically motivated student and talented player, but by his own admission had a problem with fighting off the field. One brawl in particular stood out.

The year was 1982. Reggie, age fifteen, was at an under-21 dance club on Lansdowne Street near Fenway Park with two cousins who got into a scrape with some fellow clubbers over some girls. Reggie stepped in. A few punches and one police confrontation later, he found himself badly beaten and in jail. "I was just looking out for family and the fight just exploded," he says. "Luckily, this was back in the days before every kid had a gun, so it was just fists, but it was chaos. Bouncers, security guards, cops. It looked like the whole Boston police force was there." While being dragged down the stairs and out of the club and thrown into the paddy wagon by police, Reggie was pummeled. "When I shave my head you can still see the knots and gashes."

He admits that he was disorderly and fighting the police, but also maintains that the officers used excessive force—one in particular who, with a swift smack of his billy club, gave Reggie the trademark Letterman-esque grin he'd still sport 23 years later.

"I can't say I *didn't* fight back, but if you get whacked in the head with a nightstick a few times, you're not going to just sit there and take it." But it could have been much worse. When Pearl, Stoney, and older bother Tony came to the station to bail him out, a lieutenant told them that Reggie was lucky to be alive. "They booked me for assault on a police officer, threw me into a cell, and didn't really give me any medical attention. My head was black and blue, swollen. My eye was bloodshot red. My tooth was gone, so there was blood pouring out of there, too. When my mom looked at my face she started crying and said I looked like the Elephant Man. Tony started yelling at the cops, 'Look what you did to him, look what you did to him!' That's when the lieutenant said, 'You're lucky he's not dead for attacking a police officer.' I learned a lot about how the world works right there."

Painful though it was, it was indeed a lesson. That was the last time Reggie got into a serious fight. But it wasn't over: he soon faced the possibility of being sent to a maximum-security juvenile facility for his part in the brawl. However, the police had a compromise in mind: if the Murphys didn't sue the city for the "overzealous" actions of the officers, all assault charges against him would be dropped and the incident would be forgotten. Reluctantly, they accepted. "It was my call," he says. "I didn't want to put my mother through any more drama. She had to take time off from work, lose wages, hire lawyers, and it was draining her financially and emotionally. I just wanted it done."

Unlike his Hyde Park teammate Delaney, who would be recruited by some big-name football programs, Reggie was a workingman's kind of player; he wasn't a blue-chip stud athlete fending off scholarship offers. His grades were only average at best due to part-time effort. "During football season I was an A and B student, in order to maintain my eligibility. Other than that, I pretty much goofed off." While his grades fluctuated, he was certainly no dumb jock. A chemistry teacher, amazed by how Reggie could skip class all week and then show up for an exam and ace it, urged him to attend prep school. But his family didn't have the money, nor would they be able to afford college. So Reggie, who also was about to become a father (his high school girlfriend was pregnant with the first of three children he'd have by age 23), entered the army reserves, and in 1985, a week after graduation, was sent down to Fort Jackson, South Carolina, for basic training. This was the first time the 18-year-old had ever been away from Boston's inner city on his own. "That was a real experience," Reggie says. "I actually had my 19th birthday in basic training, and I remember thinking, 'Where the hell am I? What am I doing here?'" His girlfriend gave birth to their son while he was trudging through the swamps of South Carolina. "That's one thing I regret, not being there to see him born. But I had made a commitment to the reserves and I had to fulfill it. It was just bad timing."

Reggie soon moved to San Antonio for seven months of job training with behavioral science specialists. "I was a counselor, and we'd help people get through some of the tougher parts of army life, from everyday family issues to, you know, telling someone that it's okay to see their buddy get his head blown off. We dealt with a lot of suicidal situations. In fact, on the weekends, part of our training was at institutions." Smiling, he adds, "Working at mental hospitals comes in handy when dealing with some of the dudes on the Panthers."

He had originally put off higher education to support his girlfriend and son. But after getting out of the army, the 23-year-old turned his attention back to college, in part to focus once again on his passion—football—and see if he could play at the proverbial next level. Wanting to take himself as far from his inner-city comfort zone as possible, he applied to a small school in a little town of barely 5,000 people tucked into the northeastern corner of Kentucky: More-

head State University, best known in football circles as the alma
mater of former New York Giants' quarterback and CBS football
broadcaster Phil Simms, who starred there from 1974 to 1978.

A walk-on, Reggie played his freshman year for the Eagles and
gained notice as a tough, if undersized, outside linebacker and strong
safety. "I was a lot skinnier and faster back then," he says with a laugh,
which explains how a guy who now resembled a mini Charles
Barkley could ever have been anything but an offensive lineman. "It
was a great experience. Even though I never really started, and sometimes wasn't even on the travel squad, I'd still meet the guys at the
field and go to every game. Marshall [University, in West Virginia]
was our biggest rival, so I once got to play against [New England Patriots' receiver] Troy Brown. That was cool. And that's why I'm always riding the young dudes on the Panthers to go to college. You're
only young once. Semi-pro football will always be here, but college
won't."

Case in point: Reggie lasted at Morehead for only one year. As his
sophomore year began, he learned that his girlfriend was pregnant
with his second child. So he dropped out and went back to Boston
for good, found work, and settled in. "I wasn't going to be a dead-
beat," Reggie, now a desktop technician at a company in downtown
Boston, tells me. "I had responsibilities. Looking back now, though, I
sometimes kick myself in the ass about it. Can't believe it's been almost 20 years since I had the chance to stay at college."

At about 1:00 A.M., the bar lights flickered on and off. *You don't have
to go home, but you can't stay here!* Time to head out. Leaving the bar
was like walking a wedding reception line. I said good night to Reggie,
Donnie, Delaney, everyone else, each one of my teammates, shaking
hands, slapping palms, joking, talking some more, bumping shoulders,
all with uncharacteristic ease. I felt oddly proud of my coordination.

I stumbled out of the bar—not surprising, considering the 53
beers Jeff had bought me. Squinting, steadying myself, I brought Cliff
and Khary into focus. They were smoking a couple of butts under the
neon glow of a Pabst Blue Ribbon sign. Khary, taller than Cliff by a
good four inches, wore a track suit and had sunglasses perched on top

of his head. He looked over and gave me a chin nod, after which Cliff turned toward me.

"You outta here, Mark?" he asked, blowing smoke out of his nose.

"Yup. See ya at practice Tuesday, fellas." I started forward to shake their hands but instead caught the edge of a rise in the concrete and gracefully lurched into Khary, practically bear-hugging him to keep from falling, knocking his sunglasses to the ground.

"Whoa, okay, man," Khary said with a chuckle, lifting his cigarette so I wouldn't light myself on fire.

"Sorry, I'll get 'em," I said, clawing around the sidewalk for his sunglasses and handing them back to him. "They broken?"

"Nah, man, they're cool," Khary answered, dusting off the semi-tinted gold shades and resetting them on top of his head. At that moment he was the smoothest-looking cat within 50 miles of the Drinking Fountain. It was as if Jay-Z dropped by for a visit.

"You're not driving, are you?" Cliff asked, laughing. "Don't want to be bailing your ass out of lockup in a couple hours."

"Nah," I answered. "I'll take the T."

He checked his watch. "No, you won't, it's almost two-fifteen." *Two-fifteen? Christ, it was one o'clock like 10 minutes ago.* Dropping his cigarette and snuffing it out with his foot, Cliff walked over to the curb, hailed a cab for me on Washington Street, and poured me in. I waved out the back window as we pulled away. Cliff shot me a peace sign.

I was still good and drunk when I climbed into bed 20 minutes later. I think I remember Celia muttering something in a sleepy, pillow-muffled tone, perhaps asking how the bar was, perhaps telling me I smelled boozy (likely the latter). And I think my response, seconds before passing out, was a slurred, nonsensical, "Just kick it."

MAN IN THE MIRROR

SO HOW WAS I physically holding up at the halfway point in the season?

First and foremost, I hadn't been carried off the field on a stretcher yet. That was a bonus. Luckily, aside from that one botched snap and subsequent hit, I hadn't been so much as *breathed on* by an opponent. Credit went to my teammates (read: bodyguards), who, as Elvis said, had my back. I sometimes felt as if I were stored in a glass box on the sideline with a "Break in case of kicking emergency" sign on it. Ah, the cushy life of a specialist.

But I was still working hard. Thanks to practices and games, I was running more every week than I ever had before. I'd never worked on my abs or any other part of my body in my life (and it showed), but suddenly I was doing sit-ups, push-ups, leg lifts, and other daily staples of boot camp calisthenics that I'd *never* have done if left to my own devices. After all, I made a promise to myself that I'd do everything the other guys did short of full-contact drills, and it was starting to pay off. Forgive the R-rated hyperbole, but I was feeling *abso-fucking-lutely* fantastic (aside from some expected aches and pains in the legs and ankles, but nothing a little Advil or a beer after practice couldn't cure). I was totally rejuvenated, as if I'd been swimming in the space-pod pool from *Cocoon* for the past several weeks. I had more energy than ever before, and was running my ass off in sprints. But unlike before, my teammates now cheered me on or used me to motivate the other guys. *C'mon, now, the* kicker's *beating y'all!* Between you and me, not to sound immodest, I was looking and feeling better than I had in a long, long time. And Celia had noticed.

"Your arms just don't look as potato-sticky anymore," she told me one day as I walked into the bedroom after a shower.

"That was almost a compliment."

"Seriously," she said, squeezing my arm, "there's some actual definition here now."

"Keep digging the hole," I said, "What you mean is, *You were a skinny little shit before and now you're almost male.*"

"Really," she continued, eyeing me like some bizarre science experiment. "Your stomach's flatter, your shoulders are a little broader, your chest is more defined, and you just look more, I don't know . . . *fit.*"

"Oh . . . I know." I flexed in the mirror and air-kissed my biceps.

"Let's not get carried away. But you look good. I'm proud of you for working so hard at this. I never thought you'd take it this seriously."

Kidding aside, this made me feel great. Not that she didn't think I was somewhat attractive before—*I hope* she did, otherwise we had some deeper marital issues than just the reduction in "quality time" that football was causing. But it never hurt to know that your spouse might be checking you out when you're not looking. Football was better than a gym membership.

As for my inner workings, I now had the stamina of a sherpa. Well, maybe not that extreme, but I was running strong. I could pretty much run all day if asked, and I routinely dusted almost everyone but the fastest guys in sprints (I could live 20 lifetimes without beating the receivers or D-backs). I could now do 60 or 70 push-ups and 100 sit-ups without breaking a sweat. I didn't quite have Pee Wee's 12-pack abs yet, or even a six-pack, but I was at least on my way to having a two-pack. And I owed it all to the Boston Panther Diet. If I could have shrunk it down to pill form, bottled it, and marketed it on QVC, I would have made a fortune. I was the living, breathing, kicking "Before and After" picture.

All that said, one morning in mid-August, right after getting out of the shower, the too-bright light over our mirror revealed a shocking, totally unprecedented sight: curling out of my right sideburn was one, single, solitary gray hair. I almost shrieked. It was as if God were saying, "All this football fitness stuff is nice and all, but let's not get cocky and think you're defying time, okay, Dick Clark?" It was just a barely noticeable gray nub, something you'd see plucked from a cartoon chin in a multiblade razor commercial, but it mocked me. I know it did. Before you knew it, I'd look like Andrew Jackson on the twenty-dollar bill. At least I might get a Grecian Formula endorsement out of it.

I found Celia's red-and-white-striped makeup bag, grabbed some tweezers—the gray hair's natural enemy—and plucked it. "See you in hell," I hissed, holding him in the light for one last second before turning on the faucet and sending him to his watery grave.

But it was a Pyrrhic victory. Deep down, sadly, I knew that football or no football, he and others like him would be back someday. With a vengeance.

PRESSURE KICKS

ON AN UNCHARACTERISTICALLY cool August night, Pitt of all people got me back to feeling young again.

We were gathered around him at the 50-yard line after warm-up calisthenics and sprints. That's right—I said *50*-yard line. We were finally practicing at English High, on a real field with lines, end zones, and (most important for me) goalposts. *Fare thee well, chain-link backstop. You served me honorably.*

"Look, gentlemen," Pitt began, "we're four and two. Only four games left. We control our own destiny. No one can stop our receivers. D-block is holding teams to maybe 13 points per game. Southie has been offensive player of the week, what, four times already? Amos is averaging close to a 100 yards a game. The line is controlling the game. Special teams are hitting and filling lanes. And

Mark—where's Mark?" He craned his thick neck and located me kneeling next to Reggie and Donnie. "Mark, stand up."

I did. *Now is when he finally orders everyone to stone me to death.*

"Look at that leg." Pitt grinned and laughed heartily. "He's got *dynamite* in that skinny white leg, best damn kicker in the league far as I'm concerned! With all this talent, we shouldn't lose another game. And we keep it going at Charlestown this Saturday. Am I right?"

Yes, sir! we answered in resounding unison.

As I stretched out a few minutes later, Donnie's big, bald head appeared above me. "I got a surprise for you at the end of practice."

I sat up. "Should I be worried about this? Is it rookie hazing time?"

"Nah." He grinned devilishly. "But it's good. Pitt will tell you at the end of practice."

"Does this involve me being taped to a goalpost and covered in shaving cream?" I yelled after him as he jogged away.

"You'll see," he called back to me.

O'Neal was standing nearby. "What was that all about?" I asked him.

O'Neal shrugged. "He's probably going to rape you like a prison bitch. I wouldn't worry about it."

"Cool." I nodded. "That sounds fun."

We laughed and O'Neal began lighting up a cigar. "Hey, Mark, been curious. What do your friends and family think about you playing football?"

"Celia is a little nervous that I might get killed, but she has a blast at the games, and my parents think it's great."

He put on a mischievous smile. "They probably think you're conducting some kind of Dian Fossey football experiment. Panthers in the Mist." Before I could even say anything, he was off.

"'Dearest mother and father,'" O'Neal began in a pseudo-British PBS documentary accent, "this is day 23 of my immersion into the natural habitat of the American football-playing Negro. So far, my observation has concluded that while occasionally peaceful and docile, the common American football-playing Negro is an aggressive creature. As a mere kicker, and a Caucasian one, I try not to look the darker males in the eye, for it is a sign of aggression and I might be attacked. I will write again soon if I am not killed and eaten by these savages."

We laughed until I could barely breathe. A few guys doing drills looked over, curious . . . or maybe just annoyed that they were working their asses off while we were kicking back drinking piña coladas and giggling like schoolgirls.

"What are you crack whores lookin' at?!" O'Neal yelled, stabbing his cigar at them and still laughing. "Get back to work!"

As practice wound down an hour or so later, Pitt blew his whistle and gathered everyone at the 30-yard line. "Okay, gentlemen, time for sprints. *But* we have a little twist today."

Donnie grinned at me. Christ, what was he up to?

"We're either gonna run a little or a *whole* lot. How much isn't up to me tonight. Because of an ingenious idea Donnie had, it's up to one of you." Everyone looked around, confused. Then Pitt found me in the crowd, lasered me with a challenging glare, and pointed at me like Jacob Marley's ghost pointing at Scrooge. "It's up to Mark."

Everyone turned.

Me? I thought. *The whole team's end-of-practice-torture fate was up to* me? Pitt explained how it was going to work.

"Mark, you'll get 10 tries from the 30–40-yarders. If you hit eight or more, the team runs 10 50-yard sprints, end zone to midfield."

"Only eight?" Elvis said, waving derisively at Pitt. "Mark'll hit that in his sleep."

"But if he misses three or more," Pitt continued, grinning at Elvis, "so even if he makes seven, your penalty is doubled, and you run 20 sprints. And not just 20 *50*-yarders, but 20 *100*-yarders, end zone to end zone. We'll stay all night if we have to."

Everyone groaned. A few whistled, impressed with the high stakes. Someone in the back of the pack yelled, "Oh, shit, no!" Some guys, however, jumped up and down, reveling in the pressure in which I was now buried neck-deep. Despite possibly having to run twice as much, this challenge certainly added some intrigue and casino-like electricity to practice.

Donnie, standing beside me, leaned over. "I told you this was gonna be good, Mark," he said, practically giggling. "About time you kicked under some real pressure."

"Go fuck yourself," I responded, grinning the frozen, faux-confident grin of the damned.

"Don't screw this up, Kick! It's all on you! Don't choke!" Brandon, always the anticheerleader, yelled over to me.

"Why you ridin' him?" Derek, the chiseled defensive end, groused at Brandon. "You *want to* run extra or something?"

"Hell, yeah, I want to run," Brandon replied. "Look at the fat asses here. We *need* to run. Dynamite leg my ass. *No way* Kick hits eight. In fact, I got 10 bucks he only makes *five*." Brandon, grinning sadistically, challenged the rest of the team. "Ten bucks against the kicker? Who's in? Anyone think he hits six?"

Through all the amused laughing and chatter, most everyone I could see shook his head *no*. No one here thought I'd make more than five out of 10? Wow, that was pretty goddamn depressing. But then a deep, raspy voice from the back of the pack spoke up.

"Bitch, I got 10 bucks on Vina-tizzy!" Ace burst through the pack of players and, nodding confidently, playfully shoved Brandon in the shoulder. The smaller D-back stumbled backward a few feet, nodding himself, grinning. "All right, big man. Done. Anyone else?"

"I'm in!" shouted Elvis. "Baby boy hits six in his sleep, and three more just to make you cry."

Guys cheered and whooped. Game on.

Hearing Brandon write me off—and, more than that, receiving a bolt of energy from Ace and Elvis's public endorsement—I discovered that not only *wasn't* I nervous anymore, I was pissed. Insulted. Annoyed at the sheer gall of Brandon—the balls on this kid!—suggesting that I was only 50-percent. I felt confident, almost cocky, and, more than anything, defiant.

"All right, let's do this," I said, nodding confidently. I then looked at Brandon. "I hope you brought your ATM card, sister."

"*Whooooooooaaaaaaahhhh!*" the group howled. Brandon laughed, and beckoned more abuse. "Bring it on, bring it on!"

As Donnie and I set up for kick number one, Pitt interrupted with a jovial, almost taunting tone. "Oh, Mark, forgot to tell you, one more little rule: you only get four kicks from the middle of the field. You have to take three from the right hash and three from the left. And Mohammad, Brandon? Get over there. You guys are going to distract him. These are real game conditions. Still think you can make eight?"

I shrugged. "You can make me kick from the stands if you want, Coach. Bring it on."

"*Oooooooooooooooooooohhhhhhh!*" everyone hooted, turning back to Pitt, watching the two of us volley back and forth like a Wimbledon match. Pitt grinned, perhaps enjoying the confident position I'd taken. He nodded, "All right, big man, we'll see . . . we'll see."

Chelston and Chezley, the Twinkies, ran down to the end zone and set up behind the goalpost to shag the balls. There would be no snaps, but Donnie would hold.

I took a deep breath and looked at the goalposts, the little flags on top of each barely swaying in the breeze. I started forward. "Don't choke, Kick!" Brandon yelled, but I barely even heard him. I connected and sent it flying long, straight, dead center.

One for one.

"Vina-*tizzy*!" Ace yelled, high-fiving everyone around him. He then jokingly threatened Brandon and Mohammad. "Don't be distracting him or I'm gonna have a serious beef with you two bitches. I got 10 large ridin' on this!" Donnie held the second kick, waiting for me.

"Hey, Scott Norwood . . . wide right!" Mohammad screamed as I stepped forward and kicked number two, but no worries: it, too, sailed long and straight, and would have been good from 50. Chelston caught it on the fly, did a brief celebratory dance, and spiked it.

"THAT'S TWO!" the team cried out in unison, stomping their feet and high-fiving. This had become a circus sideshow. *Step right up and watch the kicking freak!*

Donnie moved to the left hash mark. As Brandon yelled "Miss it, miss it!" in my ear on kick three, I did just that: I hooked it left. A groan filled the English High night. One missed. I could afford only one more. If I missed the next one, I'd have to hit six straight to make eight. And that's what happened: I popped up kick four, and it fell a few yards short of the crossbar.

"Uh-oh," Mohammad yelled, "pressure's getting to him! Only two for four! Can't miss another one or we're running hard . . . and he's the goat!" He was right—if I missed one more I'd have about 40 large, tired men very angry with me. That could not happen.

Two more kicks from each spot: center, right, and left. Those left-hash ones were a bitch . . . but not impossible. I hit kick five long and through from the left.

"THREE FOR FIVE!" they yelled.

"No more misses!" Elvis cheered. "You got it, baby!"

Rolling now, I belted kicks six, seven, eight, and nine: beautiful high strikes into the night from all three hash marks, all right down the middle. Brandon and Mohammad taunted me before each one, waving their arms, calling me every name in the book: "bitch," "punk," "crack whore" (O'Neal's signature favorite), you name it. But it was as if I were wearing Bose QuietComfort headphones: I heard nothing. It was only me and the ball. *Just me and the ball.*

"One more, Kick. I'm smelling a choke," Brandon teased, and Ace playfully got him in a headlock.

I was now seven for nine. One left. There was a palpable electric current running through everyone. More than any in-game extra point, more than any real-game field goal (even the 43-yarder the previous week), this one kick—in practice—was suddenly the most vital undertaking in my 37 years on the planet.

And then Donnie raised the stakes even more.

"Hey, Pitt, I got an idea," Donnie said, grinning like Satan himself. "We move back to the 35. If Mark hits a 45-yarder, we only run five half-field sprints. If he misses, we run 25 full-field."

Pitt considered the suggestion. "Okay, Mark, you can either still kick this last 40-yarder and stick with the original deal. Or you can accept Donnie's wild-card challenge, and if you make it, you guys only have to run five."

"I like the sound of that," KFC chimed in.

He stared at me. I stared back at him. Right then, we were the only two men on the field. I swear I heard the *Good, the Bad, and the Ugly* theme. "So," he said with a smile, "you have the balls to up the ante?"

"Fuck yeah," I said before I could even think about it. But I meant it. I was *not* missing.

This sent everyone into absolute delirium. Guys were practically falling over each other.

Donnie moved back to the 35-yard line and got set, 45 yards away from my target.

"Shhhhh," Ace said, holding the laughing, nerve-racked pack of players back like an official at a PGA event. "Yo, shut up, y'all, let the man concentrate!" Everyone but Brandon and Mohammad heeded Ace; they let loose with a torrent of distracting taunts. But like with the previous made kicks, their voices soon faded out as I paced back and over.

I stepped forward and swung and it wasn't even close. Close to missing, that is.

It was the single most perfect kick I'd ever unleashed, flying right down the middle with room to spare. Before I could even raise my arms, I was lifted off the ground.

"*Vina-TIZZEEEEEEEEEEEE!!*" Ace bellowed, carrying me on his shoulders along with countless others. I lay prone, arms outstretched, flying, as if crowd-surfing at Lollapalooza. As the guys carried me around the field and down to the end zone for our measly five half-field sprints, I looked over at Pitt. He stood defiantly, arms crossed at his chest. But he wore a small smile of satisfaction.

Donnie's challenge had worked. I was a money player now.

LIGHTS OUT

AUGUST 20. My allegedly dynamite-filled leg and I made the short drive over the Gilmore Bridge to Charlestown for our seventh game of the season. We'd won four straight and were sending a message to the EFL: the Panthers were for real.

There was barely any grass on the Townies' home field; it was a torn-up disaster area with dirt patches, rocks, mud puddles. The uneven white lines were the only things that gave this gravel death pit even the vaguest resemblance to a football field. Even by semi-pro standards, which were inconsistent at best, this field was barely playable.

"What a shithole," I said to Jeremy as we stood in the pregame sprint line. As a firefighter, he'd found himself in worse places than this. But just barely.

"You're not kidding," he agreed, laughing and shaking his head. "I won't be diving for any balls tonight."

But the field was all we had, and we had to work with it. That was just the EFL. That was semi-pro ball. Sometimes things just weren't up to snuff. Fans got into games without paying. It was pulling teeth finding kids to work the chains on the sidelines. Guys on the same team often had mismatched helmets or jerseys. And, aside from our home field at English, you never knew what kind of playing surface you'd get. But no sense bitching: both teams had to play on this disaster area, so there was no advantage either way. You still had to put the ball in the end zone.

We did have one advantage, though: Charlestown was relatively undermanned and, if our first game was any indication, just less talented overall. They had some good, hardworking players, no doubt, but they just didn't have our speed. Their offense was pounded and bull-rushed by D-block, which more or less systematically beat the fight out of them. Southie hit Sam for a touchdown pass. Chezley had a beautiful 66-yard interception return for a touchdown. And when their starting quarterback was knocked out of the game on a savage (but clean) hit by Gary, aka "T. O.," a reserve receiver-turned-cornerback, they were done.

As far as the kicking went, however, I wasn't comfortable at all. Not only because of the horrible surface, but also because Donnie was finally informed that week that he'd be suspended for his earlier altercation at Midddlesex. So Delaney, who dressed for games and played some situational receiver (despite the bad knees), volunteered to hold. Not that I didn't trust Delaney's athletic skill, but he was no Donnie. He hadn't caught one snap all season until pregame warm-ups, and had a couple bobbles then. Being a holder, contrary to what most people probably think, is more than just slamming the ball on the turf and holding it with one finger: it requires maximum hand-eye coordination, timing, and a delicate, impeccable touch. Delaney just hadn't practiced enough to get that down.

After Sam's touchdown catch, we lined up on a barren patch of gristle. Reggie snapped. Delaney, wearing gloves for some reason, bobbled the ball and, before he could regain control, it squirted away a few feet, forcing Todd, the up man, to pounce on it before Charlestown could recover. And following Chezley's touchdown, Delaney got the ball down, but it was still moving and spinning, laces *in*, and I hooked it a good five yards left of the upright. I should never miss an extra point, and I blamed myself more than anyone . . . but the shaky hold didn't help. Nevertheless, Delaney and I turned it around later in the half, connecting on a 30-yard field goal and hitting the point after our third score (an Amos run). Things were falling into place kickingwise and, most important, we were routing Charlestown 22–0.

As the half wound down, we were about to score again to put us up 29–0. And that's when we were all reminded that—despite surviving for 40-plus years—the EFL was sometimes not the most organized league. Suddenly—poof!—the stadium lights went out.

One second Southie is standing under center, hands ready for the snap, calling out "White 15! White 15!" in our "Seattle" three-wide-receiver set that was virtually unstoppable that night; the next, we're all standing in complete darkness.

"They snuck inside and pulled the plug on purpose! Okay, we got it, you surrender," Ace called across the darkened field to the shapes milling about on the Townie sideline, as confused as we were. "Just wave a white towel next time!" While that might have been a logical explanation considering the beating we were dishing out, the real story was that the Charlestown owner had forgotten to—or just didn't bother to—pay the city for the use of the lights. So the city shut down all electricity to the field at exactly 9:00 P.M.

The refs and captains conferred out at midfield, nothing but huddled outlines. Finally, Insano jogged back over to our sideline. "They forfeit," he said, shrugging. "Lights ain't coming back on."

We were now 5–2, winners of five straight. Though this last win was more "semi" than "pro," we'd take it as we looked ahead to the Randolph Oilers, who'd be visiting English High the following weekend. I hoped that Delaney remembered to pay our electric bill.

All season long, Reggie had been posting messages on the Panthers' official website, www.bostonpanthers.com. Motivational thoughts. Pregame speeches. Stuff like . . .

> The Night Before your emotions are all over the place. The Night Before is a hard time for you, your girl, your kids, and the family pet! Tension fills the air, the music you listen to gets you amped and ready to ball! You don't hear

the music, you FEEL it! The Night Before, your dinner tastes like grass, your drink tastes like sweat with a touch of blood, the salty taste one gets when throwing their body into an opposing player for that crushing block that will free your running back for the long one! You spend two days a week going to practice, four days in the gym, one day at chalk talk. Now the time has come for all of your off season training to pay dividends!

But as we prepared to face Randolph, Reggie posted a different—and, in my mind, far more important—message:

> Some of you young dudes are wasting your time being out here playing in this league. Next Tuesday at practice, a re-cruiter from a school down south will be watching and giving out information to anyone interested in going to college to play football . . . and get an education! Some of you dummies need to take advantage of what he is offer-ing. I will do all that I can to get you into school and play-ing ball for real so you can get that diploma and do something REAL with your lives.

"We have a lot of kids on this team," Reggie explains. "I urge them to use this level of football to get into college. Yeah, it's about getting physically and mentally ready to compete at that level, and maybe beyond. But let's get them into college so they can get *an education* first and get a good job, rather than waste valuable time playing in this league at their age. This league will be here for them when they get out of college with that degree. They don't need to be here now, playing with us old guys who maybe already had the chance to go to college. I want them to learn from our experiences, our mistakes."

Reggie's commitment to guiding the younger kids into college got me wondering: What *do* college scouts think of semi-pro ball? What kind of players do they look for? Have they ever found hidden gems in the EFL? Are the semi-pros a viable source for college-level talent?

Byron Beaman, 36, married with an infant son, is a scout for Elizabeth City State University in Elizabeth City, North Carolina. ECSU lies halfway between Norfolk, Virginia, to the north, and, to the south, Kitty Hawk, North Carolina, where the Wright Brothers made their historic first flight.

While by no means a football factory, the school has a proud tradition as a member of the Division II Central Intercollegiate Athletic Association (CIAA), the oldest African-American athletic conference in the United States, competing against such D-II stalwarts, and historically African-American colleges, as Livingstone College, Virginia State University, Virginia Union University, and Winston-Salem State University. Never claiming to be the Big 12 or the SEC, the CIAA has nevertheless produced such NFL players as former Pittsburgh Steeler/Tennessee Titan receiver Yancey Thigpen; former New England Patriot/Baltimore Raven All-Pro tight end Ben Coates; and former Miami Dolphin receiver Orande Gadsden.

A Mattapan native who quarterbacked Reggie and Delaney's Hyde Park High team, Byron played college ball (Western Connecticut State University) and then joined the semi-pros (the Boston Bandits of the New England Football League), playing for seven years in the '90s. In other words, he has valuable experience to pass on to his potential recruits. "Knowing what it takes to get to that next level, I can pass that on to these kids," he says. "I can give them a realistic perspective on things."

The MIAA—Massachusetts Interscholastic Athletic Association— has strict rules that dictate when scouts can and can't contact high school recruits. During the summer, it's okay to call, write, or e-mail, but there can be no personal contact. As the April signing period approaches, however, when student-athletes typically sign letters of intent, personal visits are allowed. That's why, Byron says, the semi-pros, not under MIAA jurisdiction, give him more recruiting flexibility. Might the Panthers produce a couple diamonds in the rough? "I have a lot of respect for leagues like the EFL and NEFL. Semi-pro used to *not* get a lot of respect in the football world, but that's changing. It's definitely a place where you have a lot of talented guys who respect each other on both sides of the football. The mentality is, *We all have to get up and go to work in the morning, so let's play hard, but fair*. I just say God bless everybody in semi-pro football. I'll do whatever I can to give some of these guys a chance they might not have otherwise."

Byron scours the semi-pros throughout the summer and fall.

Should he get lucky and find a player of college age or one with re-maining college eligibility (like the postarmy Reggie), Byron will en-courage him to apply in time for the January semester rather than the following fall. That's because if a player gets to school in the winter, he'll not only arrive in plenty of time for spring football camp, he'll also have more time than the average freshman to acclimate to what is often a drastic life change. "Some of these guys have never left their neighborhoods before, let alone the state," he explains. "Some have never even flown on an airplane before, so it's a lot for a young kid to take in. If a student-athlete is able to [enroll in January], he can get settled academically and socially even before getting into all the rig-ors of a football schedule. The average freshman, coming out of high school and enrolling in the fall, doesn't have that benefit."

Surprisingly, Byron's sales pitch first focuses not on football, but on academics. He highlights eventual benefits that don't necessarily have to do with improved 40-yard-dash times—specifically, how a college degree can increase one's earning potential *outside of* football. He praises the relatively small Elizabeth City student body and class-room sizes, meaning more individual attention than at larger universi-ties. "Gone are the days of the 'dummy football player,'" Byron explains. "If you can't swing it academically, it'll be hard for you to play at the college level. You don't want be the next 'woulda, coulda, shoulda' guy from the block; you want to be remembered as a kid who went off, did it right, got his degree, came back home, and made things better. You want to be a role model for the younger kids. If a kid wants to play semi-pro *after* college, great," Byron adds, echoing Reggie's message board sentiments. "Play when you're twenty-six, not when you're eighteen. Go to college, get that degree, and come back a better person."

The school's location in rural North Carolina is a bonus. There are fewer distractions and temptations than in the inner city, and Byron has had success bringing kids down south, where there aren't as many negative influences. "Some guys might even have extended family down here, giving them a built-in support system they can trust," Byron says, before adding, with a laugh, "At ECSU, there isn't a whole lot else to do *besides* play football and go to class, and maybe go cow-tipping on weekends. So these kids are here to play football and, more importantly, get that degree."

Byron scours the northeastern semi-pros for players, due in part to the intense competition for North Carolina in-state talent. "The really big-time athletes can go to UNC, Wake Forest, NC State," he explains. "There are also smaller Division I-AA schools nearby who are after the same players. Then you have all the black colleges like ours. And *then* you have the D-Two and D-Three schools, too. And that's just North Carolina," he says, adding that the circle of geographical competition widens to include Virginia, Virginia Tech, Virginia Union, and schools like Division I-AA Norfolk. And, of course, if a player is a *real* blue-chipper, he'll be hawked by southern powers like Florida, Clemson, Auburn, Alabama, Florida State, and Miami.

And there's yet another hurdle that scouts like Byron have to leap: parents. Like Donnie, Byron believes that most kids in the inner city and poorer neighborhoods simply don't consider college a viable option after high school. "For a lot of kids in the inner city, a lot of their parents didn't benefit from education themselves, so education isn't pushed. The athletic part will be pushed because [of] the old cliché that the only way out of the ghetto is through music or sports. All the parents see are dollar signs, even when their child is like 13 years old! Sure, he's good in Pop Warner, but his body will change, he might not develop, he might get hurt—and then it's over.

"And then they say, 'College is four years, maybe five, that's a long time.' That's because in the inner city," he says, "everyone wants everything now. The mentality, unfortunately, is *I'm not promised tomorrow, I might not even be alive tomorrow, so I want it now.*"

But Byron doesn't place all of the blame on the parents; the coaches also deserve some. Today's young players, he says, have too much of the "superstar syndrome," fueled by coaches who force teachers to give star players preferential treatment to maintain their eligibility. Hence players think that if they're naturally fast or strong, everything will be handed to them. "I got news for you: speed goes away," he says. "Talent and strength go away. I don't want to waste my time on a kid who takes his talent for granted." The local superstars have a tainted view of their talent because they've had their egos built up to unrealistic proportions by coaches and hangers-on. "Every kid in the inner city thinks he can play for Florida State or Miami. The reality is, Florida State and Miami don't even have to leave their *counties* to recruit, let alone the state."

So what's Byron's solution to the superstar syndrome and the mishandling of goals and dreams? To get communities to understand that everybody can't dance, sing, run, catch, or jump-shoot their way out of the neighborhood. "Somebody's got to do it the academic way, the good, old-fashioned way. There are very few LeBron Jameses in the world. That's why I do what I do. I can't guarantee anyone a million dollars, but I can guarantee you that you'll be able to get a good job and have a means to provide for your family even if football isn't an option. You can't cut corners in life because it gets you nowhere.

"Bottom line," Byron concludes with a somber chuckle, "I've yet to see a gangsta with a 401(k). At the end of that rap video, the gangsta who got shot by the police is going home to dinner with his family. He's an actor. In *real* life, the gangsta who gets shot isn't going home—he's going to the morgue."

It was September when I chatted with Byron. After another month of attending semi-pro and high school games and practices in and around Boston and Rhode Island, he would head back down to ECSU to watch the homecoming game and get one last look at the football team to gauge its primary need areas, and how those needs would fit in with the student-athletes he had been targeting up north. Then he'd return to Boston and start assembling his final list of recruits. From that point it'd be up to the kids. Knowing now what he offered, I sincerely hoped some of my younger Panther teammates would choose the Byron Beaman retirement plan. Not the gangsta one.

PUT ME IN, COACH

WITH THREE REGULAR-SEASON GAMES to go, we were firing on all cylinders. That was unfortunate for the Randolph Oilers. Randolph had always been one of the best-run, more buttoned-up teams in the league, and to their credit, always played hard and had some talented guys, year in, year out. But we had zero intention of losing that night at English High. Not in our house.

It was during that game that I started to notice a change in my behavior. *Was I, a measly kicker, becoming of all things, cocky?* If an incident at the end of the first half was any indication, the answer was yes.

We'd beaten the Oilers up and down the field for most of the first half, but only led 7–0 as halftime approached. With under a minute left, Southie and the O had driven down to the Oilers' five, but the drive stalled there when a holding call brought it back 10 yards. After an incomplete lob touch pass to Sam in the corner, we now faced fourth and goal from the 15. No chance for a first down. It was score a touchdown or turn the ball over on downs. With a kicker as hot as I was, Pitt's decision was easy: send me out there and go up 10–0. But just as I was snapping on my helmet to head out with Reggie and Donnie, Pitt called a time-out. The coaches huddled on the sideline. Southie soon trotted over to join them.

What's there to even think about? With the way I had been kicking, *no way* Pitt doesn't take the points here. I stretched out, did some practice kicks on the sideline, and when the coaches broke apart, I started heading out to the field.

And that's when I saw Southie running back out.

I turned around and held up both hands to Fink, who sat high up in the stands at home games, calling plays from the superior vantage point, our low-tech version of the coaches' booth at NFL stadiums.

"Fourth and 15?! C'mon, Fink, we take the points!"

He either didn't see me, or ignored me. Angrily unsnapping my helmet, I paced back and forth like a caged animal, hands on my hips, fuming. *Why would we* not *take the goddamn points?!* As Southie and the guys lined up for the play, I found myself having unprecedented, unsportsmanlike, and, worst of all, un*teammate*like thoughts: I wanted them to fail. I wanted this to blow up in the coaches' face. I wanted them to realize that when you have a chance to keep sticking a dagger into an opponent's throat, you do it, even if that knife is only three inches long (the field goal) rather than a lower-percentage six (an unlikely touchdown). Why did we *always* have to go for the goddamned ESPN highlight reel play?! We could slowly bleed them to death rather than going for the jugular every time!

"What the fuck?" I said loudly enough for most players around me to hear, kneeling down and slamming my helmet on the turf. "Fink thinks he's at home playing *Madden* again!"

Elvis and Gio, standing nearby, shook their heads. "I hear you," Elvis said. "We should take three here. Sometimes I think these guys get a little caught up in trying to be flashy instead of making the smart call. But hey, what do I know?" He shrugged. "This is my first year."

Elvis was right. And I got my wish—my totally wrong, selfish, antiteam-player wish. From the second Southie caught the shotgun snap, the play was a disaster: the blocking collapsed, he was forced out of the pocket, couldn't find a receiver, scrambled some more, and finally fired a desperate bullet to the corner, where a leaping, double-covered KFC couldn't reel it in.

Randolph whooped and hollered, amped by the defensive stand. We should have gone up 10–0, kicked off, and forced them to drive the length of the field against D-block, who'd allowed them only 42 total yards in the first half. But no, the cocky, reckless play call had given them hope, life, reason to believe they could still win this game come the second half. Hell, they had a good kicker of their own, a tall lefty who was booting long ones in warm-ups; they could easily have driven close enough to get them a half-ending field goal and cut it to 7–3.

Christ almighty, I'd already hit a 43-yarder this season. This one was a 29-yarder. A chip shot, the way I'd been kicking. *What the fuck did I have to do to prove myself?!* I turned around to Fink and defiantly held up three fingers. I shouldn't have taunted him like that, rubbed his failure in with the benefit of my 20–20 hindsight, but I couldn't help it. He glowered down at me and held up a finger of his own: his middle one. If I wasn't so pissed off it would have been pretty god-damned funny.

After a halftime spent listening to Pitt rail against the offense for missed opportunities (I held my tongue about the one they blew with me), we came out in the second half and took control right away. A Southie-to-Jeremy bomb in the third quarter put us up 14–0, and another touchdown (a pretty Amos option pass to Sam that caught them totally off-guard in the fourth) made it 21–0. I hit two dead-center extra points. Meanwhile, D-block was as dominant as they'd been all year. *D-blocccccccccccccccck! D-blocccccccccccccccck!* came the chants every time Insano, Pee Wee, Derek, Ace, and Caleb stifled Randolph on key third- and fourth-down attempts. When not on the field or conferring with coaches, the big twins always stood side-by-side, bookends, their numbers 68 and 69 stretched wide on their broad backs. They were always the first to start chants, pounding their thigh pads for emphasis. *Dee-fense! (thud, thud), Dee-fense! (thud, thud).* "I'm a workingman and I'm out here to have some fun!" Jason, a construction worker, yelled at one point to no one in particular, walking up and down our sideline, waving his arms to the crowd to get them psyched up, bashing guys on the shoulder pads. "You hear me, good people? I'm a workingman and I'm out here to *have some fun*! Get it up for the defense! Wooooooo!"

The only Oiler score came on a well-executed flea-flicker that caught our secondary flat-footed, but they missed the two-point conversion. It was now 21–6, and it stayed that way until the final few minutes, when on fourth and long—I guess Pitt and Fink must've remembered we had a kicker—I added an in-my-sleep 32-yard field goal.

Final score: 24–6. We were now 6–2 on the season . . . with six straight wins. With two games remaining, we were in sole possession of third place behind Middleboro and Brockton and a lock for the EFL playoffs. On the season, I was now 14 of 16 on extra points, and three for three on field-goal attempts. In fact, I felt like I'd never miss again. But I wasn't happy with myself for how I'd acted when my number wasn't called. I'd *never* wanted the ball in crunch time in my entire life, and now, here I was, getting pissed off because I *wasn't* called upon in a pressure situation. Amazing what simply putting on a football helmet and playing a game where emotions and adrenaline run higher than Ricky Williams during his NFL "sabbatical" could do to a guy. It was that switch that turned Darrell Jones into Insano. Freud would have had a field day with Fink's reckless call and my subsequent reaction. Had Siggy been standing there alongside me watching me rant and rave—ignoring the fact that he was Austrian and wouldn't have understood a single word—he would have determined that Fink's "football id"—the id being the part of one's personality that wants whatever feels good at the time, with no consideration for the reality of the situation—and my "superego"— the part that dictates our belief of right and wrong—had collided. The problem is, both of our egos failed us, considering the ego's job is to satisfy the selfish needs of the id while not upsetting the superego. That's just my amateur psychologist's take on the matter, anyway. I was probably way off. After all, I was just a dumb, overly emotional football player now.

SNAKEBIT

WE HAD A BYE the following week. It was hell. Sure, we had practice Tuesday and Thursday, and we worked just as hard as we would have otherwise. But, alas, there was no game that weekend, no reward. It was like having sex without a climax. As such I was edgy, a little short with Celia, leading her to treat me like the whiny little child deprived of his new favorite toy. "Why don't you go run around outside," she suggested at one point, having grown tired of my moping and sighing.

My behavior in public was less than normal, too. While walking through the Boston Common or down Beacon Street, I would occasionally stop, back up two steps, sidestep two more, and then kick an imaginary ball through nonexistent uprights. Anyone passing by would have seen a man gazing at something off in the distance and muttering to himself, probably never thinking, *No, he's not an escaped mental patient—he's just a semi-pro kicker on bye week who is merely counting off how many yards it might be from here to that tree over there and determining whether he can kick it that far,* which was exactly what I found myself doing. All the time. I was suffering from serious withdrawal. Sadly, however, I wouldn't be getting my football fix anytime soon.

Even though the interminable bye week finally ended and our rematch against the defending champion Middleboro Cobras at Battis Field in Middleboro, aka the "Snake Pit," would take place that following weekend, I wouldn't be there. My first book—*Committed: Confessions of a Fantasy Football Junkie*—had just been published, and on the September 11 weekend of the Middleboro game, I was already long scheduled to be out in Vegas to do some publicity and participate in the World Championship of Fantasy Football, or WCOFF, the largest big-money fantasy football league in the world. It was a business trip of sorts that I simply couldn't miss, no matter how important the Cobra game was. I felt I was letting my teammates down, especially with our six-game winning streak on the line. I hated the thought of us possibly losing by a field goal or, worse, an extra point. It killed me to miss that game. It turns out, however, if there was one game I *wouldn't* have wanted to see in person, it was that one.

First off, the weather was brutal. Rain, slop, mud. "Every time we started to get something going, we'd literally get stuck in the mud again and get stopped," Kelly reports. "It was the most frustrating game I've ever seen."

It was also too close for Middleboro's taste. We quickly went up 7–0, with Mohammad and his left-footed toe booting the extra point. The Cobras were used to dominating in the Snake Pit, and didn't like any team coming into *their* house and making a game of it. According to Sean Wilson, a linebacker from Braintree who'd played for Randolph the previous season, the cheap shots were pouring down as hard as the rain. "They were punching us, grabbing our nuts, and the refs were just letting them get away with murder," he says. "You could just tell something was about to jump off."

In the second quarter, with the score tied (Middleboro had tied it up on a long series of plodding runs through the mud), Southie hit KFC on a beautiful bomb to put us up 13–7. However, when KFC spiked the ball in the end zone—as wide receivers in all levels of football had been doing after scoring touchdowns for, oh, decades—the ref threw a flag for, of all things, taunting. The touchdown stood, we still led 13–7—we missed the extra point on a botched hold—but the ridiculous penalty shook us up and gave Middleboro an extra 15 yards on the kickoff they'd taken back to our 40-yard line. With the extra 15 tacked on, they started from our 25, and powered through with runs to go up, 14–13, which was the score at half.

"It was pretty nasty out there . . . rain, mud—just ugly," Kelly tells me. "Every time we started to get something going, there was a terrible flag or the weather kicked up, or we'd take some stupid penalty. It was just the longest, most horrible game." But O'Neal adds that it wasn't *all* the refs' fault: the Panthers dug their own graves, too. "When you're always getting up in a ref's face, yelling, screaming, cursing, the refs don't respect that. When you make a bad reputation for yourself, it follows you, the refs go looking for things to penalize you for. That's something I always tell these guys: don't sink down to the other team's level; you have to play up and be the better man. Clearly they didn't listen."

Making matters worse, according to Sean, Middleboro continued with the dirty play. They may have been what most EFL teams aspired to—a successful, profitable, well-run organization—but their allegedly underhanded style of play brought things to a head on a punt return that set the stage for, as Sean predicted, something to blow.

"I hit the guy in bounds on a punt return—a legal hit—and we crashed into our guys on the sideline, but everything was cool," Sean recounts. "I got up, the other guy got up, that was that. But then, out of nowhere, four or five seconds after the play ended, another Middleboro guy flies in and blindsides me, BAM!" At that point, he says, Donnie, standing nearby, grabbed the late hitter by the face mask and started pulling his helmet off. A scrum broke out. Yelling. Pushing. Shoving. "And then one of their guys drops the n-word, even though he's surrounded by like 20 black guys," Sean recalls. "At that point someone shoved the guy and he falls back on his ass and his helmet comes flying off. Of course, the refs, who took their sweet old time getting over there, only saw the *second* guy into the fight, the one who retaliates, so they flag us for the fight . . . *only* us! I couldn't believe it!" And that's when Sean saw Donnie pick up the stray Cobra helmet and casually walk over to a fence separating our bench from the woods. Like an Olympic hammer-tosser, Donnie reared back and chucked it as far as he could. The helmet flew into the woods and rolled into a small creek that trickled behind our bench.

Meanwhile, there was another storm brewing back on the field:

Ace. "He must have been tired of being punched in the nuts and the stomach all game, and the refs doing nothing about it, so he just snapped," Sean recalls. "He was taking on two, three Cobra players, just going batty. He probably would have been charged with murder if a bunch of us didn't run over there and pull him away. It was ugly." And it got even uglier.

Back on his own sideline now, Ace apparently began fighting with everyone who came into his limited vision: coaches, teammates, friends. It was absolute chaos. The fans were horrified. Delaney, who always imagined Ace on a short leash anyway—"Guys sometimes call him 'Nine Lives' because he's been kicked off and comes back so many times," he says—told the volatile defensive end to take his uniform off right then and there. He was off the team. Far as Delaney was concerned, there would be no 10th life.

Ace angrily stripped off his jersey, shoulder pads, and helmet, hurling them in all directions. "Fuck *all* y'all. I'll go play somewhere else and come back and destroy you! I'll go play for Brockton, Randolph, Charlestown, anywhere but here!"

The refs took several minutes to get the game back under relative control and assess all the penalty yards—*all* against the Panthers, utterly mind-boggling considering it had allegedly been the Cobra player's late hit that had started the melee. "When the smoke cleared, get *this*," Sean says, "the Cobras had the ball on *our 10-yard line*." They scored on an easy run to go up 21–13, and they scored once more, while we barely moved the ball across midfield. The fight and subsequent ejections and internal chaos had done us in.

Final score: Cobras 28, Panthers 13.

While I was 2,000 miles away in a desert oasis where people's hopes and dreams tended to come crashing down around them from time to time, the Panthers, *my* Panthers, also had gone bust. The six-game win streak? Over. Donnie? Suspended . . . again. Ace, for whom playing for the Panthers was more important than his eyesight? Kicked off the team . . . again. Just like that, all the positive steps and great play were washed away in the early September rain. We'd let the veteran team lure us into the one trap that always caught us: a game of mental toughness. Other teams had it; we didn't. We were too young, too volatile, too easily thrown off our game. In the time it took for Donnie to throw a helmet, Ace to throw punches, someone to allegedly throw a racial slur, and the refs to throw their flags, we'd regressed to the clueless, wide-eyed, confused 0–2 team of old.

After hearing the Panther point of view at my first practice back, I e-mailed Chris Leonard, a veteran Cobra offensive lineman, to get Middleboro's take. Not surprisingly, it differed from Boston's.

> The Panthers organization, regardless of the tremendous turnaround made from 2003 to this season, is the laughingstock of the league. You may not know this, but the Panthers are thought of as the DIRTIEST, MOST UNSPORTSMANLIKE, DISRESPECTFUL group of grown men to ever grace the EFL. After that debacle down in Middleboro, where one of your players threw the helmet into the woods, and while waiting for the helmet to be found another Panther player walked by one of our guys and hit him square in the nuts. You may have a better record this year, but the 2–8 Panthers in 2003 were a better T-E-A-M and representative of the EFL than this year's laughingstock.

O'Neal had a more succinct explanation: "We were overwhelmed by the idea of coming into the Snake Pit and playing the champs, and Middleboro took advantage of it. No one in this league can beat us if we keep our heads; we're just too talented. But I'm beginning to think that this might be asking too much of these guys."

Fink, who'd watched the melee unfold from his spot up in the grandstand, agreed. "Other teams do cheap stuff against us because they're afraid of us. They know that no one can match up with us, skillwise. But they also know that all it takes is a cheap shot here, a 'nigger' there, or some other kind of mental bullshit, and we'll collapse."

But the game, Ace, and Donnie weren't our only losses that night. Jason, aka "Doc," who had played a steady, under-the-radar reliable safety for us since arriving on his rice burner from Florida, quit the team—not after the game, but during. As Ace tussled with teammates and refs and players tried to pry each other apart, without a word, Doc simply walked off the sideline, undressed in the parking lot, hopped onto his motorcycle, strapped his pads and helmet to his back, and buzzed off into the Middleboro night, never to play for the Panthers again.

BITCHES AND APOLOGIES

WHEN I RETURNED FROM VEGAS, I discovered that whoever was in charge of football weather—God, Mother Nature, the ghost of Vince Lombardi?—had suddenly flipped a switch, shutting off the sweltering humidity and turning on the crisp, cool, lung-biting air for which New England in the fall was renowned. Soon, leaves from Vermont to Rhode Island would begin their miraculous transformation from simple greens to Crayola-on-acid—eye-twitchingly beautiful reds, oranges, yellows, and the elusive burnt umbers that lured foliage "peepers" to the region every season. The leaves, the far-off smell of burning firewood, the cool air pinching your skin: *now* it was officially football season.

This being the case, nearly everyone at practice that Tuesday after Middleboro now wore skintight Under Armour long-sleeved shirts under their shoulder pads. Some of the braver souls still wore shorts, but most wore sweatpants. Jeremy, Sam, and KFC wore thin leather athletic gloves. And a few guys—like the Twinkies, to whose tropical genes the crisp, 55-degree air must have been positively Arctic—actually wore ski hats . . . under their helmets.

"You get to any strip clubs out in Vegas?" Reggie asked me as we sat on the FieldTurf, stretching out our groins Buddha-style.

"Nah." I smiled. "We had the wives with us."

He winced as if I'd told him I was quitting the team to play field hockey. "Wives? How can you go to Vegas with your wives? And even *with* the wives there, how can you *not* go to the strip clubs?" He turned away, shaking his clean-shaven head. "I'm disappointed in you, Mark."

"So I hear all hell broke loose in Middleboro."

"Same old bullshit," Reggie replied, shaking his head. "These bastards act like a few wins are going to change who they are, but it's the same old Panthers. Guys show their true colors when things aren't going right."

"And Ace really got kicked off the team?" I asked.

Reggie nodded. "Kicked off *again*, you mean. Getting in fights with the other team is one thing. I mean, this is football, tempers flare; it happens. But you can't be fighting with your own teammates and coaches. He was out of control, swinging at everyone who came near him. We could have won that game, too. Bunch of stupid bastards. That's all we got here, Mark: a bunch of selfish, stupid bastards who think that you win a couple games and everything's gonna just keep going like that automatically, that you can just relax and get lazy."

He then echoed Byron's sentiments about the *now-now-now* mentality that you sometimes find in the inner city. "That's the problem with some of these young guys: they get a job for like eight bucks an hour, get a few dollars in their pocket, and they think that they've got it made, that they're on top of the world. So what do they do? They stop trying to work harder, or trying to get better, or trying to move even higher up the ladder. They start thinking, 'Wow, this shit is *easy*, life ain't nothing, I got some pocket money for some beer, or maybe some weed, I can take my girl out for a nice dinner, it's all good.' But next thing you know, they get so fat and happy and complacent that pretty soon they start coming in late to work, and then stop coming in at all, and then what? I'll tell you what—they get their ass fired, and they're right back to square one where they started: unemployed and broke as a motherfucker.

"And that's what the Middleboro game did to us," he concluded. "As a team, we're back to being broke, unemployed motherfuckers."

Coach Pitt called us all to midfield. We took a knee and received an all-too-familiar verbal bitch-slap, like we had after Brockton. But there was one difference: it wasn't Pitt who laid into us, it was O'Neal.

"I'm embarrassed to be associated with such childish, selfish motherfuckers! Do you know, or even care, that you erased everything we've accomplished this season—*everything*—with that shit you pulled up in Middleboro? The whole league is laughing at you now. Do you even care? You're a joke. A disgrace to the great game of football. And all you did was justify all the stupid, ignorant shit those assholes always yell at you. You want to act like a bunch of niggers, then fine, that's what people will think you are: nothing but a bunch of ignorant niggers! You call yourselves men? You think that getting in fights and acting up makes you men? It doesn't. All it makes you is a bunch of whiny, selfish little bitches."

He reached into his pocket and removed a roll of stickers of some sort.

"And that's why we got you these to wear, because if you want to act like little bitches, you're gonna tell the world that you *are* little bitches!"

O'Neal held up the roll, covered with round, bright-pink stickers that said BITCH in large, black, block letters. He handed them all to Pitt.

"Brand these little bitches, Mike," O'Neal hissed.

Pitt peeled off the first sticker.

"You're a bitch," he said to reddish-haired Stanley, a polite, hard-working 23-year-old who was planning to take the Police Academy entrance exam and, unluckily, happened to be standing closest to Pitt's firing range. *Thwack!* The slap of Pitt's palm against Stanley's helmet sounded like an executioner's gunshot and sent Stanley stumbling forward a few steps. Perhaps in preparation for a future as a police recruit (who'd likely endure some rookie hazing), Stanley quickly righted himself and stared ahead without a word of complaint. Pitt then moved on to the next guy. And the next. And the next.

"And you're a little bitch." *Thwack!*

"Here you go, bitch." *Thwack!*

"And one for you, little bitch." *Thwack!*

Through it all, no one said a word. We knew he and Pitt were right.

After giving probable concussions to nearly three dozen other guys, Pitt stood behind me. I could almost hear him growling. I hadn't even been at Middleboro. But, like Stanley and everyone else who'd gotten their punishment, I stared ahead and awaited mine. And I didn't want Pitt to ease up on me, treat me any differently just because I hadn't been at the game. Frankly, I wanted him to smack the shit out of me *because* I hadn't been there.

Pitt slammed my "Bitch" sticker onto the back right corner of my helmet, hitting me so hard I thought he'd knock my head clean off, still attached to my spine, and send them skittering across the turf like the fossil of some prehistoric lizard suddenly come to life, making a run for it. Like Stanley, I stumbled ahead a couple of steps but quickly righted myself. No way I was going to be the one to fall down.

"Good," Pitt said, glaring at each of us. "Go ahead, look around. All you see is bitches, right? Get used to it. That's how the rest of the league sees you, and that's how *we coaches* see you, so get used to it. Those stickers stay on until you prove otherwise. If we see one of you bitches taking off your sticker without permission, I swear to God it'll be the last thing you ever do."

He turned to O'Neal. "Anything else?"

"Yeah, I got something else. Most of you guys"—he hissed and looked around at us, struggling to find the right words—"I wouldn't use as *a shield in a shit fight!*"

There was a beat of total silence.

Then another.

Then a third.

And then I heard a snicker behind me. Then a stifled laugh. Then everyone just exploded. Howling, doubled over. Even Pitt and O'Neal reluctantly gave in, cracked smiles and began to laugh.

"*Shield in a shit fight?*" cackled Southie, who was normally a pretty quiet guy but now was wiping tears from his eyes and nearly hugging KFC to keep from literally falling onto the ground, laughing. "What the hell does that *even mean?*"

O'Neal started chuckling despite himself. "Hey, it was the first thing that came to mind," he said with a shrug.

"But this doesn't mean you're not all little bitches," Pitt added. "Circle it up, and then defense over with me, offense down there with—"

Pitt paused and looked behind us. We all turned to see a tall, lean figure in baggy jeans and a hooded sweatshirt, blue bandanna wrapped over his forehead, making his way down the stairs and onto the field.

Without so much as a word to anyone, he walked right into the middle of the circle of players. Head lowered, hands jammed into his front pockets, he took a deep breath and finally looked up to face each and every one of us. There were already tears in his eyes.

Ace, the team's self-proclaimed engine, had broken down.

"I just wanted to come here and step like a man and apologize, tell y'all that I was wrong for how I behaved last game," Ace said, his normally deep, booming baritone voice now faint, cracking with emotion. "I been going through lots of stuff with my son lately. He's keeping me up all hours. I try to handle my business off the field and take care of my business on the field. But I couldn't do it no more." Ace paused and tried to collect himself, his eyes welled up even more, and his voice dwindled to a near-whisper. Khary, perhaps his best friend on the team, grabbed Ace by the shoulder and shook him gently back and forth. *I got ya. I'm right here. I got ya.*

"So when Middleboro started beefin', and that guy punched me in the stomach, everything I been goin' through lately just exploded outta me," Ace continued, a tear now running down his cheek, which he wiped with a brisk, backhanded swipe. "I couldn't stop it. But I had no business takin' it out on all y'all who was trying to pull me away. This ain't just a football team to me—y'all are my family, straight up. I always say I got two families: the one I was raised with, and the one I play ball with. I'd die for all y'all out here, because right now, football is the only good thing I got in my life. The *only* good thing. I'd be dead or in lockup if I couldn't play ball no more, but knowin' that you got my back, and I got y'all's, and knowin' I can come out here every night and play this game—that's what keeps me goin.' And seeing y'all down here while I was alone up there, just watchin' and thinkin' that I might not ever step on this field with you anymore, I didn't even want to keep goin' on. Football, and my kids, are what keep me goin', and if I lost one of them I don't know what I'd do."

He paused and looked around, took another deep breath.

"So I just wanted to come here and stand in front of all y'all like a man and apologize, and let you know that shit'll never happen again. I don't know whether I'll be allowed back on the team again, but

whatever y'all decide, coaches, and Delaney, it's cool, you gotta do what you gotta do. I understand that.

"But whatever y'all decide, I'll always be a Panther."

There was total silence at first. It was the only time I can remember all of us gathered in a huddle like this at a practice or game where someone wasn't yapping about *something* to someone else while someone was trying to talk. I think it was Mohammad who started clapping first. And soon everyone else was, too. Pitt and Ace walked off to one side. Most were impressed with Ace's honesty.

"Took guts," Mohammad, almost 10 years Ace's junior, says, sounding more like a proud older brother than a younger teammate. "I was real impressed that he stepped up like a man and admitted he was wrong, and to open up like that in front of *this* group? That's not easy for a cat like Ace to do. He's proud, and he's stubborn, but he's a good person underneath it all, know what I'm sayin'? A lot of these guys talk tough, and a lot of them have gone through some shit, but they're all good people underneath."

Some, however, like Delaney, didn't quite buy the contrite act because they thought it was just that: an act. "I've seen this a thousand times before," he says of "Nine Lives." "He'll go off, get in fights, come back, apologize, say he's going to change, but you know what? He'll never change. He might be better for a while, and act like the model player, but he'll be right back in the middle of some shit before you know it, you watch. And it only makes the organization look bad. I'm trying to change the image of this team, so whenever Ace goes off, it sets us back. I'm sick of it, you know? We need less guys like that, not more."

Me? I was torn. I agreed that it took guts for one of the toughest guys out here to expose himself raw in front of his peers, especially in a part of society where a tough veneer is sometimes the only thing keeping a guy alive. And to cry in front of teammates like that was unheard of in a sport like football. So in that respect, I was impressed with the way that Ace stepped up and had the guts to admit that he was wrong. And he'd always been nothing but cool to me. Right before my kicking showdown at practice a few weeks back, in fact, he'd been the first one to step up in front of the entire team and actually put money on me. I'd always remember that. But I also couldn't ignore the fights and the explosions and the countless stories of past transgressions and expulsions from the Panther team. Still, maybe this was just the wake-up call Ace needed. Maybe this time he realized that his actions might finally cause him to lose the one anchor in his life.

Pitt, Delaney, and Ace conferred away from the rest of us. After a few moments, and contrite nodding, Ace walked back over to us. Without a word, he stepped into the huddle with the rest of us.

"Team on three, team on three," Insano began. "One, two, three—!"

"TEAM!"

MUDDERS

OCTOBER WAS A GREAT TIME to be a sports fan in Boston.

General Manager Theo Epstein and his Red Sox, after a brutal July swoon that included the hated Yankees running away with the AL East, the Sox almost losing the wild card, and the controversial trading of fallen local hero Nomar Garciaparra, had made the play-offs and were about to begin an American League Divisional Series at Fenway Park against the Anaheim Angels.

The New England Patriots, fresh off a Super Bowl win over the Carolina Panthers, had begun the 2004 season with an exciting win at home against their own biggest rival-in-the-making—Peyton Manning and the Indianapolis Colts—and were now heading into the second month of football undefeated, with Tom Brady, Tedy Bruschi, Richard Seymour, Corey Dillon, and the rest of Bill Belichick's gang (including my namesake Adam Vina*tizzy*) trying to accomplish something virtually unheard of in this modern NFL era of rampant free agency and salary caps: repeating as Super Bowl champions. The Eagles of Boston College, alma mater of Doug Flutie, in their final Big East season before defecting to the more prestigious ACC, were also in full swing, drawing tens of thousands of people to the Heights of Chestnut Hill. And, of course, even farther down the local sports food chain, with one regular-season game left to play, the EFL's Boston Panthers, despite the recent meltdown against Middleboro, were 6–3, and about to face the Clinton Irish Blizzard in their season finale.

The top six teams in the regular-season standings made the EFL playoffs. As it stood, 8–0 Middleboro and 8–1 Brockton would receive first-round byes as the first and second seeds, respectively. We were currently third, and if we beat Clinton to finish 7–3, we'd hold the third spot and host a first-round game against the number six seed, which would be Randolph; Clinton was a spot below us right now at number four, with the Shamrocks in the unfamiliar position of a number five seed. A win today and we'd be assured of a home playoff game against Randolph. The Panthers, in their short history, had never hosted a playoff game. A loss today, however, and we'd still make the postseason, but would likely play on the road. Needless to say, this was a pivotal game for the franchise.

I met the guys at Franklin Park and we filled a bunch of cars with players and equipment and caravaned up to the game. An hour northwest of Boston, rural Clinton, of all EFL hometowns, was the most different from the world most of our guys lived in. "Where are we— Nebraska?" marveled Sean, riding in my Jeep's passenger seat as we wound our way past algae-covered ponds, cow-filled barnyards, and fruit- and vegetable-stacked farm stands. The smell of manure permeated the rolled-up windows. Sugar Bear, meanwhile, was in the backseat slumped against the window dozing, and had barely said three words since we left Franklin Park; his newborn daughter's 3:00 A.M. feedings were sapping his reserve energy. Sean, a light-skinned guy with racially mixed parents, added: "Man, I bet *I'd* even stick out like a sore thumb out here."

It had been raining off and on all day long. Not just a lazy drizzle, either . . . I'm talking downpours, the kind of rain that can turn a nice, grassy field into a mud wrestling pit, which is exactly what happened to Fuller Field. And the conditions inside weren't much better. We dressed in a cramped, damp janitor's closet-turned-locker room in the corner of a squat, brick maintenance shed behind one end zone. Outside, barely audible over the rain beating on the metal gutters, the hometown announcer's tinny voice ran through both rosters: names, numbers, positions. When he got to mine, he said, "Number six, kicker, Mark Saint . . . Saint . . . Saint Almond?"

Unlike Boston, where there were a plethora of entertainment choices battling for the attention and dollars of its citizens, Clinton was one of those towns where there simply wasn't a helluva lot going on every weekend. Irish Blizzard games had long been a staple of the community, a Friday or Saturday night town block party, residents near and far coming to cheer on the Blizzard, playing in their green, white, and gold uniforms, and Notre Dame-esque gold helmets bearing what looked like the Chicago Bears' "C" on each side. However, while there normally would have been a packed house, the inclement weather now made the stands more or less barren, with only a few diehards—girlfriends and other family members, most likely—braving the elements, huddled under umbrellas, cloaked in ponchos and other hard-core rain gear. There were 20 people, tops. And they all looked miserable.

Maybe it was the weather, or the long drive, or the less-than-playoff atmosphere. Maybe it was the fact that Donnie had once again been suspended (for his part in the Middleboro melee) and wouldn't be there to hold. Maybe it was because I was at the end of my first long, mentally and physically exhausting football season. Whatever it was, I felt miserable, too. Just . . . *off*. The vibe in our locker room was lethargic. You could just sense it: despite the importance for playoff seeding, this was going to be an ugly, ugly game.

And boy, was it—just a clumsy, mud-soaked, mistake-filled comedy of errors played between the 30-yard lines; neither team was able to advance the ball much beyond that "too far for a field goal, not close enough for a touchdown" point. The only ones doing their jobs with any consistency were Khary and the Clinton punter, but that had more to do with the offensive ineptitude.

"Are you guys actually *trying* to lose this game?" Pitt begged the offense at one point as they skulked off the field after another listless, fruitless three-and-out. Pitt's question was almost rhetorical: we may not have been trying to lose, but we certainly didn't appear to give a shit about winning.

Finally, however, after countless punts, young Chezley, playing cornerback, got us going. He snared an errant, wounded-duck pass—

not easy, considering the ball was as slick and squirmy as a harbor seal—and returned it for a TD. However, my bad pregame mojo stuck with me as I lined up for the kick. I'd never seen the future *that* clearly before—I just knew, *knew* I was going to miss, and miss horribly. As Delaney caught Reggie's snap and got the ball down perfectly, I literally had a flash-forward and envisioned myself two seconds later, badly hooking the ball left, a good 10 feet wide, just a horrific display of poor technique and lethargic effort. And that's exactly what happened: I clumsily planted my left cleat into the thick mud with a sickening squish, swung my soggy right cleat, which felt like a cinder block tied to my ankle, and lazily hooked the ball a good 10 feet wide left. Hands on my hips, I hung my head, the raindrops cascading from the top of my helmet into my eyes. Where, normally, a teammate would have given me an encouraging head slap or told me not to worry about it, no one said a thing as they passed by me.

Panthers 6, Irish Blizzard 0. As I passed by Pitt, he stared at me, baffled, his eyes wide with concern, befuddlement, rather than the anger and/or frustration that would have greeted me a few weeks back. He expected me to make kicks now. And I'd let him down.

"What happened?" he pleaded.

I could only shrug. "Hooked it." Then I kept walking, right past him. Frankly, I didn't have an excuse. And there was no point in explaining that the overall pre- and in-game lethargy from the other players "above" me had trickled down and seeped into the machinery that housed my competitive drive, bringing the gears to a grinding, gritty halt, rusting the innards beyond repair. That would have sounded like an excuse.

We scored again in the second quarter, but again, it was off a Clinton miscue. Their running back fumbled near their own goal line, and after Insano recovered, Amos dove over the top for a one-play, one-yard TD plunge. This time I somehow managed to boot the extra point, putting us up 13–0. On the ensuing kickoff, the Clinton return man brought it back through our flailing special-teams coverage and took it home. After the PAT, they were within six, 13–7. Thus ended a sloppy first half. Trudging to the janitor's closet, I began to fear that my missed extra point would come back to haunt us.

The locker room at the half was part mausoleum, part battle zone. I sat in a trance and listened as the defensive players, who felt they'd been carrying us most of the season, unleashed their pent-up frustration on the offensive players.

"Come on, O. How many times we got to do all the work out there?" a frustrated Brandon implored, banging one fist on a flimsy locker door, which rattled loudly. Brandon was a pretty quiet, reserved guy (when he wasn't talking shit to me, that is). If he was speaking up, it was a sure sign that the defense as a whole had simply had enough. And frankly, I couldn't blame them: they'd held opponents to a stingy 13 points per game, while the offense, unfortunately, hovered just above that, scoring 18 points per game. Sure, Fink and Southie's crew had scored more than 20 points in four of the last five games, but they were utterly ineffective against Middleboro and were just as weak tonight. Compare this to Middleboro and Brockton, who had been blowing teams out by 30 or 40 points all season long. Translation: the defense *was* carrying this team, while the offense might have been headed in the wrong direction at the exact wrong—read: playoff—time.

"Yeah," Derek chimed in. "Both our scores were ours, a pick and a fumble recovery. All you did was run it in from one yard, and you ain't done shit else all day besides fumble and go three-and-out. What we got, like 20 total yards of offense?"

"Man, shut up, no-tackling motherfucker!" yelled Todd, who had already fumbled once, a costly one as we were getting close to a score. "How many times you and the supposed 'D-block' gonna let [burly Clinton running back Daron] Brown into our secondary? Dude's got like a hundred yards already! If that's how tough D-block is, I'll do time there any day!"

"Stop fumbling and I'll make a tackle," Derek countered, and the two stood up, ready, it appeared, to start throwing punches, defensive guys backing Derek, offensive guys backing Todd.

Sitting on the cold, clammy cement floor, I leaned back against a locker and watched, partly concerned, but mostly not caring if they beat the shit out of each other. I was just too tired. I looked over at Jeremy, who smiled at me and shook his head, as if to say, *Can you believe this shit is happening again?* "I was supposed to go to an Arena tryout down in New York today. Insano, too. But our ride fell through," he said, chuckling at the sad irony. A day that began with dreams of playing football at the next level had ended here, sitting in a broom closet, covered in mud, watching teammates about to have an intrasquad steel cage match. "Glad I showed up tonight," Jeremy added, nodding, still laughing to himself. "This is real fun."

Coach Pitt entered, followed by O'Neal, Fink, and Mark. With one whiplash motion of his Popeye forearm, Pitt slammed the door behind him, nearly ripping it off the hinges in the process. He hadn't had an explosion in a while, so he was due. "Quiet, all of you!" he yelled, glaring at us pathetic excuses for football players. "I am flat-out *disgusted* with what I saw out there in the first half! But I'm even more disgusted by what I heard outside this door just now. If I hear one more defensive player calling out the offense, or an offensive player calling out the D, you're off the team, period. No questions, no arguments. Just pack your shit and leave. This 'offense against defense' bullcrap ends now. This is a team. We win as a team, and we lose as a team. And if we lose tonight, we could lose a chance at a home playoff game. Do you want that?"

"No, sir," about half the room responded listlessly. Some guys had towels over their heads. Others leaned against lockers, looking like they'd rather be somewhere else. Pitt looked around the room, taking the time to stare at each one of us. He just shook his head and left. No door slam. No more yelling. He, too, had had enough. As we silently filed back outside into the drizzle, Donnie (who'd come to the game but didn't dress) turned to me. "Mark," he said with an amused grin, "you follow these guys around with a camera for a week and you'd have the funniest reality show on TV, hands down."

Our play in the second half remained anything but funny. The offense went three-and-out on nearly every series throughout the third and most of the fourth quarters. And the defense didn't do much better, allowing the Clinton offense to penetrate as deep as our 10-yard line on three or four occasions before they, too, either fumbled or got flagged for some untimely holding calls, knocking them out of field goal range. If they had even an ounce of luck, they would have been up 21–13 or 28–13. As it was, we still led 13–7 as the fourth quarter dwindled down.

After the Clinton offense stalled once again deep in our territory with under two minutes remaining, we took over on downs. All we had to do was run out the clock. But on the first carry, Todd, who'd had trouble holding on to the ball all day, was hit by the Clinton defensive end and lost control of the ball. There was a mad scramble in the mud, body on top of body, arms flailing, legs kicking. The refs unpeeled the pile layer by agitated layer, and the defensive end who'd made the initial hit emerged on our seven-yard line with the ball clenched in one meaty fist. Covered in filth, he leaned back and let loose with a victory howl, looking like some kind of feral, mud-covered Viking berserker. The 10 or so remaining diehard Clinton fans went as crazy as 10 soaking wet people could.

Holy shit, they're gonna score, go up 14–13, and I'll be the goat for missing the lazy extra point! Out of all the gaffes, miscues, bonehead plays, untimely penalties, and idiotic mishaps to choose from, mine will be the *only* thing everyone remembers! I'll be *solely* responsible for losing us a home playoff game! I wanted to dig a hole in the mud right there on our sideline and burrow until I reached downtown Peking. I didn't breathe as I watched Clinton set up and, in what felt like slow motion, run three quick plays.

First and goal: incomplete slant pass across the middle.

Second and goal: a surprise/trick call—a delayed quarterback sneak up the middle—sniffed out by Derek and Pee Wee, who dropped the quarterback for a two-yard loss.

Third and goal: fade/timing pattern to the corner, Brandon and the receiver got tangled, no flag, overthrown, ruled uncatchable, well out of bounds.

Fourth and goal.

Fourteen seconds left.

The quarterback faded back and tried the exact same fade pass.

This time Brandon momentarily slipped in the mud, leaving the wide receiver open in the corner for what would be an easy catch. The ball floated in slow motion. The receiver leaped up. The ball hit his fingertips. He grabbed hold, cradled it safely in his palms. Then pulled it down into his stomach, where one of his raised knees inadvertently jerked up. The ball sprung back up in the air. Panic in his eyes, he juggled it. Had it. Lost it again. It hit off his shin. Deflected away. Fell to the ground. The ref waved off the catch. The receiver crouched, curled into a ball and grabbed both sides of his helmet, and then pounded the mud with both fists. The referee blew his final whistle as the clock hit zeroes. Game over. Panthers 13, Irish Blizzard 7.

I was officially spared. And we had stumbled into the first home playoff game in team history. Sean, Sugar Bear, and I stopped at Wendy's on the way home and celebrated our semi-enjoyable win with a semi-enjoyable meal.

POETIC JUSTICE

ACCORDING TO the final standings, we should have actually been playing Marlboro in the first round of the playoffs. The Shamrocks were the number six seed, while Randolph had climbed to the number five spot with a win on the last weekend. This meant that Clinton, the number four seed, was supposed to play Randolph while we hosted Marlboro. However, the league honored the Irish Blizzard owner's unexpected request to switch the matchups and host the Shamrocks in the first round. It made sense from a business standpoint. Clinton and Marlboro were close and therefore had a rivalry, so the crowd was more likely to be larger, and the teams would make more at the gate. Money talked. But that was okay. We were hosting regardless and had beaten Randolph handily, 24–6, earlier in the season. That said, after the Clinton game we had no business taking anyone for granted. We needed something to get us back on track. Who would have guessed that "something" would be poetry?

> *If you can keep your head when all about you are losing theirs and blaming it on you; If you can trust yourself when all men doubt you, but make allowance for their doubting, too; If you can wait and not be tired by waiting, or being lied about, don't deal in lies or being hated. Don't give way to hating, And yet don't look too good, nor talk too wise. . . . If you can talk with crowds and keep your virtue, Or walk with kings—nor lose the common touch, If neither foes nor loving friends can hurt you, If all men count with you, but none too much; If you can fill the unforgiving minute With sixty seconds' worth of distance run—Yours is the Earth and everything that's in it, And—which is more—you'll be a man, my son!*

That wasn't the entire poem that Coach O'Neal handed out to us on a chilly Tuesday night in mid-October, but it was most of it. Rudyard Kipling's "If." He had printed up about 50 copies and handed them out to each of us as we gathered under a clear sky, a remarkable number of stars visible above the field despite the intrusive glow of city lights.

"My father gave this to me when I was younger and I thought I knew everything there was to know about life," he told us as we gathered at midfield after our prepractice calisthenics, our breath visible for the first time that season. "I was headstrong, cocky, thought I had all the answers, and it turned out I didn't know a damn thing. And now I'm passing it on to you. Look, I *still* don't pretend to know everything, but I've played my share of big games, and I've maybe seen and learned some things that you guys haven't yet. This is the first home playoff game this team's ever had, and for most of you guys, it's probably the biggest game of your lives. I just wanted to pass on whatever I can to help you put it all in perspective. For what it's worth, even though we've had our bumps and beefs along the way, and—"

"And you wouldn't use us as a shield in a shit fight?" Mohammad interrupted, causing a round of laughter. O'Neal would never live down his now famous insult.

"—and yes, even though I wouldn't use you as a shield in a shit fight." O'Neal grinned. "I'm real proud of all of you. The team that showed up against Clinton wasn't the real Panthers. The *real* Panthers is the team that won five straight, stuck together, and lifted his teammate up when he was down. The *real* Panther team has more talent than anyone in the EFL. *That* is the team the Randolph Oilers have the unfortunate job of playing on Saturday. We have to make them pay for how we played last week."

Pitt, nodding along with his old friend's sentiments, was about to blow his whistle and split up the offense and defense when Coach Cliff chimed in.

"I got something to say, Coach."

He took a few steps out in front of the entire group, much like Ace had just a couple of weeks earlier, and faced everyone, a sad smile on his face. "Not sure how many of y'all know this, but, um—" he cleared his throat—"I might be going away for a while. I've had a situation come up again and I don't know how it's gonna turn out." Apparently he had been accused of an assault. With his prior record, if convicted, Cliff would no doubt be sent back to prison. My heart immediately sank. All season long, I was pulling for Cliff to keep following that more spiritual path and control the temper that, he admitted, had gotten him into trouble so many times before. It crushed me to hear that he might be locked up again.

"I have a court date in December, and if it doesn't go my way, like I said, I'll be going away again for a while. If that happens, fellas, I just hope you'll write, and maybe come visit. Last time I was inside, all y'all coming by to see me, and writing me and letting me know what's up, you know, that kept me going. I felt like I was still a part of the team. I got my kids, but I need something else to keep me going on the inside, something I know is waiting for me when I get out, and that's football. That's this team. If I don't know that I have y'all, and this team, waiting for me when I get out?" Before answering his own question, he paused and took a deep breath, perhaps imagining a life without football. "Well, I don't know if I'd survive, know what I'm sayin'?"

As we ran through our drills over the next couple of hours, and I kicked field goals and extra points, there was initially a subdued, almost melancholy vibe, a combination of O'Neal's poetic challenge to us and Cliff's sobering news. But as the adrenaline started flowing and the focus returned to the task at hand—football, in just a matter of days against the Oilers—there also was a lot of chatter about how much smack the Randolph players had been talking that week.

"They said, and I quote, 'We're gonna come up there and beat your monkey asses,'" said a chuckling, incredulous Mohammad, who spent a good deal of time on the EFL league website's message board (I'm sure talking his own share of smack).

"Fellas," he concluded, "if that's not enough incentive to kick the shit out of them, I don't know what is."

BANANAS

ENGLISH HIGH was packed that night, our first Friday night game of the season. The barbecue was fired up, and the southern-sweet smell of fried chicken and burgers wafted over the field. The drill team from the home opener was back, the band cranking out endearingly off-key renditions of various football fight songs, and the young dancers doing their sequin-covered best with reckless disregard for the limitations of the human spinal column and bone structure. And what the fans saw that night was the single most complete football game we'd played yet that season. I'd never seen our offensive line—the big twins, Mohammad, Big Paul, and the rest of the guys—control the flow of a game like that. They opened holes at will, bashing the Oiler defensive line back on their heels time after time, allowing Amos to slash his way for 15 or 20 yards at a time. It was almost unfair. When the first impressive drive—starting at our own six-yard line—ended at the Oiler 25, I was called in for a field goal.

If I missed, a great drive would be wasted. But I wasn't going to miss. Calmly forgetting any and all remnants of my blasé Clinton performance, I took one last glance at the plastic flags twitching in the breeze on the tips of the goalposts, focused on Donnie's hold— thankfully, Donnie was back—stepped up, and cranked it. Forty-two yards. Panthers 3, Oilers 0.

After D-block shut down the Oilers on their first possession, we scored right away on a Southie-to-Sam TD pass. But Randolph, in our only breakdown of the game, promptly returned the kickoff for a TD, putting them down by only three, 10–7. That was as close as they got. We took control, scoring two more touchdowns. We could have put up 40 or 50 points if we'd left our starters in. We were *that* good that night.

Better yet, we held up mentally. When Randolph realized that the game was out of reach and their week-long smack talk was all moot, they started in with the cheap stuff that would normally make us snap, retaliate, and end up getting penalized. On more times than I could count, the big twins, typically the first to get personal-foul calls, simply held up their arms while an Oiler defensive lineman kept hitting after the play, frustrating Randolph even more and causing *them* to get flagged. One time an Oiler even ripped Jason's helmet clean off. But Jason, to his credit, just picked up his helmet, snapped it back on, and went back to work. And on the next play, he pancake-blocked the lineman, landing on him with all 300-plus pounds and driving him into the turf. Revenge.

Late in the game, after a running play down near the Oiler goal line, Todd emerged in agony and ripped off his helmet, both his hands clasped over his eyes. Apparently someone had eye-gouged him in the pile. But other than Big Paul, who wanted to take on the whole Oiler team by himself (and probably could have), we kept our cool. Big Paul was quickly dragged away by both of the big twins so he wouldn't be suspended for round two. And on the very next play, Todd, half-blinded by the cheap play, took the handoff and, behind a bulldozer block from Big Paul, pounded it home for the score and spiked the ball right next to the guy who had eye-gouged him. Revenge.

I added a late chip shot 25-yard field goal to put us up 27–7. But the exclamation point on the day came late in the fourth quarter when Derek, "speaking" for the entire team, rushed in untouched on a blitz, literally picked up the Oiler quarterback, and body-slammed him onto the FieldTurf, WWF-style. Our sideline erupted as Derek, standing over the writhing quarterback, flexed his massive biceps and, mimicking a man with a shovel, began to dig imaginary dirt out of the turf and "bury" the quarterback with it. That was as showy as we got, but the Oilers deserved it. They'd taunted us at the wrong time and had to pay.

Final score: Panthers 27, Oilers 7.

After his postgame prayer, O'Neal and I walked off the field, his arm draped over my shoulder pads. "This was the best game I've ever seen you guys play. But there *is* one thing I regret," he said.

"What, the kickoff return?" I guessed. Honestly, aside from that, I couldn't think of one thing we'd done wrong.

"Nope. I wish I'd bought a whole bunch of bananas," he replied. "And when we went through the handshake line, I would have gone, 'One for your monkey ass . . . and one for your monkey ass . . . and one for *your* monkey ass. . . .'" We both cracked up and, after getting into dry clothes, headed over to the Drinking Fountain for the first home playoff win celebration in Panther history.

The partying lasted into the wee hours. Again, Delaney brought in trays of wings and pizza. We had the Red Sox and Angels in Game 3 of the American League Divisional Series, and the Sox, going for the sweep, were ahead. Todd, who didn't drink but enjoyed the bar scene as much as anyone, brought his Xbox and set it up right on the bar. Guys kidded, heckled, and taunted each other in an impromptu *Madden 2004* tournament that included Panthers and Drinking Fountain regulars alike. Life was good.

Celia had, of course, come to the game, and brought her friend Cynthia, visiting from Baltimore. The two of them kicked back and watched us boys with restrained amusement as we did boy things like high-five, chug Heinekens, and awkwardly man-hug, savoring the victory. Sam, the Head Start teacher and former sideline smack-talker extraordinaire, was off his crutches now and walked with a slight limp toward me, holding out a Corona.

"Great win, Mark," he said as we clinked bottles. "It kills me not to be out there, but I'm with you guys in spirit. And I'll be cheering you boys on next week, wherever we're playing. I'll be there."

I asked him about his rehab.

"It's going good," he said, bending and straightening the knee. "I'll be ready for training camp. I'll be ready."

Cynthia, a young, smart, attractive, outgoing woman, and a clinical social worker, was receiving more than a little attention from my not-exactly-shy teammates. Coach O'Neal alone must have chatted her up for an hour, talking with her about their common fields of study in psychology and sociology.

"Get 'em up for all my Panthers!" Cliff yelled somewhere between two and 57 times throughout the evening, precariously balancing himself on a bar stool and raising his bottomless glass of Courvoisier. When the dust settled in the wee hours of Saturday morning, he had spent more than $500, no small feat in a bar where beers are two bucks and the house delicacy is Corn Nuts.

Jeff, as usual, was playing the role of Panther goodwill ambassador to the Drinking Fountain/de facto mayor. He hugged, high-fived, and pressed the flesh more than the old school Boston Irish politicians who had prowled these very neighborhood streets for decades. The J. P. neighborhood kid, when not hugging, kissing, or, well, hugging, spent most of the night standing behind the bar, keeping a genial but hawklike lookout on the crowd just in case someone, anyone, ever faced the horrible proposition of running out of beer.

"Mahhhhk, baby!" he yelled over to me at one point, and tossed me a Bud Light bottle before coming over to meet Celia. "To the best kickah I evah played with!" he toasted, and we clanked bottles. He hugged a stunned but amused Celia and Cynthia with both beefy arms, almost getting them both in headlocks. "Cecelia," he said, turning her name into a Simon and Garfunkel song, "your hubby is good people, real good people! You ladies need anything tonight, lemme know!" He then muttered something indecipherable and, red-faced, wobbled back through the crowd to spread more good cheer.

But the highlight of the night for me was when I was chatting with Insano, Pitt, and Donnie about our opponent in the semifinals: Brockton. We'd found out that they'd absolutely demolished Rhode Island 54–0 in an unofficial warm-up/bye-week game, and would be hosting us the following week back down at Marciano Stadium for the right to move on to the championship game. Marlboro, meanwhile, had upset Clinton on the road—beware what you wish for, Irish Blizzard owner—and would now face Middleboro in the other semifinal, a battle of EFL dynasties past and present.

It was only fitting that our road to the EFL Super Bowl once again went through Brockton. After all, that was where it'd all begun for us as a team what now seemed like three years ago—and for me as a baggy-jersey-wearing, scared-shitless rookie.

"We're gonna win, no question in my mind, no question at all we're gonna beat those cocky Buccaneer fucks," I told everyone.

"We're a different team now than we were back in June. We're smarter, we're more under control, more disciplined. The only way anyone in this league can beat us is—"

"—*is if we beat ourselves*," they all cut in, laughing, parroting the mantra the coaches had beaten into our heads all season.

"But this time, I'll let our secret weapon actually play," Pitt said, alluding to his (justifiable) benching me in the first game. He then raised his Coke (like Todd, he didn't drink). We toasted—perhaps an unofficial signing of a peace treaty that, whether we'd known it or not, we'd been working on all season long.

Right then, the bar erupted in shouts of glee, cheers, and chaos. We looked up to see David "Big Papi" Ortiz, who was fast becoming a New England folk hero, rounding the bases, clapping his hands, having just launched a Jarrod Washburn pitch into the left-field Green Monster seats to beat the Angels 6–5 and clinch the American League Divisional Series. All the Sox rushed out of the dugout, and in from the bullpen. Ortiz rounded third, approached home, flipped off his helmet, and hopped with both feet onto the plate, where he was mobbed and playfully beaten on the head by his jubilant teammates. It was now on to face the Yankees, just like we were now moving on to face our own nemeses, the Buccaneers. This was a good omen for Boston teams, I thought. A good omen indeed.

As Celia, Cynthia, and I waited for a cab out front, we saw Cliff and Khary each smoking a cigarette under the glow of the Drinking Fountain's neon Pabst Blue Ribbon sign, just as they had been that night in late July when I'd received my "Just Kick It" *nom de kick*. I walked over and gave each one a handshake-shoulder bump good night.

"Stay safe, fam," Cliff said, using one of his favorite terms, "fam," which was his version of "family." I always liked hearing him call me and the other Panthers "fam." It just sounded . . . sincere.

"See ya Tuesday, fellas." When I pulled back from Cliff, I noticed he was crying. I figured it was just the gallon or so of Courvoisier he'd ingested that evening. But I was wrong.

"Yeah, I was drunk and actin' the fool, but it wasn't the booze," he would tell me later when I asked him why he'd been crying. "But it wasn't because of my legal situation, it was because I knew that whether we won or lost in Brockton, the season was almost over. We had two games left at the most. When a football season ends, something inside of me dies. It means I gotta get back to my real life. And real life just ain't the same without football."

LAME DUCK

AFTER THE RED SOX dispatched the Angels in three straight, Boston was buzzing with nervous excitement, readying for another ALCS blood feud between the Red Sox and the hated Yankees. Meanwhile, another bitter (albeit less noted) rivalry was about to be reignited. Boston vs. Brockton. The Panthers and the Bucs. Together again for one last showdown.

At the start of what might have been our final practice of the season, Thursday night before our Saturday Brockton game, Pitt asked us to take a knee at midfield. I thought he, or O'Neal, or one of the captains was going to launch into one of the typical pregame speeches that we'd all come to know so well. So when he dropped the bombshell he did, it left us all if not stunned, then at least baffled by the timing.

"After thinking about it a lot over the past week," Pitt solemnly informed us, "I've decided that I won't be coming back next year as head coach."

Huh? Now? He's telling us this *now*?

He went on, his eyes displaying an unemotional, dead calm. "There's just been too much bullcrap this season, all the petty bickering, and selfishness, and 'me first' this and 'me first' that. You guys don't respect the game, and if you're not going to take it seriously, I'm not going to waste my time. If I have to work all day and then come out here and work some more, then you have to, too, and I'm just not seeing it anymore. No one is above the team, but lots of you act like you are, and I'm just tired of wasting my time on people who don't want to give 100 percent."

I wish I could say there was a collective gasp, or a thunderous round of protests, considering our head coach and stern, guiding force had just announced his resignation before the most important game in franchise history. But there wasn't. Honestly, I don't think anyone was very surprised. Everyone just nodded, or stared ahead, resigned to the fact that we'd be playing our next game—and possibly our last, if we lost to Brockton—for a lame-duck head coach. Not exactly a "win one for the Gipper" moment.

With that, we headed into the EFL semifinals. If we beat Brockton in their house, we'd move on to the first EFL Super Bowl in Panther history. It was only the most important game of our lives.

LIGHTNING STRIKES

EVEN THOUGH thunderstorm season in New England was typically reserved for August, the forecast for our late October EFL semifinal game against Brockton called for some volatile weather: rain showers, torrential at times, and possible lightning storms. It was also oddly humid. As I pulled into the Marciano Stadium parking lot, the summerlike weather took me back to that Sunday afternoon in June when I had purposely delayed my entrance into the stadium.

Now I simply parked, gathered my equipment, and calmly walked in through the front gate with a purpose, confident that the team of which I was now an integral part was going to avenge its season-opening loss. I had no doubt that despite Pitt's odd, abrupt news of his resignation, we were ready to handle the challenge. We had the best-skilled players in the league, bar none. And, now, finally, after our convincing round one playoff victory, we seemed poised to step up to the enormity of this game.

Pausing before heading under the grandstand to the locker rooms, I placed my duffel bag on the ground, hopped a small chain-link fence, and walked onto the field. Marciano, like English, had Field-Turf. And it also had the more modern yellow upright goalposts, rather than the throwback H-shaped goalposts on some of the fields. I hated the H-shaped ones. Charlestown and Clinton had those and—no coincidence, I think—I'd missed extra points on those fields. Hey, whaddya know? I now had neurotic mental quirks! I guess I was a real kicker after all.

I stood on the 10-yard line—the spot, exactly 20 yards from the crossbar, where Donnie held for my extra points—took two steps back, two steps to the left, exhaled, and briefly looked at the uprights. They stood tall and still against the cloudy skies. The little flags on the tips occasionally fluttered in a breeze, which, while not stiff, seemed to be picking up, an ominous sign of weather to come.

Some barely postlarval butterflies hatched and began to rumble and flutter in my stomach. I stared at the goalposts and was reminded of a scene in the greatest sports movie of all time, *Hoosiers*. Before the climactic basketball championship game against inner-city powerhouse South Bend Central Bears (in real life it was the Muncie Central Bearcats), Gene Hackman takes his small-town Hickory players into the empty arena, which is more massive and intimidating than any they'd ever been in before. He gives Ollie, his smallest player, a tape measure and asks the biggest player, Strap, to hoist Ollie onto his shoulders. Hackman then asks Ollie to hold the tape measure against the rim, and drop it down to the floor.

"Ten feet," says Strap upon reading the tape. Hackman then asks another player to measure off the distance between the foul line and the hoop. "Fifteen feet," says the player.

"Ten feet. And 15 feet. I think you'll find that these are the exact same measurements as the gym back in Hickory," he reminds them. The team collectively grins. All intimidation of being the small-town hicks in the big city are erased. And, as you know, on Jimmy Chitwood's "I'll make it" jump shot, they go on to win the legendary Indiana High School Championship.

Okay, so maybe it was a tad corny for me to be going all *Hoosiers* on myself. But so be it. These goalposts were just as high (10 feet) and just as wide (18½) as the ones back at English. And, right then, I knew that if it came down to it, which I hoped it wouldn't—not be-cause I couldn't handle the pressure, but because I'd rather we win comfortably—I would make the kick to put us in the Super Bowl.

I nodded at the imaginary Donnie crouched on the 10-yard line; anyone watching would have assumed I was high, crazy, or both. Leaning slightly, arms dangling loosely by my sides, I watched as Don-nie raised his hand up to the imaginary Reggie, who fired the ball back. Donnie placed it down, twirling it laces-out under his index fin-ger, balancing it with delicate, loving care as if it were a Fabergé egg. I stepped forward and, in slow motion, kicked a smooth, crisp extra point high and straight.

It's good.

I was ready.

Our visitors' locker room was surprisingly subdued. Everyone was quiet, sitting on the cool concrete floor with their backs against lockers, just staring into space, lost inside their own heads while en-visioning tackles, patterns, coverages, schemes, and the like. That, or they were so intimidated by the game just minutes ahead of them that they were shocked mute or, dare I say, scared. After all, most of these guys (myself included) had never played in a game of this magnitude. Over the course of the season, I'd heard talk of a city championship game here and there, but they were rarely spoken of with any real zeal or nostalgia. Plus, that was high school, when they were kids; this was semi-pro, against grown men, *as* grown men. Even the youngest Panthers had had to grow up really fast over this one season.

After a full season I still didn't have a set pregame routine, like I heard many manic, superstitious pro kickers did. Before every single game, longtime Baltimore Ravens' kicker Matt Stover, according to John Feinstein's *Next Man Up*, "lies flat on his back on the locker-room floor before each game, legs on a stool, eyes closed, shutting out the world until it's time to brush his teeth (yes, brush his teeth) and go out on the field." I wasn't that insane. Yet.

The tearing of tape outside the locker room door, where Kelly was busy stabilizing knees and ankles, was the only sound. Todd, in Buddha position, stretched his groins in a far corner, wearing massive headphones—pulsating, silver, high-tech earmuffs—and a slit-eyed glare, bobbing his head to the beat. On a bench just above him sat Donnie, wearing just black football pants and a white tank top under-shirt over his ample upper body and gut. I saw that he was pulling on—for the love of Brian Boitano—sparkly, sequin-covered cleats. I pointed at them.

"Does Earth, Wind & Fire know you raided their wardrobe closet?"

Donnie smiled. "This is to go to the Super Bowl, Mark. I gotta bring out the 'A' cleats tonight."

"The stadium lights better not reflect off those disco balls and blind me," I teased.

"If they do, I'll switch back to the fur," he assured me.

Pitt asked everyone to face the far end of the room, where he and the other coaches stood near the blackboard, on which were scrawled X's, O's, arrows, and other hieroglyphics that, even after months of football immersion, didn't make much sense to me. Which was fine. I was glad my duties were more robotic—head down, kick, repeat. Maybe someday I'd throw myself into learning more about the X's and O's and the finer nuances of the game. But, for now, I had to live up to my nickname and just kick it.

"Nothing I can say that you don't already know, gentlemen, so I'm not going to bother with all that rah-rah stuff," Pitt said. "We owe this team. We're going to run the ball down their throats today. That number 99? He's big, but he gets tired real quick. We're going to run everything at him, tire his ass out, and then keep running some more. We'll wear 'em down." He paused and looked around at all of us. "This season hasn't been easy. For any of us. We've had our share of problems on and off the field. But I'm proud of you guys. No matter what's happened, you've come together when it counts. Now let's just go out and execute, and then go home and start getting ready for the Super Bowl."

Unlike that first Brockton game, where I nearly drowned in the sea of enraged, excited humanity that carried me out the door, this time the captains simply stood up and led us out the door. Thunder rumbled off in the distance as we exited in single file. Gravel crunched under our cleats. We split into two lines under the grandstand and waited at the mouth of the tunnel. All I could hear was guys' breathing, evenly, coolly, and then faster, a steady adrenaline rush ready to be cranked up and unleashed as pure rage. Looking out to the field, bright green under the stadium lights, I could already see raindrops starting to pepper down. All the way across the field, the fans who'd arrived on our sideline early were popping open their umbrellas.

We stretched and warmed up as usual. As the captains gathered at midfield, we stood along our sideline, facing them, holding hands, waiting for the coin toss. The ref flicked a silver dollar into the air. The Brockton captains and our guys then shook hands one last time, and then they split off on either side of the 50-yard line. The ref made the "receiving" gesture in front of our captains. We won. We'd receive.

"Offense get ready!" Pitt yelled. "No penalties, gentlemen. The running game is our bread and butter today. No penalties."

Brockton lined up to kick off, and the stadium announcer updated the "other" playoff game going on in the Boston area that night. "Hideki Matsui, two-run homer, Yankees lead the Sox 3–0 heading into the bottom of the first." The crowd groaned, as did both sidelines. Our collective love of the Red Sox may have united us for a brief moment, but there was no getting around one fact: we hated Brockton, and they hated us. No mutual Red Sox love was going to stop this war.

The refs blew their whistles. Both teams lined up. Brockton kicked to Jeremy at our own 15-yard line. He burst through the coverage, a black-and-silver rocket, and was about to make one last cut outside . . . *he's gone!* . . . when one of their other special-teams guys dove, slapped his ankle, and tripped him up. He rolled out of bounds at our 49, where he was mobbed before heading back onto the field with the offense.

Great kick return aside, right from the start this game eerily resembled the first Brockton game. Amos, our Warrick Dunn-esque "scatback," wasn't able to penetrate the Bucs' thick defensive front, mostly because our O-line wasn't able to get any push, particularly against the considerable bulk of number 99—the same Warren Sapp clone whom Sam had once taunted with "cheeseburger" and "fat" smack talk. On third and 11, Southie overthrew a wide-open Sam. Three-and-out. The offense trotted off the field. Frustrated, Southie unsnapped his chinstrap and slapped his own helmet. Khary punted.

Throughout the first quarter, however, the Bucs weren't faring much better. Even with a talented, veteran, scrambling quarterback named Anthony Comer, they weren't able to pick up a first down. Punt. Us? Three-and-out. Punt. Back and forth we went like this, barely moving the ball and boring the hell out of the fans. Heading into the second quarter, there were maybe three first downs between both teams, 50 total yards. It might have had something to do with the rain, which alternated from sprinkles to downpours, creating a slippery mess of the turf. The wind kicked up a notch, too, turning spirals into wounded ducks, and high, arcing punts into wobbly squib kicks. But every so often, an odd quiet patch would arrive. The rain would stop, the wind would die, and the clouds would part, revealing a swath of stars and a radiant harvest moon. It was beautiful and eerie, like the eye of a hurricane.

"Un partido feo," a frustrated Elvis said to Lenny and Gio as the three of them kneeled at one end of our sideline, watching the action (or lack thereof) as I kept my leg loose behind them, doing air kicks and stretching out. Damn right, Elvis: *an ugly game.* Which got those butterflies all stirred up again because in an ugly, field-position game like this, it could come down to a kick. The thing is, though, they weren't butterflies of fear or nerves; it was excitement. I was glad the game was going this way. I wanted the team on my shoulders. They'd picked me up more than once this season, so I wanted to return the favor, help them up if I had to. That's what teammates did.

While I flirted with visions of kicking a game-winner, however, Brockton drew first blood in the middle of the second quarter. Comer scrambled right, as he'd been doing almost every play, and momentarily tucked the ball under his arm and started to head upfield, causing Brandon, playing corner, to step up to cover the run . . . and that's when the quarterback stopped—freezing Brandon, springing the receiver—and floated a long pass over Brandon's head. We groaned in unison as the receiver caught it in stride and sprinted to pay dirt past a diving Keon, a safety who'd arrived a split second too late.

D-block moped off the field, bickering about blown coverages and assignments. "What happened there?" Pitt asked Brandon, the whole defense, anyone, everyone. No one answered. "Anyone?"

"I thought I had safety help," Brandon finally answered, removing his helmet and spraying some water into his mouth.

"You did have safety help, he got there," Pitt said, nodding at Keon. "Comer's gonna run nine times out of 10, that's what he does. You all made the right reads, he just made a good play. Now we'll have to make some plays. Someone, please, go out there and make a play!"

We did make plays. Bad ones. Every time we started to gain some momentum, someone would do something stupid to kill it. Holding calls. Late hits. You name it. I can't even list them, there were so many.

Even Insano, the rock of the defense if not the heart and soul of the entire team, was atypically out of control, reckless, and, it seemed to me, even nervous, like a rookie. Toward the end of the second quarter, D-block had stuffed the Brockton offense on three straight run plays deep in their own territory and forced them to punt from their seven-yard line—into the wind, no less. Though we were down 7–0, we could feel the momentum shifting. Unless the punter was a BALCO client, we'd get the ball back inside the 50, maybe even closer. We just *knew* we were about to reclaim control of the game.

"Make a play, fellas!" Elvis screamed, smacking the top of his helmet with his palm as Jeremy set up near midfield. "This is it! This is the time to step up! This is where we separate the men from the bitches!"

The long snapper let it fly, but the ball bounced a few feet in front of the Brockton punter and ricocheted off his shin.

"*Ball!*" we all yelled from the sideline.

The punter darted to his right, recovered the ball, and, while running, just barely got the kickoff from the five-yard line, mere inches over the outstretched hands of Insano. It was a low, fluttering kick that traveled no more than 25 yards. Jeremy sprinted forward to the Brockton 30, and with 20 yards of momentum behind him, fielded the punt and just kept running. He didn't even break stride, not even a momentary thought of juking or breaking outside to either sideline—he simply tore through the heart of the Bucs' coverage, right up the gut. It wasn't even fair. The flat-footed Bucs looked like they didn't even see him for the first 10 yards, and by the time they realized where he was, it was too late—he was already leaving them in the dust.

"He's gone! He's gone!" Elvis and I screamed together, giddily racing down our sideline, following Jeremy's relatively short scamper to the end zone, our helmets raised in the air. Elvis high-stepped in anticipation of Jeremy doing the same. "Go baby go baby go baby go!"

Jeremy crossed the 15, then the 10, and was about to score when both Elvis and I stopped our victorious gallop, almost simultaneously. Maybe it was just an inherent reflex, a negative sixth sense we'd all developed by that point in the season, having seen too many spectacular plays negated by penalty flags. We looked back at the spot of the punt. I mentally rewound the play a few seconds and remembered seeing Insano rushing in slightly out of control, but I'd lost track of him all in the Jeremy excitement. That, or I'd purposely ignored Insano's involvement, knowing that I'd eventually see what I saw: Insano standing above the punter, whom he'd absolutely leveled with a late hit. Elvis and I let out an anguished groan. Sheer sports misery, in stereo.

"Noooooooooooooooooooooooooooooooooo!"

"OhhhhhhhhhhNooooooooooooooo!"

"Yeaaaaaaaaahhhhhhhhhhhhh!" cheered several Bucs' players on the field, all of them making the "it's against them" motion with their hands and arms, letting their sideline know that the flags that now littered the field were due to Insano's overzealous rush.

If you'd just walked in to witness this one scene in any walk of life *other than* a football game—outside a bar, in a Roman gladiator movie—and you saw one man lying prone on his back while another man loomed above him, you'd think that the man still on his feet was the victor, the one on the turf the vanquished. If this *were* a gladiator movie, Insano would be just seconds from plunging one last sword thrust into the heart of his mortally wounded enemy. But this wasn't any other walk of life; this was football. Nine times out of 10, when a player found himself standing above a punter whom he'd just leveled, it was the man lying on his back who had won. The Bucs' punter knew this. As the yellow flags came flying in from all directions, one of them actually hitting Insano in the thigh, the punter stopped writhing on the ground, smiled, and enthusiastically pumped one fist.

Seeing my special-teams counterpart acting like he'd done anything special *other than* just act like Marcel-friggin'-Marceau faking an injury—well, this enraged me. I'd have had more respect for him had he broken out the "man trapped in a box" routine.

"Ref, no, he took a dive!" I found myself screaming. This guy was doing a disservice to all kickers, perpetuating the stereotype of us being nothing but pratfalling little dandies.

Dropping my helmet and pushing through a couple of my teammates—*okay, what am I doing, what am I doing?*—I angrily strode toward the side judge, who was running back to his spot near the sideline after retrieving his infernal flag. As I reached him, I began serenading him with mock applause. "Way to fall for it, sir! He was probably practicing that ballet move all week!"

The ref, a stocky man of about 50, chuckled at my misguided point of view. "Five-four drilled him, son. Took four extra steps just to get there."

"He barely grazed the fucking drama queen!" *Had he, though? Had Insano not played as much of a role in the late hit as I wanted to believe?*

"Watch the language, son," he said, turning around briefly to see who the mouthy pest was, and looked me up and down as if to say, *This is the tough guy giving me so much grief?*—"Keep it up, 6, and I'll tack on another 15."

Even though every fiber of my being confirmed that Insano had clearly committed the late hit, I kept badgering the ref. I don't know what came over me. I just snapped. "Come on, you were *dying* to give them the ball back. How long have you lived in Brockton?"

This time the ref wheeled around and gritted his teeth but was smiling slightly, as if relishing the idea of throwing me out of the game; that, or he was amused by a kicker gone bonkers like this. "Coach, get him away from me or I'm flagging your whole bench." It was then I realized that O'Neal had had me by both shoulders and had been trying to pull me away from the ref the entire time. Well, he wasn't trying *that* hard. If he'd wanted to, O'Neal could have picked me up and slung me over his shoulder as if I were Charlie McCarthy.

"Whoa, settle down there, cowboy," a grinning O'Neal said while practically carrying me away feet-off-the-ground through a few teammates. "They made the right call," he confirmed. "Insano just decked that guy. *Stupid* play. Don't know what the hell he was thinking."

"I know," I conceded, regaining control of myself. "I just wanted to yell. I'm so sick of us doing stupid shit to lose games."

"Yeah, but it isn't going to make anything better by getting us a bench misconduct. I thought you were the quiet, composed, mature writer," he teased. "You've been hanging around these crack whores too long."

The punter picked himself up, smugly patted Insano on the right shoulder pad—*Thanks for the dumb-ass penalty, pal!*—and trotted off the field toward his waiting teammates, who happily gave him high-fives and slaps on the helmet. As the players left the field around him, and the offenses trotted back on, Insano remained absolutely still. He stood with his hands on his hips, head lowered, clearly realizing that his ill-timed, completely unnecessary hit had just cost us the tying touchdown. He didn't move. I had to think that what he'd just done was already beginning to devour his season-long leadership role like a flesh-eating virus, a cancerous, rookie-level mistake. He still didn't move or so much as raise his head or look over in our direction. For the first time, even from a good 30 yards across the field, I looked at Insano and saw not a tireless, indomitable warrior, but a mortal young man just dreading having to face his teammates.

Jeremy, laughing at the absurdity of it all, flipped the ball to the refs and disappeared into our sideline. The refs brought it back to the seven-yard line—the spot of the original snap—and subsequently marched it one giant stride at a time 15 yards upfield to the 22, where Brockton would now start another fresh series.

All the while, Insano didn't move. He just stared down at the empty spot on the turf where the wily punter had been lying just seconds before. The rain was steady now, but seemed to be particularly heavy right over him, as if he had his own personal thundercloud. For all we knew, he might stand there for the rest of the game, overnight, for the rest of the fall, and on through winter—just a snow-covered statue of ill-timed failure. Hopefully he'd thaw out in the spring.

He finally snapped out of it and trotted back to our sideline. He walked right through a cluster of players, who parted to let him pass. He sat down on the bench, paused, and then slammed the side of his helmet with his palm. And then did it again. And again. After giving him some time alone, Cliff walked over, knelt in front of him, and lightly grabbed his face mask. "Cap, you've been carrying us *all year long*," Cliff reasoned. "You've been picking us up when we needed it, and now we're gonna pick you up. Forget it, baby, it's done. Play's over. Ain't nothing you can do to change it now. Just move on."

Insano nodded, but still just stared out at the field.

Both teams lined up near the new line of scrimmage. The referee made the official announcement to the stands. "We have a personal foul, late hit and unsportsmanlike conduct, number 54. Fifteen yards from the spot of the foul, loss of downs." He then dramatically turned and with a gunlike flash of his right hand, pointed toward our end zone. "First down, Brockton!"

The home crowd cheered, and I seethed, sensing that the ref enjoyed his dramatic little presentation to the Buccaneers' fans. Meanwhile, the few fans on our side who were still braving the increasingly dismal elements—including Celia and my in-laws—just shook their heads, sensing that even though there was more than one half of football left to play, Insano's penalty had reached right into our collective chests and ripped our hearts out.

Channeling the adrenaline of unexpected new life, Comer wasted no time dropping back and firing a bullet to a wide-open receiver cutting right to left across the middle. He caught the ball and, in a cruel irony, turned and raced right up the gut of *our* defense, just like Jeremy had moments earlier. Gone. One play. Seventy-eight yards. One flag. A 14-point swing.

Brockton 14, Panthers 0.

They kicked off. Jeremy fielded it, but handed off to a reversing Sam, who brought it back to the Bucs' 48-yard line. But we didn't even have time to set up for a last-second Hail Mary. The clock ran out.

It was a very ugly, uninspired first half. We had managed only four first downs, maybe 70 yards of total offense. Our running game was ineffective. And Brockton was jamming our speedy receivers at the line, slowing their patterns and allowing the defense to record a handful of "coverage sacks" after Southie, a good-running quarter-back but no Comer, was forced out of the pocket. As for me, I hadn't so much as sniffed the field. The only one getting any work was Khary, punting. That said, Brockton wasn't doing much better offensively. D-block was more or less containing them. They couldn't run on us at all. The touchdown passes were two of only about seven completions Comer had all half. If we didn't commit the stupid penalties, this was a 7–7 game, a whole different story. As it stood, we had only 30 minutes to reverse our fate or our season was over.

The rain beat down as we trudged off the field and under the grandstand, the drops making metallic pings on the benches above us. "Update from Fenway Park," the by-now very depressing stadium announcer crackled, "Yankees lead the Sox 11–3." The home crowd, although happy that their Bucs were winning, groaned loudly, with scattered boos, ill-tempered by the prospect of the Red Sox losing yet another ALCS to the hated Yankees. "Looks like it's another 'wait till next year' for the Sox, folks," the announcer added glumly, in true pessimistic Sox fan fashion.

"Unless you got some good news, shut the hell up," someone muttered behind me, speaking for all of us as we filed into our locker room.

"This team sucks! *Sucks!* They ain't shit, and we're letting them do anything they want out there! When are all y'all gonna start acting like men?!" Todd challenged us, stomping around the room with as pained an expression as I'd ever seen. "None of y'all motherfuckers are playing with any pride! Hell, I'd take Insano over all y'all in a heartbeat . . . at least he's out there *tryin'* to make a play!" He slammed a fist into a locker door and kicked over a green Gatorade squeeze bottle that had been sitting on a bench. But no one else was really biting. This was as subdued as I'd seen us all year. The only one who rivaled Todd on the "fired up" scale, in fact, was Kelly.

"Okay, who stole my tape?!" the diminutive, red-haired trainer yelled after bursting into the room. No one responded, which only seemed to agitate her further. "I said, *Who stole my tape?!* My supplies are not there for you to take whenever you damn well please! They are *my* supplies, and they cost money, even a stinkin' roll of tape. I'm going to turn the lights out and when they come back on, I want my tape on this table! I don't care—"

"Someone *please* tell her to shut up," a voice complained from the back of the room. "We down 14–zip. Who cares about the stupid tape?"

But Kelly was made of Teflon when it came to insults from football players. She'd just spent too much time around this team, and others, to get rattled. "I don't care who took it, I just want it back!" She flicked the lights off. Waited a beat. A second. A third. And then flicked the lights back on. Nothing. No tape. A few guys snickered. It was at that moment—upon hearing the useless sense of moral victory in whoever had snickered—that I wanted to take a flamethrower to the entire room. Seriously. I wanted to torch it and everyone in it. If the only thing that these guys cared about at that moment was mocking the trainer—if that's the type of "victory" they were satisfied with—then screw it. We weren't cut out to be EFL champions.

"Fine," Kelly said, chuckling ruefully and shaking her head. "You win. Have it your way."

As guys dried off as best they could with towels and sweatshirts, Pitt gathered the defense over in one corner near the chalkboard, and, in subdued tones, went over some adjustments. Fink conferred with Southie, the two of them sitting next to each other on a bench and looking at some plays diagrammed on Fink's clipboard.

Pitt then walked to the front of the room and leaned against the wall, arms crossed at his chest. "Either you want the season to end tonight, or you don't. It's that simple. You all know what you need to do. We've been fighting from behind all year, even when we're ahead.

No one expects us to come back 14 points against this team. Do you expect to come back and win this?"

A few guys nodded. A few—Mohammad, Todd, Insano, myself—shouted "Yes, sir!" But there was just something . . . missing. It didn't sound convincing. Pitt stared at everyone, perhaps seeing these Panther faces in a locker room for the last time. Everyone stared back.

"Insano," Pitt finally said, "line 'em up, lead 'em out. We have a playoff game to win."

As the third quarter began and the thunder that *had* seemed several miles away now roared and rumbled much closer to the stadium, a funny thing happened on the way to losing miserably without putting up a fight: we began driving. With conviction. Straight down the field. Finally, perhaps with big number 99 and the rest of the Bucs' defense tiring, we began running the ball effectively, our original game plan. With Southie rendered more or less ineffective for the entire first half, Pitt and Fink decided to sink or swim with the running game. After we kicked off, held them to a three-and-out, and downed their punt at our own 20, Amos slashed ahead for five, seven yards at a time. Southie didn't fire a single pass. We were rolling.

"We ain't dead yet, gentlemen!" Cliff yelled, pacing up and down the sidelines, trying to spur on a new round of enthusiasm on the bench. "Wake up, we ain't dead yet! The Panthers still got some fight left in 'em!"

Yes, we were alive. On life support, but alive. The Bucs, on the other hand, seemed lethargic and, more than that, downright stunned by our inexplicable turnaround.

"Stay loose, baby, stay loose," an excited Jeff said, bustling past me on the sideline as the offense ran another draw play, this time to Todd, who burst through the line for another gain of about four, taking us down to the Bucs' five-yard line. A palpable electric current had returned to our sideline, causing our once-deflated reserves to stand up and cheer on the offense. There was no doubt we'd score; 14–7 here we come. From there it'd be anybody's game.

Another angry symphony of thunder bellowed just outside the stadium fences. And now the rain was driving, almost spitefully.

Southie lined up behind Big Paul. "White 15! White 15!" he barked, looking at both sides of the line. It was a run play, and the way we'd been bashing our way ahead at will, there was no doubt that Amos would take it in. Another nearby thunderclap—the weather was rolling in fast and furious now—provided an appropriate, timely sound track for the hurting that our offensive line was about to lay upon the Bucs' front four. But just before Paul snapped the ball, thunder's more excitable counterpart, lightning, made its first appearance of the evening. The sky behind the Bucs' end zone exploded in a crackling flash of white light.

"Whoa!" Gio, standing next to me, marveled at the Pink Floyd laser light show Mother Nature was putting on.

"Holy shit, did you see that?" Jeff exclaimed, pointing to the tree line just behind the stadium. "That was, like, 50 feet away!"

"Ooooooohhhhhhhh," the spectators on both sides of the field cooed in unison, as if watching a Fourth of July fireworks show. The elements let loose again seconds later, and another jagged streak of lightning zapped down to the horizon. But the referee crew wasn't as impressed. "Okay, that's lightning, fellas. Off the field!"

In football, rain, even driving, pounding rain like what we'd already played through, was acceptable. Almost cherished. It was football, after all, not badminton. This game was *supposed to be* played in harsh conditions. But lightning? That was a different story. Lightning was football's kryptonite, and referees always halted games when lightning made an uninvited appearance, no matter what the game situation—*even when a team that was as good as dead five minutes ago was about to score and get themselves right back into the goddamn game! Gee, thanks, God!*

The side judge whom I'd harassed after Insano's penalty ran over to our sideline. He conferred with Pitt and the other coaches. "Get your guys into the locker room, Coach, we're gonna wait this one out." Pitt nodded, and he and O'Neal began spreading the word down the sideline. But Fink, whose offense had finally been clicking, protested.

"No! Not now! One more play, Mr. Referee! All we need is one more play and we're in!" Fink yelled.

"Sorry, Coach." The side judge shook his head while trotting off. "League rules. Everyone off the field, *now.*"

Fink just shook his head, and I even thought I saw him chuckling. He wore a look of absolute comical resignation, a facial cry of *Uncle!*

that said to whomever controlled our fate, "You win . . . we give up . . . do whatever the hell you want." Whether it was an act of man (Insano's late hit) or an act of God (lightning) that did us in, we were clearly cursed, period, and there wasn't a damn thing we could do about it. The Red Sox and the curse of the fat-ass Bambino had nothing on the Panthers.

"Why does this shit *only* happen to us?!" Fink yelled to no one in particular and slammed his clipboard to the turf. "*Only* us." Several pages covered in X's, O's, and arrows came unclamped and blew away down the sideline right past me. Without even thinking about it, I sprinted after them, lunged, and caught a few stray sheets under my cleat. But by the time I was able to stomp on a few to thwart their watery escape, they were nothing more than soggy paper fragments, blue ink smeared and running, as if my cleat had severed an artery. When I picked them up, they practically disintegrated between my fingers.

"Here." I handed Fink what was left of his playbook. He just stared at them, and then, with each of us holding mushy clumps of former plays, we looked at each other, the rain streaking down our faces. We didn't need to say it, but we were thinking the exact same thing: *There goes our season, dissolving right between our fingers*. And, oddly, we both laughed. It wasn't funny at all but, in a sick way, it sort of was, too, in that *Isn't life a bitch?* kind of way. Sometimes, if you didn't laugh at life, you'd go insane.

Tossing aside the pulpy mess, we jogged back toward the grandstand and into the locker room.

This being the end of my story, I wish I could fictionalize the rest of the Brockton game. I wish I could write that after a rousing, emotional locker-room speech by Pitt or O'Neal or Ace or Donnie or Reggie, my fired-up, reenergized Panthers hoisted the hopes and dreams of Boston's inner city onto their shoulders and emerged from the locker room an unstoppable force. I wish I could say that after the utterly improbable lightning delay, we picked up right where we left off: driving with authority, patience, control, confidence. With all that we'd been through that season, I honestly wish I could give this story the rousing triumph of the human spirit, the feel-good Disney movie ending that my teammates, for all their many faults, truly deserved.

That version would have the skies clearing after a brief delay. And have us immediately scoring under a bright, full moon to make it 14–7. Then we'd quickly score again to tie it up with only seconds remaining. Then, on the ensuing kickoff, after our heroic captain and fallen leader, Insano, redeemed himself by blasting the Bucs' return man, jarring the ball loose, and recovering the fumble, *that* version would have me, the unlikeliest of Panthers—this is my book, after all—booting a 50-yard field goal as time expired to put us into the EFL Super Bowl. I'd be carried off the field by my joyous teammates as, like the ending of *The Natural*, lighting struck the stadium lights and sent sparks cascading onto the field around us, like so many falling stars upon which wishes come true.

That ending, I really want to write. *That* ending is what my teammates earned with the trials and tribulations of the 2004 season. But I can't give it to them. This is real life, not Disney. In real life, sometimes things just don't work out the way you want. Sometimes the bad guys win. Sometimes lightning strikes at the wrong time. Sometimes it's better to be lucky than good. And, unfortunately on that October night, aside from a few glimpses, we were neither.

What really happened is this: by the time the refs finally poked their heads into the locker room—nearly a half hour later—and told us play was resuming with us on the Bucs' five-yard line, the damage had been done. Any momentum we'd regained at the start of the third quarter was gone. "Everyone relaxed again," a despondent Insano would tell me later, still sitting on a bench in a near-empty locker room in the filthy, soaking-wet uniform he didn't want to remove, not yet, because removing the black, white, and silver jersey and black pants would have meant it was time to return to life without football, a life that, as Cliff had said, just wasn't as sweet.

Alas, in the non-Hollywood version, when we reset at the five-yard line, Southie took the snap from Paul, but it wasn't clean, and he bobbled it. He regained control of the ball, but stumbled a bit trying to turn and hand off to Amos. Just as he attempted the exchange, a Bucs' defender flew in, drove his helmet into Southie's right shoulder, and sent the ball skittering away on the wet turf. A second Bucs' lineman pounced on the loose ball. After peeling away the layers, the refs signaled that the Bucs had recovered.

Game over. Again.

Sure, okay, we *did* finally manage to score that night. But, fittingly, it was on a fluke play in the middle of the fourth quarter. Jason, our backup quarterback who'd played sparingly all season because Southie just happened to be on his way to the EFL offensive MVP award, had come into the game because Southie had injured his throwing shoulder on the hit before the fateful, postlightning storm fumble. He could barely lift his arm above his shoulder, and Kelly said it was not good. His season, whether or not we made a valiant comeback, was over.

On his first series, Jason got us on the board, but not directly. With a great arm but limited mobility, Jason, six-three, fired a slant pass at midfield to Sam, who had a defender draped all over him. However, Sam, while trying to drag the defender for an extra yard or two, fumbled. The Bucs' guy recovered, but was immediately hit by one of *our* players, and subsequently fumbled the ball right back to Sam, who sprinted untouched into the Bucs' end zone.

Bucs 14, Panthers 6 with about 10 minutes to go.

As I approached the ball on the PAT, I saw that big number 99 had bulled through our front line, right up the middle. His right hand, the size of a manhole cover, caught a chunk of my kick, and it fluttered well off to the right of the post.

No good.

I trudged back to the sideline, feeling small, insignificant, ashamed, as if, despite all the good things I'd done that season, I'd regressed to square one—that one goddamn missed extra point washing all my successes away like the violent shake of an Etch A Sketch. Even though there was already an air of defeat permeating our entire team, I didn't want to contribute to the loss. I didn't want my last kick of the season to be a blocked extra point. I didn't want to think about that all winter and spring.

Our ensuing onside kick failed. The Bucs recovered and ran off large chunks of the clock until their drive stalled with about five minutes left in the game. Still, they believed the game was in hand, and were already celebrating. "Look at them," Cliff, gesturing to the Bucs' sideline with his helmet, said to anyone within earshot. "Look over there and remember that for next year, fellas. I hope no one forgets that image over there. That's what victory looks like."

Jason, who was perhaps the only one of us that night playing with any fire, led us on one long, final drive to the Bucs' 16-yard line. But we stalled there. Fourth down. Pitt, I was sure, would go for the touchdown, what with so little time remaining. So you can imagine my surprise when I saw him holding up three fingers. "Field goal!" he shouted.

Jogging onto the field, I didn't feel any pressure. All I felt was sad. Not just because I knew this kick, even though it would put us within five, wouldn't make a difference in the game, but because I knew this might be the last kick of my first and only football season. The time, the effort, the emotions, the physical toll: I just didn't know if I had another season left in me.

"Let's end on a high note, Mark," Donnie said. "This ain't nothing."

I nodded. As a steady spritz of rain sent drops cascading down my mask and into my eyes, I waited for the snap. Left hash mark. Twenty-three-yard line. A 33-yarder. He was right. It was nothing. However, it came off my foot low, more of a line drive, and I was sure it'd be blocked again. But it kept rising, rising into the drizzle, not a pretty kick by any means, but just high and long enough to fly over the crossbar by five or six feet. The refs raised their arms on either side of the uprights. It was good.

Brockton 14, Panthers 9.

While I felt personal relief, there was little celebrating after the kick. It was a bittersweet consolation prize, if that.

Brockton recovered our onside kick and ran out the clock. The refs blew their whistles. The Brockton crowd cheered. We walked the "Kumbaya line" at midfield—even Donnie did, breaking his personal rule. We all slapped hands—*Game . . . good game . . . good game . . . game*—and grudgingly wished the Bucs luck in the Super Bowl. O'Neal led the prayer at the 50-yard line, the two teams mixed and mingled, kneeling, heads bowed, grown men who'd just outright hated each other now holding hands. Same as always. Except this time there would be no practice on Tuesday, no game for which to prepare next Saturday. Our season was over.

There were tears in the locker room afterward. And swears. And complaints. But, more than anything, there was a general feeling of regret, draped over each one of us like an itchy burlap blanket. We could have easily won—it's not like Brockton had dominated—and we let it slip away.

I got undressed, changed into some dry clothes, zipped up my duffel bag, and slung it over my shoulder. I knew that once I stood up and walked out of this locker room, I might not see most of these guys ever again. I walked across the room, saying brief good-byes to everyone I passed. I didn't want to make a long, drawn-out, dramatic thing out of it. I just wanted to leave and remember the good stuff: the joking, the laughter, the Drinking Fountain after big wins, the new friends I'd made.

Ace, in a voice far more subdued than his usual one, looked up as I passed by. "Vina-tizzy, way to hit that last one," he said.

I shrugged. "Wish it was a game-winner."

He looked at me a moment and then shrugged. "Better than *not* making it. Next year that kick gets us into the big one."

He was right. We had lost but we'd still get to play again if we wanted to. Many people weren't so lucky. Hell, Ace was probably the luckiest to be playing at all. If a guy who might go blind playing football could see that—at its basest, most innocent level—football was just a game and that there's always next year, then shouldn't I?

I slapped and shook more hands as I made my way toward the door. I then reached the three guys who'd first ushered me onto the field all those months ago—Reggie, Delaney, Donnie, the veterans, the elder statesmen, my benefactors. Amazing to think that those first few kicks led to where I now stood, in the losing locker room full of grown men wistfully, reluctantly removing the football equipment that they likely wouldn't wear again for several months. Some of them, like me, perhaps never again.

"Take it easy, Donnie," I said, extending my hand.

"You playing again?" he asked. I hadn't been prepared to answer this question, mainly because I didn't know the answer myself. I had a lot of thinking to do between now and April, when 2005 Panther training camp was scheduled to open.

"We'll see," I replied. "Not sure yet. You?"

"Naw, this is it for me," Donnie said, yanking off his Elton John-in-*Pinball Wizard* cleats, which smelled like wet dog. "I'm done, man. I'm too old for this. I'm retiring."

Reggie, standing nearby, rolled his eyes. "He says that every year."

Donnie laughed and nodded. "He's right. I do."

I exchanged cell-phone numbers with Reggie and some other guys, and we promised to keep in touch and meet for beers in the off-season. I looked around the locker room one more time, taking in the sounds, the sights, everything. Aside from the sound of tape being torn off ankles, knees, fists, or the metallic rattle of a locker door, or an odd, rueful laugh here and there at some joke intended to make the miserable feel a little less so, it was quiet again. Guys had already started to move on.

I headed out to the parking lot, where guys had wasted little time cracking open some postgame beers. The rain, our tormentor all evening, had finally left us alone, the sky now a mix of clouds and patches of stars. Jeff, the Big Twins, and a couple of other guys were gathered around an open car trunk in which sat a Styrofoam cooler of iced Bud Light cans. Pulsating hip-hop bass pumped from the subwoofers and brought me back to my very first Panther practice, kicking in the dark with similar music blasting out of a low-riding Honda.

"Mahk, heads up, buddy," Jeff called out, and tossed me an icy can. Honestly, I didn't really feel like a beer. I just didn't think we'd earned it. I didn't even feel like eating. I just had a bad taste in my mouth. We could have—should have—won. But maybe we didn't have to earn it by winning? Maybe just coming out here and competing, giving it everything we had, playing this game we loved was enough to earn any semi-pro player a cold beer afterward? Seemed fair. I snapped open the can and the beer went down fast, cool. As I finished it, O'Neal sidled up alongside me. We just shook our heads, wearing reluctant half smiles.

"We should be playing Marlboro next week," I said with a sigh. The Shamrocks had upset the Middleboro Cobras at the Snake Pit in an epic overtime shoot-out, 35–29. Despite finishing the regular season in the middle of the pack, they had stepped up in the playoffs and returned to the Super Bowl for the umpteenth time in the team's history.

O'Neal nodded. "Yeah, we could have won, but I think we were beaten even before we stepped on the field. We might have the best skill players in the league, and the fastest guys, but it comes down to this, for me anyway: the moment was just too big for us. Most of these guys had never played in a game this important before, and they just couldn't handle the enormity of it. You could see it in their eyes before the game, at halftime, on the sideline. We thought we were ready, but we weren't."

O'Neal and I exchanged cell numbers before he hopped in his car and took off. I hoped to keep in touch with him regardless of whether

I ever kicked again. You could learn a lot from a guy like Mike O'Neal—football was the least of it. He was just a good man.

For the last time that season, I drove home from a Panther game, listening to the last dreadful innings of the Red Sox game. The Yankees had widened their horrific lead to 19–8, and were about to go up 3–0 in the series, an insurmountable lead from which no team in baseball history had ever come back. Just a depressing night for Boston sports all around, with two seasons on two very different levels of sport suffering anticlimactic, non-Hollywood endings.

A NEW DAY

UNLESS YOU WERE PART of an underground biosphere experiment in the fall of 2004, you know how the Red Sox responded to that 19–8 ass-whupping from the Yankees. Down to literally their last out of the season. Bottom of the ninth. Dave Roberts steals second. Bill Mueller singles him in with the tying run off Mariano Rivera, only the most dominant closer in baseball history. Extra innings. Back and forth, two exhausted heavyweights playing rope-a-dope. In the 12th, "Big Papi" Ortiz slams a Paul Quantrill pitch into the right-field seats, instantly cementing his place alongside Russell, Orr, Yaz, Bird, Brady, Belichick, and Charlie on the MTA as Boston legends. Sox win. They live to fight another day. And another. And another. And a few days later, they're spraying champagne in their former house of horror, Yankee Stadium, and soon after *that*, in Busch Stadium after sweeping the mighty St. Louis Cardinals for their first World Series championship in 86 years.

As Keith Foulke underhanded to Doug Mientkiewicz, I stared at the TV as if it had just sprouted vestigial wings and started flying around the room. Not knowing whether to laugh, cry, dance, or soil myself, I hugged Celia, who, while not a long-suffering Sox fan like I was, reveled in the moment. I watched replay after replay on every possible TV station until the sun came up, like Oliver Stone breaking down the Zapruder film. It was then that I decided that 2004 was not just a one-year football experiment, a mere "book thing." I would definitely play for the Panthers again in 2005.

The Sox' improbable World Series win showed me that no matter how bleak things might seem, there's always a glimmer of hope. There's always another day to fight. If the Sox could exorcise the near-century-old demons that had haunted them, my Panthers—the following year or the year after that; against Brockton, Marlboro, or Middleboro—could purge their demons, too. It wouldn't be easy. Not much in life is. But when the Panthers *did* win an EFL title, I wanted to be a part of it.

Dorchester, Roxbury, Mattapan, Jamaica Plain. Until June of 2004, these were neighborhoods I'd never really visited before. They were just names on newscasts, maps, places you were told to avoid if you were smart. But like my teammates themselves, while sometimes conflicted and imperfect, these places were also so lively, honest, real, and energetic that it was always a bit of a letdown whenever I returned to my relatively subdued neighborhood. It was quieter on Beacon Hill. Safer. But, if anything, my unlikely foray into football taught me that the safe route isn't always the best route to take in life. If I'd never turned off my computer and TV, gotten off my couch, and started playing football, I never would have met these guys. If I'd never pushed my athletic—and geographical—limits to get an inside look at this great game in its most pure, stripped-down, raw level, I never would have become an integral part of this team, or developed an unconditional love of this sport. I never would have learned whether I had what it took to stand alone, a man on an island, and look a lifetime fear of sports failure right in the eye and say, *Bring it on*. That kid who once cried on the sidelines of a soccer game was finally banished from my psyche. It took about 30 years, but he was gone.

Now, I'm not naive enough to believe that a few field goals, postgame beers, or fun sports nicknames are going to save the world. Not everyone wants to walk life's Kumbaya line. But I did recognize— and my teammates and coaches might have, too—that as we battled together week after week for four straight months, spending as much time with each other as we did with our *other* families, we at least avoided the unfortunate fate of living our entire lives mere miles apart, yet never once meeting. That would have been the worst defeat of all.

Football had given me a lot over the years: countless hours of entertainment; the pride of two Patriots' Super Bowl titles; and, for one incredible season, the unexpected thrill of actually playing the game. But as I looked back on that 2004 season with the Panthers, I realized it gave me something even better than all of that put together: a smaller Boston, and a fuller life.

EPILOGUE:
THE POINT AFTER

SINCE 1976, either the Marlboro Shamrocks or Middleboro Cobras had advanced to the EFL championship game, and 2004 was no exception. Despite finishing the regular season in the middle of the pack, Marlboro won its first playoff game against local rival Clinton and then upset Middleboro in an epic 35–29 overtime semifinal, advancing to face Brockton in the championship. There, experience prevailed and Marlboro topped the Bucs 14–7 to win its umpteenth Eastern Football League ring.

When the EFL's 2004 postseason awards were announced, our quarterback, Anthony "Southie" Ravenell, was named Offensive Player of the Year. Not surprising: he led the league in passing yards, passing touchdowns, and was the catalyst of the league's second-ranked offense. Also not a shock, several Panthers—Insano, Derek, Jeremy, Sam—were named to the league's All-Star team. What was surprising, however, was that an author who shall remain nameless (hint: he was a rookie and has a pretentious French-sounding name) finished as the league's top-scoring kicker. I knew I'd had a pretty good season, but there were several good kickers in the league, so I was pleasantly surprised to discover that I'd outscored them. Obviously, it was a testament to our offense's proficiency. But I was still pleased.

While we didn't win that ring, the 2004 season was a step in the right direction for the Panthers. The team finished number 24 in the Minor League Football News Eastern Regional top 30. Never before had the Panthers ranked so high.

For the first time ever, I found myself in the midst of a football off-season. No more practices. No more games. Five long months, November to April. *What do football players typically do in the off-season?* I often wondered. *Sit submerged in giant tubs of ice? Run up and down mountains carrying telephone poles on their backs? Guzzle raw egg shakes?* I kept in touch with the guys after the season ended, occasionally meeting Reggie, Donnie, Delaney, Insano, Cliff, and others at Victoria's Diner on Mass Ave. for a Sunday morning breakfast here or after-work dinner there. We'd laugh about all the craziness of the past season and talk about plans for the upcoming one. Delaney and Reggie asked me to join the team's board, where I'd hopefully use my advertising background to grow the Panthers' profile around Boston. (I eventually pitched a story idea to a local nightly news show, *Chronicle*, that, come summer, would devote a full half-hour feature to the Panthers and semi-pro football, sort of a condensed, video version of the book you just read.) But the football-less winter dragged on. Minicamp wouldn't open until mid-April, and I wanted to put the free time to good use.

I decided to finally get some real kicking instruction.

When I started researching, the name that popped up over and over was a man named Doug Blevins. *The New York Times, People* magazine, *The Washington Post, Fast Company*, HBO's *Real Sports with Bryant Gumbel*, practically everyone had profiled him. Blevins, 42, had an impressive résumé to say the least—coaching/consulting jobs with the New York Jets, New England Patriots, Miami Dolphins, Minnesota Vikings; kicking coordinator for NFL Europe—and a long list of successful clients—Philadelphia Eagles All-Pro David Akers, Miami Dolphins team record-breaker Olindo Mare, and perhaps his greatest "find," an undrafted rookie free agent out of South Dakota State whom NFL personnel "experts" dismissed as not having what it takes to kick in the big time, yet would go on to make a clutch kick or two for my beloved Patriots: Mr. Adam Vinatieri. But what makes Doug's story even more compelling is something else entirely.

Doug has cerebral palsy.

He has spent most of his life in a wheelchair, needs help getting dressed, and has no use of his left arm. And he most certainly has never kicked a football. Yet, while growing up in Abingdon, Virginia, a tiny colonial burg just west of the Blue Ridge Mountains where football, as it is everywhere down South, was more religion than sport, Doug was a worshipper from the age of four, reeled in by the famous Dallas Cowboys–Green Bay Packers Ice Bowl game in 1967.

"For as long as I can remember, the only thing I wanted to do was coach in the National Football League," he says in a friendly, southern drawl. "I'm inconvenienced, not handicapped. Things could be worse. A lot of people with certain handicaps have speech impediments, and as a coach you're finished if you can't communicate with your players. I've been very blessed to do what I do."

Doug's story is worthy of its own book, recounting his amazing journey from wheelchair-bound youth to NFL kicking guru. Suffice it to say that Hollywood has come calling on several occasions with ideas for movies based on his life . . . and he has turned them down every time. "They always wanted to start the movie with some bullshit scene of me sitting in my wheelchair on the sidelines and bawling my eyes out because I could never play football like the other kids," he scoffs, almost insulted. "I never cried. Not once." This is a guy who, as a kid, once broke a kneecap . . . playing *tackle* football . . . *on crutches*.

"He is so precise on the fundamental part of it, so sound," Vinatieri, godfather to Blevins's son and his most famous client, told *Fast Company*. "But every time he goes out on the field, he is the most excited, slap-you-in-the-head, fired-up coach." And Mare, in the same article, said that Blevins taught him a whole different type of lesson: "I haven't told him this," Mare said, "but his life provides a whole different level of motivation for me on the field."

Given his high profile, I was shocked by how accessible he was. I simply called the number on his website, www.dougblevinskicking.com, expecting to go through handlers or assistants. But he himself picked up on the third ring. I introduced myself, explained that I was a semi-pro kicker writing a book and wanted to interview him about the position.

"I can do ya one better than an interview, Mark," he told me. "I have an opening next week, why don't you come on down and go through my program?"

I almost choked up a kidney. *Me? Train with the guy who coached Vinatieri?* I was wayyyyy out of my league. But before I could even think about it, I heard myself give him the same answer I'd given to Reggie all those months before.

Sure, why not?

A few whirlwind days later, I found myself on a prop plane straight out of *The Buddy Holly Story*, bouncing and rolling through heavy wind gusts over the southern foothills of the Appalachian Mountains, sweating profusely, and white-knuckling a duffel bag containing my cleats, some athletic tape to flatten the laces, a couple of changes of clothes, a dop kit, a football, and an orange rubber tee.

Doug, as promised, met me at the tiny regional airport in his customized minivan, and the next day we drove to a remote, country high school football field where I went through a condensed version of his program.

I won't detail everything he taught me that day under the blazing hot April sun—don't want to give away any trade secrets—but one moment stood out.

I hit a few kickoffs, all of which had landed somewhere around the 20-yard line. Not great.

"First, you're using the wrong tee," Doug said and reached into an equipment bag hanging on the side of his rugged, thick-wheeled motorized wheelchair—this was no nursing-home chair; he could have entered the Paris-to-Dakar Rally—and he pulled out a flat, black rubber tee and tossed it over. "Those orange ones are for straight-on toe kickers. These are better for soccer-style."

I teed a ball up on the 35-yard line, leaning it just-so on my new tee, and started backing up for another kickoff. But Doug stopped me.

"This time," he instructed, sizing me up from behind mirrored, wraparound shades that reflected sunlight under the bill of his Dallas Cowboys mesh-backed baseball cap, "try eleven steps back and five over. And run like a train on rails, perfectly straight, but not straight to the ball—straight to your plant spot just left of the ball. Keep running and explode through the kick. You've been pulling up short. Explode right through it so you're still running downfield even after you kick."

I did exactly as he said and the ball flew and landed—in the middle of the end zone.

"There ya go, boy!" Doug exclaimed, buzzing over and giving me a high-five with his good right hand. "That felt better, right?"

Holy shit! Better? Damn right it felt better? I'd seen Vinatieri and other NFL kickers not reach the end zone on some kickoffs! Sure, they kicked from the 30 and I kicked from the 35, but still . . . *holy shit!*

"How'd you know that was the right number of steps?" I asked, incredulous, worried he might in fact be a warlock.

"I don't know, I just . . . visualize it," he said with a shrug, the way Mozart might have shrugged when asked how he knew exactly which notes should comprise a requiem. "I used your first few kicks to gauge your stride, examine your body type, leg length, whatever, and it just came to me: eleven back, five over."

We worked out for the rest of that afternoon. I kicked more balls in a few hours than I had in my entire life. More kickoffs. Field goals from all distances and hash marks. Each time, Doug adjusted a step here, an angle there, a follow-through here. He then put me through his running regimen, customized just for kickers—short, sprinting bursts rather than long, cardio-building jogs—after which it felt like my legs were overcooked pieces of linguine, my lungs covered in wet wool.

We had dinner and a few drinks that night. And by "a few" I mean somewhere in the neighborhood of 50. Doug is a local celebrity of sorts; everyone in Abingdon knows Coach Blevins. I don't think we paid for a beer all evening, a night that ended with us having a semi-drunken pancake dinner at a highwayside Perkins (or was it Denny's?) sometime around 4:00 A.M.

Doug (not hungover, damn him) dropped me (totally hungover) off at the airport the next day. We shook hands good-bye.

"You know, Mark, most writers I've had down here usually suck, so I was pretty darn skeptical of you, too," he admitted. "But I gotta say, I was very impressed. You still have good leg speed for a guy your age. I wish I'd gotten hold of you 15 years ago," he added, shaking his head with a semi-rueful smile.

He then dropped this bombshell on me: "If I found you when you were just out of college, you could have been in the NFL."

My jaw practically came unhinged. This was both profoundly depressing and amazingly exhilarating: the former because I wouldn't have minded an NFL paycheck all these years, the latter because—how do I put this delicately?—*Doug Blevins just told me that I could have kicked in the fucking NFL!*

I flew back to Boston with Doug's shot of adrenaline-filled kicking confidence surging through my veins—just in time for Panthers training camp.

True to his word, Coach Pitt didn't return for the 2005 season. But he wasn't done with football by a long shot. He got an interview with the new Cleveland Browns head coach (and former Patriots' defensive coordinator) Romeo Crennel, and hoped to land a position doing something, anything on Crennel's staff. While nothing came of it, just getting the interview was quite an accomplishment, and sitting down with such a noted professional coach must have lit a spark under Pitt. He eventually returned to the Panthers, but "only" as defensive coordinator, which wouldn't be as demanding on his time.

Like his old friend Pitt, Coach O'Neal didn't return to the Panthers in 2005. Initially, anyway. He had temporarily put aside one love, football, to work on his other love: cigars. He became the part owner and manager of a cigar bar on trendy Newbury Street in the Back Bay, where his good humor and knowledge of the product most certainly made him a success. But like Pitt, he couldn't stay away from the Panthers entirely; he started attending games about halfway through the season and soon found himself back on the sidelines again in his Panther polo shirt, sleeves rolled up, chomping his cigar, helping out with the defense, and keeping practices loose with the occasional cry of "keep running, you crack whores!"

Donnie, despite having claimed "this is my last year" after Brockton and at the end of nearly every one of his 16 semi-pro seasons, actually did retire. And with the head coaching position now vacant, he took over for Pitt. The private eye and former navy man (not to mention Halle Berry paramour) was now the Alpha Panther.

Reggie returned for his 15th semi-pro season after having been named the EFL's Sportsman of the Year for 2004. Having lost half of my field goal team when Donnie hung up his fur and/or sequin-covered cleats, it was a relief to have Reggie still long-snapping. His old high school teammate, Delaney, remained as owner and continued to foot the bills. He watched with delight as, one night at practice during minicamp, I demonstrated my new, Doug Blevins–improved leg, booming kickoffs into the end zone, or close to. I would most definitely be handling the kickoffs in 2005, a relief to Khary who had also returned and would still be playing safety and punting.

Cliff, who had an impending court date (December) hanging over his head as the 2004 season ended, avoided a return to jail. But that wasn't the only highlight of his off-season: his oldest son, Ant, graduated from high school. "Seeing him get that diploma was the proudest moment of my life," Cliff says of Ant, who, along with being a key member of his football team, also won an English award at graduation. "The football stuff is cool, and I hope he keeps playing if he wants to, but when he won that academic award I couldn't stop smiling because I know he's on his way to doing what I've always hoped he'd do: grow up to be a better man than his dad." Ant was off to Springfield College in the fall. Meanwhile, Cliff took a job that combined his love of music and his religious leanings: he became the sound engineer for a church in Dorchester.

D-blocks's heart and soul, middle linebacker Darrell "Insano" Jones, got married and became a dad again before the 2005 season. His wife, Inita, gave birth to a girl, Khoral, who joined older brother Khesahn. But even late-night feedings and long days moving furniture couldn't keep him away from football, and he was once again back in front of the calisthenics lines that April, leading us in Panther jacks. He'd had another tryout with the Manchester Wolves of the Arena II League and said it went well, and that he might hear from them. But for now, all he had to show for it was a complimentary T-shirt reading "Manchester Wolves Open Tryouts" and his cattle call number, 296. He might never get a shot at the next level, but I doubt there were 295 players there that day with more heart and desire than Insano.

Ace, as is the rule for someone occasionally called "Nine Lives," of course came back. He looked fit and trim and bounded around with the same energy he always did, saying that he'd changed his diet and was all about salads and water now, not "all the fast-food crap that too many of these dudes eat every day." But not everything had changed. In the first day of minicamp, he got into a scuffle with some rookie who was looking to make a name for himself and picked the wrong guy to start jawing with, calling Ace washed up and old. Shoving. Pushing. A few punches. Same old same old. The "engine" of our team was back to drive; whether that meant drive us nuts or drive us to a title remained to be seen, but I personally couldn't imagine the Panthers without Ace. He'd always been in my corner and I'd be in his if it came to that.

Not everyone returned, however. Amos, our starting tailback, was nowhere to be found—he had reportedly moved to South Carolina—but he was replaced with a big, bruising back named Calvin Bryant, so we were set in the backfield. If Amos did come back, well, we'd have a "thunder and lightning" thing going on.

Then there was Elvis. The good news: he had gotten a new job within Comcast and was moving up in the world, as a hard-working team player like him should have been. The bad news: his new schedule would have him working nights during the week and on weekends, so he wouldn't be able to make practices or games. Reluctantly, he had to give up playing entirely. "I miss just being out here with the guys, bro," he said one night after briefly stopping by in his Comcast van, dressed in a crisp white Comcast polo shirt and khakis. He patted his stomach. "And I miss staying in shape, too." His brothers-in-law, Lenny and Gio, were back, however, making sure the Panthers didn't lose the entire Puerto Rican contingent.

Southie, the reigning EFL player of the year, was also a victim of a new weekend work schedule and would have to miss the first several weeks of the season. But some new blood arrived at quarterback in the form of Valderamo "Val" Teixeira, a tall, lanky, left-handed gunslinger who'd played at UMass–Dartmouth. We'd miss Southie, no doubt, but Val had talent that would hopefully make up for his lack of semi-pro experience.

Most of the other familiar faces returned: Coach Fink, Mohammad, Todd, Jeremy, Caleb, Sam, KFC, Jeff, the Big Twins, Big Paul, Jeff, Derek, Jug, Aaron, Keon, the "Twinkies" Chelston and Chezley, Brandon, you name it. Kelly, our athletic trainer/therapist/taskmaster, was also back. Jim "Jimbo" Murphy returned for his 25th semi-pro season, blaring rap from his sparkling Jaguar. Then there was Pee Wee. He returned as buff and ripped as ever, a walking fitness magazine cover ready to wreak havoc on EFL offenses. I'd witnessed his considerable football skills firsthand throughout the previous season, but I was still as curious as ever about his past off the field. On countless occasions I tried to get up the nerve to just flat-out ask him whether the rumors were true: Had he, in fact, served a long stretch at one of the toughest prisons in the area? But I never did because (a) even though he'd been nothing but friendly to me, I was still intimidated by the guy (who wouldn't have been?); and (b) even after one full season as his teammate, I wasn't yet comfortable with just cornering him and butting into what might be highly personal and sensitive areas. Not only would that have been rude, it might have come off as disrespectful, and I had nothing but respect for all my teammates. Still, I couldn't ignore what I'd heard throughout 2004, and, as the preseason wore on, I simply couldn't shake the feeling that there was far more to Pee Wee than sacked quarterbacks and crumpled running backs. So, one Thursday night practice, I finally got up the nerve to remind him that I was writing a book on the team and had interviewed several other players, and asked if he had any time after practice. "I have to leave early tonight. I have a meeting about a third job, trying to buy a house down in Quincy," he replied, and for a moment I thought he was politely blowing me off. But then he added, "You got a pen? I'll give you my new number. Call this weekend, or whenever."

That following Saturday I called him, and for more than an hour I finally heard Pee Wee's story told not merely in whispers from the periphery, but in open, honest, introspective tones, straight from the man himself.

William Holliman was born and raised in Dorchester, the fourth of seven children. His father was never around, so Pee Wee turned elsewhere for guidance. "Drug dealers, gang members, those guys were my father figures," he says. "I started working for them just to get money, to buy clothes, stuff like that, and I just got deeper and deeper." His teen years were filled with gang activity, notably with the Columbia Road Boys and Castlegate Road Gang, one of the oldest and largest, and most violent in Boston. Luckily, while he had his share of fights, Pee Wee was able to avoid some of the more deadly violence. "I never shot no one, never stabbed no one, never been shot, never been stabbed, I always just used my fists," he tells me. "I didn't need no army to fight my fights for me. I've always been alone, on my own."

While drug dealers were his de facto father figures, his older brother Charles (seven years his senior) was the one who encouraged him to give football a try. Pee Wee had always been the lone athletic talent in his family, always the fastest and most gifted player on the block, whatever the sport, yet he'd never played organized sports through high school. So one day in 1991, Charles told him to stop getting into trouble, stay away from the gangs, and try out for the Dorchester High football team.

Sadly, this advice came on the day Charles died. "He was murdered. Shot," Pee Wee tells me, adding that they never prosecuted the person or persons responsible. While he initially heeded his late brother's advice and, in his senior year, made the team as a punt returner—"I wasn't as big then, but I was still real fast," he says—he was unable to avoid gang activity and the many pitfalls thereof. A year later, he and his other older brother (the same brother who would eventually be shot prior to the Middlesex Mayhem game in 2004) were arrested for drug trafficking and possession of firearms. Pee Wee, now 18, was tried as an adult and sent to Walpole State Prison (later renamed Massachusetts Correctional Institution at Cedar Junction). He would spend the next nine years of his life being shuttled around to various maximum-security facilities (Walpole, Concord, Gardner) where he was introduced to life behind bars.

It was at Walpole that he really began to craft the Mt. Olympus–like body he sports today. He won several statewide, inter-facility powerlifting competitions, and was soon benching and squatting more than 600 pounds and fast becoming a legendary figure among prison workout circles. His almost religious training regimen did not go unnoticed. "You remember Frank 'Cadillac Frank' Salemme?" he asks me, referring to the former head of the Patriarca family and associate of James "Whitey" Bulger. "I trained him. He saw me working out one day and asked me to teach him my technique on pull-ups and dips." Pee Wee also worked out with another notorious Winter Hill gangster, Stephen "The Rifleman" Flemmi, and played on a prison softball team with Brookline (MA) abortion clinic shooter John Salvi (this before Salvi was found asphyxiated in his cell in 1996, an apparent suicide).

But life behind bars wasn't all weight training and softball games. Quite the contrary: it was a daily fight for survival, even for someone as intimidating as Pee Wee. "Guys tried to test your manhood right away, especially when you're new somewhere, so I had to crack a few skulls," he admits. "You've seen me play football, Mark, I go all-out. That's how I fight. Like I said, I never needed no army, it was always just me taking care of me. I fear no man but God, and I did just what I had to do." But as much as he could handle himself, he soon realized that violence inside prison might work for inmates serving life sentences and having nothing to lose, but it was a quick path to a life sentence of his own. He knew that he'd made some mistakes and would have to pay for them, but he also knew that his life was not supposed to be behind bars like so many of his fellow convicts. "So I corrected myself," he says. "I went to school, got my high school diploma, and I found God and promised Him to follow the path of good."

Pee Wee was released from the Massachusetts penal system in

2001. He was 27, having lost nine years in the prime of his life. But it's not what Pee Wee did before, or during, his life behind bars that makes his story so compelling. Rather, it's what he has done after getting out of prison. Today, at 31, Pee Wee counsels young gang members to help them avoid the traps he fell into fourteen years ago and help realize their potential. "Mark, we're all born stars," he says with calm, almost soothing conviction. "People just have to realize that potential. That's what I'm trying to do with these young guys, help them realize that they have as much potential as anyone else out there, no matter what kind of home they come from, and no matter what they have to overcome. And I try to steer them toward sports, toward football. Kids that age have a lot of adrenaline to get out, and sometimes they let it out in the wrong time and place."

He also works in less "public" ways. If you're ever around, say, the Park Street MBTA station late at night, you might see a hulking figure sitting among the homeless who have crept inside to seek shelter from the elements. He listens to those who always receive a deaf ear. He sees them as people when most see them as inanimate objects to be stepped over. He offers up words of encouragement or thoughts on God and religion, whatever it takes to help them get through the night and, perhaps, start getting their lives back on track, the way he did when things looked their most bleak. "They're just people crying out for help, and they need someone to listen. God changed me, and He can change them, too."

While Kelly was right all those months ago when she said that Pee Wee's parole officer suggested he play football to keep busy, it was actually the fateful words of his late brother Charles that really keeps him playing. "Every game I play is a tribute to him," he says. "I love the Panthers. I don't care about stats or how many sacks I have. I don't believe in stats. All I want is to help this team win. I'd pass out water on the sidelines if I had to. Every time I put on that number 58 and get out there with D-block, I just . . . " His sentence trails off, but he didn't have to finish the thought, I understand exactly how he feels.

It's then that I hear some footsteps in the background, high heels on hardwood floor. I figure it's his fiancée, whom he'll be marrying sometime next year. But he says his mother has arrived, and I hear him telling her that I'm the kicker and I'm writing a book on the Panthers and wanted to interview him about football, and his life. "Mark, say hi to my mom, Miss Busby."

I introduce myself to Miss Busby and tell her that while she and I don't know each other at all, for what it's worth, coming from a total stranger, she should be very proud of Pee Wee and of what he's overcome in his life, and how he's passing on his experience to the next generation.

"I *am* very proud of him," she agrees, and I can almost hear her smile. Cheerfully, she asks me about the book, when it's coming out, tells me she wants a copy, and then tells me again how proud she is of the man her son has become. I promise to get her a copy of the book when it comes out. Pee Wee gets back on, and we say we'll see each other at practice that next week, and hang up.

Just like that, Pee Wee was an enigma no more.

April and May came and went. We practiced twice a week, first at English then back at Franklin Park. We had a controlled scrimmage against Charlestown. At one point, I scooped up an errant extra-point snap, rolled out, and threw a busted-play pass, and on my follow-through, I slammed my right index finger on the helmet of a Townie player who then double-hand shoved me to the ground. Being an idiot, I never had the finger checked out, but it didn't feel right from then on (and it wouldn't be until a routine physical almost a year later when I'd discover I'd played the 2005 season with a hairline fracture just above the knuckle).

By June, we were ready for our first real exhibition game, a road game, something I'd missed last year thanks to joining the team so late. And this wasn't just an away game outside of Boston, or even somewhere in New England; no, at three o'clock on an already humid June early morning, 50 Panthers, two trainers, and a few girlfriends and assorted friends piled onto a chartered bus, and we headed down I-95 to Baltimore to take on the Maryland Jaguars, a strong team in the Mason-Dixon Football League. In a Burger King at a rest stop somewhere along the Jersey Turnpike, some of our guys suddenly found themselves surrounded by a pack of wide-eyed little kids who mistook them for NFL players. The amused Panthers happily signed autographs and posed for pictures as the kids flocked and giggled, looking so excited and starstruck that our guys just didn't have the heart to disappoint them with the truth: we weren't the Patriots or Giants; we were just some random semi-pro team passing through on a crowded smelly bus. However, I have to believe that our guys also, just for that brief moment, reveled in the daydream of what it might be like if those kids had, in fact, been right.

In what felt like a thousand airless degrees on a parched field in the Maryland countryside, we won a chippy, hard-fought game, 29–26. Everything started out right for me: I hit most kickoffs inside the 10, had two touchbacks, and connected on all my kicks. I even made a 35-yard field goal despite being bowled over by a Jaguar special teamer just as I followed through, a total cheap shot that gave me momentary flashes of Lawrence Taylor snapping Joe Theismann's leg like a chicken bone. Amazingly, there was no roughing call, and after picking myself up, I stomped toward the guy who had drilled me, clapping sarcastically in his direction. "Way to go, tough guy! You hit *the kicker*!" I called over to him. "Oh, yeah, and next time," I added, pointing up at the scoreboard, "you might want to block the kick there, superstar!" Still fuming, I turned to see Todd, who had been part of the field goal unit, doubled over, laughing at me. Despite my anger, I started laughing, too. It was going to be that kind of season. Fun, but volatile, and if the first two scrimmages were any indication, definitely more physical.

We took the momentum of the Maryland win—not to mention the incredible bonding of an overnight hotel stay, a team dinner, drinks (lots of drinks), and the epic *Harold & Kumar Go to White Castle* on the bus—into Randolph to start the 2005 regular season. We were up 41–21 with about 10 minutes left. Donnie, wanting to get the reserves some playing time in his inaugural head coaching stint, pulled all the starters, the game clearly in hand. But before we knew it, they'd scored three touchdowns and were celebrating a come-from-behind win. I had missed a 45-yard field goal in the third quarter (wide right by a few inches) that didn't seem too vital at the time, but I wished I had it back. That said, I was five of five on extra points and felt good, the loss aside.

We could have let the opening defeat get us down. But after beating Charlestown the following week, we pulled off the biggest win in team history in week three: yes, folks, we finally beat the mighty Middleboro Cobras. With the Marlboro Shamrocks taking a surprising leave of absence and the Middlesex Mayhem folding because of a lack of player interest, there were now only eight EFL teams left, but the Cobras were still the biggest and the baddest. And on a hot Saturday night in late July, we fired on all cylinders and took them down in an epic shoot-out, 34–27. The Middleboro monkey was finally off our backs, and the Drinking Fountain rocked into the wee hours afterward.

But that was the high point of the season. We played sometimes brilliant, sometimes erratic ball and finished 5–3, good for third place behind Middleboro and Brockton, and just ahead of an improved Charlestown squad. This meant we'd once again square off in a play-off semifinal rematch against the Buccaneers at Marciano Stadium, which was fast becoming like Yankee Stadium to the Red Sox. We controlled the first half and led 14–0 at the break, but couldn't sustain it in the third quarter. They started chipping away. Soon, they were up 18–14, and in the final 30 seconds, we found ourselves on their 5-yard line with no timeouts and four plays to get into the end zone . . . and into the EFL title game. After one running play that tried to catch them off guard, two Val passes to Sam fell incomplete on second and third down.

Fourth down.

Three seconds left.

Val took the snap, made a quick two-step drop, and fired a slant to Jeremy on the right side. But it was a little behind him, and a little high, and most definitely had some mustard on it. Jeremy, still in stride, had to stutter-step and reach back, and for a second it looked like he'd caught it. But it ricocheted off his fingertips and deflected over his head and out of the end zone.

Game over. Bucs 18, Panthers 14. Déjà vu all over again, as Yogi Berra would say. Middleboro, who easily handled Charlestown in the other semifinal, defeated Brockton in the championship, regaining the title they'd won in 2003.

While disappointing in the end (again), 2005 was another great statistical year for the Panthers. We finished two points off the league-scoring lead. KFC had eight touchdown catches. Sam was named league Offensive MVP. Val, KFC, Jeremy, Sam, Insano, James (a lightning fast 18-year-old newcomer at receiver/kick returner), and Derek (who led the league in sacks with nine) all made the EFL All-Star team. And, yes, even yours truly (who carried his Doug Blevins teachings with him all season long) was, for the first time since Little League baseball, named a league All-Star.

But the EFL title still eluded us. Someday, man. Someday . . .

Fast forward. It's now May 2006. Training camp started a few weeks ago. Yes, folks, I'm back for my third season, and my nearly 40-year-old hamstrings are already sore as hell from crabwalks, cone agility drills, up-downs, and sprints. (I ran the 40 in 4.9 seconds . . . not Indy scouting combine worthy but not bad for an old creaky bastard like myself.) Most of the same guys are back, too, all my not-so-new-anymore friends. It's good to see all the familiar faces, especially the rickety chain-link backstop at Franklin Park field—I could tell it missed me. We have two road exhibition games in June, in Binghamton, New York, and—get this—in Montreal, and then it's time to start our EFL championship quest all over again in July.

Most important of all, Celia is pregnant with our first child—a girl. She's already kicking.

ACKNOWLEDGMENTS

FIRST OF ALL, thanks to my readers. I urge you to email me if you have any comments about the book: mark@mark stamant.com. I always try my damndest to respond quickly and semi-coherently. Also, visit www.markstamant.com for updates and information on book signings and appearances, press coverage, and/or horrendous kicking-related injuries I have sustained during the 2006 football season.

As with any good team, there are countless people, all playing separate but vital roles, who I need to sincerely thank for getting me into the end zone (and thus begins repeated overuse of the clunky football metaphor):

Reggie Murphy, for first convincing me to strap on a helmet, Delaney Roberts, Donnie Williams, Cliff Braithwaite, Darrell "Insano" Jones, Aaron "Ace" Smith, Elvis Figueroa, Mike O'Neal, Mike

Pittman, Prince Woodberry, Leon "Fink" Finklea, Jeff Julius, Kelly Walsh, Mohammad Butahi, and all my Panther teammates and coaches. Without your honesty and good humor, this book would have been a lot worse, and about four pages long.

My editor, Brant Rumble, for knowing when to be touchy-feely like Dick Vermeil and when to drop the hammer like Vince Lombardi. This book is several football fields better thanks to your tough love. Well done, Coach.

My agent, Bob Mecoy, for constantly coming up with new formations and schemes for the Mark St. Amant-as-Author playbook. If agents are in charge of designing potent new offenses, you're a bizarre hybrid of Paul Brown, Bill Walsh, and Don Coryell.

Everyone who has enthusiastically supported both my first book and this one on the publicity end and helped get the word out: Kathy Bickimer and everyone at *Chronicle* for your terrific piece on the Panthers; Morning TV personality and radio host extraordinaire Doug VB Goudie and everyone at FOX 25 Morning News; J.Dubs, El Jefe, Bateman, and all the guys in "The Hideout" in Florida for the amusing Friday night fantasy football chats; *ESPN The Magazine*'s Eddie Matz and all the other talented ESPN writers and producers who have kindly allowed me to appear on their shows, be in their articles, and babble incoherently about fantasy football and other sundry football topics; speaking of, I must thank everyone at *Classic Now* . . . it was a helluva lot of fun while it lasted.

All my F&M and Westy friends.

All my friends and coworkers at Arnold in Boston, whose good humor, encouragement, and patience helps me balance my "ad guy life" and my "author life" as best I can.

Doug Blevins, for sharing his infinite knowledge of kicking with a random semi-pro kicker, and for being one of the most unique people I've ever met. (I don't, however, thank him for making me sprint under the hot Tennessee sun until I almost vomited.)

My family and in-laws for your continued support of my insane writing endeavors and for bringing the kids to Panther games. Their hilarious, shrill little cheers added at least five yards to every field goal attempt.

Holly and Ben Raynes, and all our other friends who always cheered on the Panthers at English and elsewhere.

Kruds, I didn't mention this in the book, but sometimes before games I'd ask you to help guide the ball through the uprights if you weren't busy. Hell, you were an even bigger football fan than I am; I knew you'd be watching.

And, finally, my wife, Celia, for her always-honest and spot-on creative input, for putting up with an absent husband on many nights and weekends for most of these past two football-filled springs and summers, and for not being insulted when I refuse to look up into the stands and wave like a complete geek during games. By the time this book is out our daughter will be born, but I already can't wait to meet her . . . and buy her some tiny little cleats.